SPEKE

Speke in 1859, by J. Watney Wilson

ALEXANDER MAITLAND

SPEKE

CONSTABLE

LONDON

First published in 1971 by
Constable & Company Ltd.
10 Orange Street, London WC2
Copyright © 1971 by Alexander Maitland

ISBN 0 09 457430 8

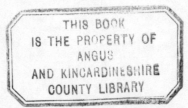
Printed in Great Britain by The Anchor Press Ltd.,
and bound by Wm. Brendon & Son Ltd., both of
Tiptree, Essex

FOR MARY

CONTENTS

ILLUSTRATIONS

INTRODUCTION

In the autumn of 1964, I began the prolonged but very pleasant task of gathering sufficient material for this first full-length portrait of John Hanning Speke.

The book has grown partly out of a lingering childhood fascination by Africa, and partly from having read Mr. Donald H. Simpson's article, 'Restoring Honour to an Explorer', which appeared in *The Times* of 12th September that same year. The late Mrs. K. W. Thom, whose brother-in-law was the co-author of my old favourite, *Wild Sports of Burma and Assam* (1900), provided me with Mr. Simpson's article and the initial inspiration. Further encouragement came early from Mr. Mark Hamilton, Mr. Wilfred Thesiger, and Mr. Quentin Keynes.

Mr. Simpson indicated a wealth of valuable source material and gave me a very fruitful introduction to the eminent East African historian, Mr. H. B. Thomas. Aided by Mr. Simpson, my wife and I 'uncovered' a cache of over a hundred Speke letters, including the original manuscript of the *Journal* and its first and second proof copies, all of which are stored with the Blackwood manuscript collection in the National Library of Scotland, Edinburgh. I have to thank the Trustees of the National Library of Scotland for permission to reproduce here extracts from these fascinating documents, and I express sincere thanks to the various members of the staff, in particular to the Deputy Keeper of Manuscripts, Mr. J. S. Ritchie, for much kindness, courtesy and generous assistance.

Mr. Douglas Blackwood, head of Messrs. William Blackwood & Sons Ltd., George Street, Edinburgh, kindly allowed me to examine several interesting letter-books and furnished much useful information.

So too the staff of the Royal Geographical Society, London:

in particular Mrs. Dorothy Middleton and Mrs. Marguerite Hughes; Miss E. Bardswell; Mrs. Molloy; Mr. G. R. Crone; Mr. G. S. Dugdale and Brigadier Gardiner, who have, over a long period, responded with unlimited patience to many requests and enquiries. My debt to them and to the Society is very great.

Mr. Quentin Keynes not only permitted me to study and draw upon his unique collection of Speke and Burton manuscripts and correspondence, but also presented me with a very fine set of *The Life* by Lady Burton. He made available the rare photograph of Burton which appears facing page 38 and introduced my wife and me to Mrs. Fawn M. Brodie, who, on page 10 of her model biography, *The Devil Drives*, has referred to the most interesting evening when, together with Mr. Keynes, we visited Burton's tomb at Mortlake.

We have received quite remarkable kindness and hospitality from all members of the present Speke family. To Mrs. Ruth L. Speke, who has been involved with the book since its inception; to Miss Nyanza and Miss Venetia Speke; Mrs. Joan Speke; Lady Milford; Mr. Nicholas Speke; and Mr. and Mrs. Peter Speke, we offer gratitude and thanks. Without their aid, what follows could never have been written. Mr. Peter Speke has provided photographs and a copy of a unique and hitherto unsuspected Memorandum written by the explorer's cousin, George Pargiter Fuller. Miss Mary Rose Rodgers helped me to determine the true whereabouts of Speke's birthplace, and Mr. and Mrs. Hugh Hanning assisted in tracing the course of his early education.

Further invaluable assistance was given by Miss Isabel Armitage; Major H. C. Webb; Mr. Stanley Godwin; Lt.-Col. Christopher Fuller; Mr. W. Chadwick; Mr. J. Ridley; Mrs. E. C. Pine-Coffin; Dr. Howard Harper; Mr. A. McK. Annand; Mr. Norman Pugsley; Mr. Francis Needham; Miss Marjorie C. S. Cruwys; Mrs. S. E. Scammell; Miss E. Armstrong, of the Royal Historical Society; and Lt.-Gen. Fahir Atabek, Head of the Turkish War History Department in Ankara.

Sir Edward Playfair, grandson of Sir Robert Lambert Playfair, has kindly permitted me to use several fascinating Speke letters from his family collection, and the wonderful photograph of Speke which appears facing page 166. The photograph, which was taken by Dr. John Adams, shows Speke holding a copy of *Blackwood's Magazine* and shows, too, the little lump on his forehead which resulted from a steeple-chasing accident in his youth.

I would like to thank the Royal Geographical Society for permission to reproduce the illustrations facing pages 23, 39, 86, 87, 102, 103, 150, and the frontispiece. The portrait of Speke facing page 22 is reproduced from *The Nile Quest* (1903) by the late Sir Harry Johnston. These illustrations were photographed for me by Mr. Rodney Todd-White. Mr. Peter Speke has kindly allowed me to use the portrait of Speke and Grant facing page 151, which was photographed by Mr. A. G. Toogood.

Mr. Gordon Waterfield and Mr. Alan Moorehead have devoted much time to discussions of Speke's personality and achievements, and have allowed me to quote very freely from their books. Philip Henderson guided my researches into Laurence Oliphant, whose biography he wrote.

I wish also to thank Professor and Mrs. Roland Oliver; Dr. Roy C. Bridges; Dr. John Allen Rowe; Mr. Ian McMorrin; Professor J. N. L. Baker; Mr. and Mrs. R. C. Wakefield; Mr. J. W. Barrett and Mr. D. W. Perkins, both of John Rigby & Co. Ltd.; Miss Brown, of Atkin, Grant & Lang; Mr. Wolfgang Pietrek; Mr. Peter Mackenzie; Miss J. Kirkpatrick, Librarian of the Royal Anthropological Institute; Mrs. Stuart Rose and Mr. Rodney Todd-White; the editors of the *Uganda Journal* and *Tanganyika Notes and Records*; and Mr. and Mrs. David Hamilton, who read extracts from the partly completed second draft. Miss Andrée Evans organised the manuscript and typed it beautifully.

Last, far from least, I wish to thank my wife, Mary Murray Maitland, for whom the dedication will say everything.

The original text of *Speke* was begun in the small house above Sligachan, Isle of Skye, in February 1967, and the final version was completed, except for several small additions, in London in September 1969.

ALEXANDER MAITLAND

FIRST FOOTSTEPS

ADEN in 1854 was held by a garrison of soldiers whose duty it was to support the policy of passive imperialism advocated by the Court of Directors of the East India Company in London. From the seizure of the port by the Company's forces in 1839, the history of Aden had been one of continual strife. A near-by Arab fortress, Bir Ahmed, had become the focus of anti-British feeling, yet the cautious Directors rejected a proposal by the Political Resident, Captain Stafford B. Haines, to destroy the fort and thereby remove the most virulent source of trouble.

At the beginning of 1854, Haines was relieved of his post and jailed on a quite insubstantial charge of embezzlement. His acting successor, Brigadier Clarke, lacked that insight into Arab affairs which Haines had possessed, with the result that during Clarke's brief term of office relations with the chieftains and surrounding tribes deteriorated badly. Nor did the situation much improve with the appointment of Colonel (later Sir James) Outram, who arrived in Aden in July of the same year, tired and ill, disgusted with his new posting and relatively disinterested in the politics of the area.

It was thus hardly surprising that by January 1855 the entire garrison of Aden, all European personnel included, was forbidden to leave the precincts of the town, so dangerous had conditions become in the immediate neighbourhood.[1]

Two months before the arrival of Outram, there came into this troubled environment Lieutenant Richard Francis Burton, accompanied by two friends from his days on the Sind Survey, Lieutenant G. E. Herne and Lieutenant William Stroyan. Burton was already a distinguished traveller and linguist, whose pilgrimage to the very core of Islam, the cities of Mecca and Medina, had earned him a considerable reputation.

In consequence of his wanderings in Arabia, Burton had developed an interest in Zanzibar, the East African coastal island which, apart from being an important centre of the slave-trade, lay adjacent to the 'eternal snows' of Mount Kilimanjaro, of which he had heard a fascinating account from the mountain's discoverer, Dr. J. L. Krapf. Neither could he forget the tales of Arab traders, which described a range of snow-covered peaks and a system of huge lakes stretching across the heart of the African continent.

These, and the meeting with Krapf in Cairo in November 1853, finally persuaded Burton for the time being to forsake Arabia, where in any case there remained only 'deserts, valleys and tribes'[2] to be discovered, and instead to explore Africa, striking out either from Berbera on the Somali coast, or from Harar in northern Ethiopia, marching south-east to Zanzibar. Thereafter he planned to travel westwards to the Atlantic shore, thus opening up two major routes by which further expeditions might penetrate and study the country in greater detail. This vast project and its corollary (a strong, private desire to determine the source or sources of the White Nile), Burton had communicated in letters to Dr. Norton Shaw, the Secretary of the Royal Geographical Society in London.

The Royal Geographical Society was in a way responsible for some of Burton's enthusiasm. It had been agitating since 1849 for the release of one or two competent officers from the East India Company's army to undertake a systematic exploration of the interior of Somaliland. Up to 1849, discounting the aborted plans of Sir Charles Malcolm, a former chairman of the Court of Directors, the only survey which had been produced was that made by Lieutenant Cruttenden of the Indian Navy, who in 1848 had journeyed along the coast, but chiefly by sea. In 1850 a Dr. Carter suggested a similar exercise, again avoiding the hinterland and using a vessel as base, but the R.G.S. would not promote the scheme, preferring to wait for someone energetic and courageous enough to penetrate the tribal areas.

Such a man was Richard Burton. In the eyes of the Society he was ideal. Possessed of insatiable curiosity and indomitable courage, he made a capable and experienced leader and an accurate observer (as amply proved by his writings on Arabia and the reports and books describing his activities in India). Against such qualities, Burton's 'deficiencies' – an excess of candour and imagination – were accepted as inevitable hazards. Although he disembarked in May 1854, sponsored by the R.G.S. and financed with a grant of £1,000 from the Government of India, Burton was forced to await official permission from the Court of Directors. The letter took four months to reach Aden, during which time he acquired an understanding of the Somali tongue, assisted by Captain C. P. Rigby's outline grammar, and some knowledge of the country's habits and geography.

The letter of permission, when it came, proved to be a rather unsatisfactory document, for the Court had taken care to absolve itself of responsibility for any accident which might befall Burton or his companions, emphasising that he undertook the venture 'as a private traveller', entirely at his own risk. Yet the shoddy paper freed him, and allowed him to snap his fingers at another individual whose opposition had conspired with the tardiness of the Court to delay the departure of the expedition.

James Outram, 'the Bayard of India', had in his youth entertained unfulfilled ambitions of exploring the Somali country, 'then considered the most dangerous in Africa', but for some reason did everything in his power to prevent Burton from doing so. It may have been that Outram's overt dislike of Sir Charles Napier, who in the forties had conquered, surveyed and administered the Sind, turned him instinctively against Burton, who was Napier's favourite and equally overt disciple. Whatever the motive, Outram's obstinacy was responsible for Burton's making a decision which subsequently proved tragic, and quite fatal to the success of the major expedition to Zanzibar.[3]

To dispel Outram's fears and protracted opposition, Burton suggested that his party should postpone its departure until the break-up of the annual Berbera Fair in April 1855. In the meantime, he promised to organise a survey of the coast around Berbera, including a study of the Fair and its trading methods, while, as a thrust at the pessimists and the faint-hearted, he decided himself to explore the forbidden city of Harar, the religious capital of Ethiopia.

Burton assured Outram that the members of the expedition

would rendezvous at Berbera early in 1855, there to make final preparations, and then, under the protection of the huge and heavily armed Ogaden caravan, which plied each year between southern Somaliland and the coast, begin the long probe into the interior.

Reluctantly Outram gave his consent.

About the middle of 1854, events took an unexpected turn. The fourth member of Burton's party, Assistant-Surgeon John Ellerton Stocks, died of apoplexy in England, just as he was about to leave for Aden. The news shook Burton severely, for he and Stocks had been close friends, and Stocks was not only a reliable contact with Government but an important figure in the expedition.

Some weeks later, in September, a P. & O. vessel from Bombay carrying army officers and sundry other officials bound for England decanted upon the quay at Aden a twenty-seven-year-old English lieutenant, whose sunburned skin betrayed a love of the open spaces and whose vast baggage, conspicuous by its heavy ordnance, hinted broadly at the new arrival's dedication to shikar.

Lieutenant John Hanning Speke of the 46th Regiment of Bengal Native Infantry had left his ship in search of sport and came intent upon finding it by crossing the Gulf and trekking unaccompanied into Africa.

That summer, Hanning Speke's initial ten-year term of military service had ended. He had quit the country immediately on furlough, the three-year-long overseas leave, partly to hunt and travel in Central Africa, partly to visit his family in far-off Somerset. His plans, made with characteristic care, but founded upon sadly inadequate information, allowed for a two-year shooting expedition followed by a further twelve months 'to be spent in indulgent recreations at home'. The trophies and specimens obtained in Africa would supplant the large collection formed already from the fauna of India and Tibet, all of which had previously been shipped from Bombay.

Speke's mother and father were apparently agreeable that much of their country seat, Jordans, was destined to become a private museum of natural history; but perhaps it is safer to add that there is no record, so far as is known, of their having objected to their son's proposal.

Directly he reached port, Speke sought the headquarters of the Political Resident and there unfolded the main details of his scheme. He wished first to cross the interior of Somaliland, and from there proceed south to the 'Lunae Montes', the range originally delineated on Ptolemy's famous map, and nowadays better known as the Mountains of the Moon. In this region he proposed to do most of the serious hunting, securing species perhaps similar to those he had killed in the Himalayas, at the same time mapping and surveying the country, just as he had already surveyed and mapped by eye untravelled sections of south-western Tibet and Chinese Tartary.

Speke readily justified his decision to visit a hitherto undiscovered part of Africa:

'My idea in selecting the new field for my future researches was, that I should find within it various orders and species of animals hitherto unknown. Although Major Cornwallis Harris, Ruppell and others had by this time well-nigh exhausted, by their assiduous investigations, all discoveries in animal life, both in the northern and southern extremities of Africa . . . no one had as yet penetrated to the centre in the low latitudes near the equator. . . .'[4]

The young officer's self-confidence was absolute, his charm and unrestrained enthusiasm a delight. And so coolly did he dismiss the difficulties of the Somali crossing, so elegantly and with such panache, that Outram, though he believed the plan to be neither feasible nor sane, felt disinclined to treat the lad unkindly.

But even a performance such as Speke's was still incapable of diverting 'honest James' Outram from his entrenched belief that private travel to Somaliland was suicidal, the tribes as he put it 'being of such a wild and inhospitable nature that no stranger could possibly live amongst them'.

Here, Speke for the first time in his life was faced with unshakeable opposition. His request for letters of introduction to the Somali chieftains was refused, and he was obliged to wait in Aden, ostensibly for the next ship home to England. For the casual adventurer, such summary treatment would have sufficed to inspire a hasty change of plan, but Speke, who in anticipation of the trek had lived his last five years in India like a Spartan, was not so easily defeated.

He continued to pester Outram, showering him with sweet words and entreaties, until in the end the Resident weakened sufficiently to palm his tireless opponent off on Richard Burton.

Although, like Outram, he found Speke interesting and immediately attractive, his lack of Arabic or scientific training made Burton wary of including him in his party. The young man's physique nevertheless impressed Burton who described him as being

'. . . of lithe, spare form, about six feet tall, "blue-eyed, tawny-maned; the old Scandinavian type, full of energy and life", with a highly nervous temperament, a token of endurance, and long, wiry, but not muscular limbs, that could cover the ground at a swinging pace, he became an excellent mountaineer'.[5]

While never doubting Speke's ability as a hunter, Burton thought his claims to 'the use of an unerring rifle' were greatly exaggerated and that the same applied to the horsemanship of which he was equally proud. But most of all, Burton was dismayed at the naivety of Speke's preparations:

'He was ignorant of the native races in Africa, he had brought with him almost £400 worth of cheap and useless guns and revolvers . . . which the Africans would have rejected with disdain. He did not know any of the manners and customs of the East.'[6]

Still more disturbing was Speke's violent motive for the journey, which was, according to Burton, that 'he had come to be killed in Africa'. Although Burton dismissed the somewhat Byronic outburst as being almost modishly agnostic, Speke's fatalism had originated in the post-Sikh War period, when he had turned his passion for 'the sport of fighting' and battle honours towards the pursuit of dangerous game and the acquisition of rare specimens, in many respects a very similar occupation.

It is almost certain that, but for the untimely death of Stocks, and Burton's failure to enlist a mysterious 'Lieutenant XXX' (referred to in an unpublished Burton manuscript owned by Mr. Quentin Keynes), Burton would not have offered Speke a place. Yet in the circumstances his furlough was temporarily cancelled, his officer's pay restored, and he, to his intense relief, was 'put on service duty as a member of the expedition'. The sole condition of Speke's acceptance was that he should cover his own expenses, 'trusting to Lt. Burton's promises in the future of being repaid', as by then the first instalment of the Government grant, £250, had been used up. Burton then suggested that Speke should explore the Wady Nogal, a valley situated in the notorious Dulbahanta territory, which cut across the north-east tip of Somaliland. He asked him to collect samples of the earth, a red substance reputed to contain gold dust, and as many camels and baggage ponies as possible for the forthcoming march to Zanzibar.

While the new recruit was thus employed, and Burton himself was en route for Ethiopia, Lieutenant Herne would collect more baggage mules in Berbera and observe the Fair. Stroyan, a native of Newton Stewart, had meanwhile been detailed to survey certain areas of the Gulf coast.

To the end, Burton could never explain his sympathy for Speke, or the predicament which he had, after all, brought upon himself. 'Why should I have cared?' he wrote, 'I do not know. . . .'[7]

Under the ingenious supervision of Herne, Speke constructed a simple camera obscura, which he added to his kit, the remainder consisting of guns, rifles and revolvers, £120 worth of cloth for barter, specimen boxes, ammunition, bags of dates, rice and salt, four thermometers, a sheaf of sabres and a sextant. While this was being assembled, Burton found him an abban, or protector, and a Hindi-speaking interpreter, both of the Warsingali tribe. In addition Speke selected a Hindustani man-servant, called Imam, and Farhan, a Seedy, as bodyguard. The bodyguard was an extraordinary-looking creature who

'. . . was a perfect Hercules, with largely developed ropy-looking muscles. He had a large head with small eyes, flabby squat nose, and prominent muzzle filled with sharp-pointed teeth, as if in imitation of a crocodile.'[8]

Strangely enough, the servants picked by Speke turned out to be faithful and efficient, just as Burton's two Warsingalis proved utterly unreliable. It may have been mere bad luck or else Burton was inconsistent as a judge of character.

The mode of dress advocated by Burton presented a more urgent problem. Contrary to the advice of Colonel Outram, he insisted that his party should travel in disguise. The procedure was familiar to Burton and, moreover, was essential for the safety and success of his journey to Harar; but for the other three disguise had little value, whilst in Speke's case, he being tall and fair, it made him appear quite ludicrous. In Outram's opinion the status of the expedition would be diminished in the eyes of the Somali, for he sincerely believed that respect and the British uniform were synonymous. Outram's point of view was shared by many, including Hanning Speke and his assistant, Captain Robert Lambert Playfair. Besides, the Arab dress felt bulky and uncomfortable; Speke afterwards complained of how he had sweated under the Aden sun, clad in '. . . a huge hot turban, a long close-fitting gown, baggy loose drawers, drawn in at the ankles, sandals . . . and a silk girdle decorated with pistol and dirk'.[9] His protests, alas, like those of the Resident, were made in vain, for when on the evening of 18th October he set sail for the Somali coast, Speke went in an Arab dhow, attired in his 'Oriental costume'.

Although he had been instructed by Burton to rendezvous with Herne and Stroyan not later than 15th January 1855, Speke did not return to Aden until the middle of February. It was only some six weeks after that, on 3rd April, that he finally met his companions at Berbera. Delighted as he was to see them, he reached the town burdened with a sense of bitter failure.

The three-month expedition to the Nogal valley had ended miserably without achieving its principal objectives. After reaching Aden on 19th February, Speke had been obliged to revisit the opposite shore to purchase more baggage animals, which he had managed to scrape together from the village of Kurrum. Before that, he had attended the trial in Aden of Sumunter, his abban, at whose hands throughout the journey he had been made to suffer continual humiliation and deceit.

It did not comfort him that Herne and Stroyan had carried

out their respective missions satisfactorily, especially as Herne had experienced similar difficulties with his abban.

As for Burton, the visit to Harar was crowned with spectacular success and resulted in the publication, in 1856, of his book, *First Footsteps in East Africa*. Burton had given Speke an opportunity of proving his worth, regardless of his slender qualifications. Speke, who had been grateful for Burton's generosity, felt deeply hurt by his failure to meet the challenge.

In order to understand this reaction, and to appreciate why the success of the Wady Nogal expedition was so vitally important to him, it is now necessary to examine Speke's background in greater depth.

He was born on 4th May 1827 at Orleigh Court, near the town of Bideford in Devon, and baptised in the church of Buckland Brewer by the Reverend Charles Davie. Although Orleigh Court was subsequently referred to both by Richard Burton and Sir Roderick Impey Murchison (and was accepted as recently as 1963 by Mrs. Dorothy Middleton in her article for the *Encyclopaedia Britannica*), Speke's birthplace has been curiously enough much disputed. *The Dictionary of National Biography* and editions of the *Encyclopaedia Britannica* before 1963 have all specified Jordans, the family seat, close to Ilminster; while an undated guide to the county of Somerset has suggested Ashill. Other sources, supposedly quoting members of the Speke family, have stated that the explorer was born at none of these places, but in Bamford Speke, near Bampton, Devon.

Hanning Speke's father, William Speke of Jordans, a retired army captain who had served with the 14th Dragoons, was the tenant at Orleigh at the time of Hanning's birth.[10] In contrast to his ancestor, William Espec, who crossed the Channel with the Conqueror, the elder Speke was a gentle, retiring man, who aspired only to a peaceful life and who seldom ventured far beyond his carefully managed estates. Even when his neighbour, the Prime Minister William Pitt, on one occasion urged him to stand for Parliament, the squire politely but very firmly refused. His wife, Georgina Elizabeth Hanning, came of a more ambitious background. Her father's family were merchants, among the richest in England, whose huge stone-built manor, Dillington, stood as the symbol of their material success.

Hanning Speke was the second of four brothers. William, the

eldest and longest lived, was born in 1825, a year after his parents' marriage. Edward, three years younger, and 'a most amiable young gentleman',[11] joined the East India Company's army (like Hanning, on the recommendation of Mrs. Speke's acquaintance the Duke of Wellington), and was killed at Lucknow on 15th September 1858.[12] The youngest brother, Benjamin became a clergyman and married his childhood sweetheart after a considerable family struggle, which he drastically resolved by running away from home. Like Hanning and Edward, Benjamin died comparatively early, but his large family was brought up by William, who inherited Jordans. It might have been the former escapade, which resulted in Benjamin's spectacular arrest by the London police after being confused with an escaped murderer, that, following upon Hanning's sudden death, prompted the verse which runs

> 'The Brothers Speke have made a stir
> Fate over each hath darkly hovered
> The one he dies the great discover(er)
> The other lives the great discovered.'

Besides the boys, there were also three sisters: Matilda and Sophia, who produced two independent histories of their family; and Georgina who later married Sir John Dorington, M.P.

From the information available, it is clear that the young Spekes were mutually much attached, and that in the years ahead, when military service, marriages and foreign travel caused them to be separated, the close ties between them were steadfastly maintained.

Unlike the pedigree of his family, Speke's education was adequate but undistinguished. He first attended Barnstaple Grammar School under the Reverend George Johnson, and after that a proprietorial college in Blackheath, London. No records of his progress in either establishment have survived, and the college in which it is believed he completed his studies was pulled down over sixty years ago, in 1908.[13]

The boy's inherent dislike of lessons was 'increased by ophthalmic attacks in childhood which rendered reading a painful task . . .'.[14] Unfortunately, the exact nature of the complaint in the early stages is unspecified, but it might have been acquired through visiting any one of the south-west seaports, or possibly from drinking infected water in the country. Ophthalmia, however, in no way impaired his skill as a sportsman and shot, although, if Burton's word is accepted, Speke overdid his shooting while in India, and was in consequence a less impressive performer in later life.

Although he liked to declare with emphasis that 'a sedentary life made him ill', his books and letters confirm that he absorbed most of the education which he found so tedious. It can only be argued that he lacked some of the curiosity which a more academic background generally inspires, and for this reason his proud 'devotion to bird-nesting and . . . hatred of book-learning'[15] denied him the benefits of company such as that of Richard Burton.

Writing in 1846 of the delicate balance between education and outdoor life, the naturalist Charles St. John noted that

'. . . this kind of education does boys more good than harm (as long as they do not neglect their books at the same time which I do not allow mine to do), as they acquire hardihood of constitution, free use of their limbs, and confidence in their own powers'.[16]

It is a pity that Speke's father did not possess a little of St. John's firmness. The boy's freedom would scarcely have been inhibited, while he would have gone out into the world, the better prepared to deal with men of alien disposition. As it was, under his mother's influence, the young man's thinking tended to develop along emotional rather than rational lines, a conspicuously feminine trait in so determinedly masculine a character.

In 1844, after his interview with Wellington, Speke left England to join his regiment in India. Sir Harry Johnston's classic *The Nile Quest* contains a reproduction of a painting which shows him at the age of seventeen, wearing his new army uniform. This portrait, the earliest known, represents a handsome youth, fresh-faced and fair-haired, with well-shaped features, a slightly prominent nose and large, light, intensive eyes. His manner is assured and his expression attractively defiant.

Judging from the introduction to *What Led to the Discovery of the Source of the Nile*, it is evident that Speke made an unwilling peacetime soldier. After the excitement and romantic anticipation of the voyage east, the routine of army life began to resemble the equally restricted existence of Barnstaple and Blackheath College. He was thankful, therefore, when the monotony of the barracks was interrupted by the advent of the Punjab War, and 'he found himself a subaltern in the so-called "Fighting Brigade" of General Sir Colin Campbell'.[17]

During the War, 'he took part in and obtained the medals for, Ramnagar, Sadullapore, Chillianwalla, and Guzerat'. He strove throughout to distinguish himself in action, although opportunity was not always in his favour. Burton recalled how '. . . on one occasion he was told off with a detachment to capture a gun; but, to his great disgust, a counter-order was issued before the attack could be made'.[18] Such indifferent luck however did not prevent him returning unscathed from the front, having risen to the rank of second-lieutenant, and with his campaign medal augmented by the addition of two clasps.

Speke afterwards served under Lord Gough in the second Sikh War, including one of its most bloodthirsty sagas, the Multani campaign of 1849. It greatly annoyed Burton, who was by then a qualified interpreter, that Speke had gone up to Multan and he had not. In spite of his fluency in the Multani dialect, Burton was mainly thwarted by an exceptionally severe bout of ophthalmia, as a consequence of which he was invalided home.[19]

Another participant of the campaign for whom Burton had, latterly, inadequate regard, was Speke's companion on a future African expedition, James Augustus Grant. Speke and 'Jim'* Grant first met in 1847. Grant, a highly talented artist, was already recognised by his fellow officers as a capable sportsman with a marked flair for botany. Not surprising, therefore, that between Speke and Grant there quickly sprang up a firm friendship, the common ground being a passionate devotion to natural history and hunting, as well as a great and lasting love for space and solitude.

---

* Speke used this familiar form of Grant's name from time to time in correspondence. See, for example, a letter to John Blackwood, 14–?–1863, N.L.S., MS 4185: 'Jim Grant intends . . .'

In other ways they were very different. Whereas Speke was frequently reckless and impulsive, Grant was the essence of the 'canny Scot', cautious, patient and shrewd. They complemented each other perfectly, but of the two, Speke's personality was unquestionably the more forceful. There is however no evidence that they met again in India, or elsewhere, until the autumn of 1859. In fact, letters written by Speke in 1860 suggest that he and Grant lost touch, possibly after 1854, but stress that there was no consequent lapse in their friendship.

The conclusion of the Sikh War was the turning-point in Speke's military career. Thereafter, soldiering grew less significant and the urge to fight gave place to the old craving for sport and solitary travel. In that year, 1849, Speke 'conceived the idea of exploring Central Equatorial Africa'.

The plan quite possibly originated as an antidote to boredom, a reaction against the truce and the lull of peace which followed in its wake. It may even have been a belated attempt to shake himself free of what he called the 'mammy strings', the inescapable domination of his mother, his schoolmasters and now his superior officers, under which he had lived continuously since boyhood.

'I had now served five years in the Indian army,' he wrote, 'and five years were left to serve ere I should become entitled to take my furlough. During this time I had to consider two important questions: How I should be able, out of my very limited pay as a subaltern officer, to meet the heavy expenditure which such a vast undertaking would necessarily involve? and how, before leaving India, I might best employ any local leave I could obtain, completing my already commenced collections of the fauna of that country and its adjacent hill-ranges?'[20]

He solved the problems by combining parsimony with his natural resourcefulness. His superiors, directed by his commanding officer, Sir William Gomm, ensured that every year Speke was granted a generous leave, in which he hunted among the hills and mountains of Tibet and the Himalayas, 'shooting, collecting, and mapping the country' wherever he went. He gained experience, while saving his money by travelling alone except for a few porters. Denying himself the doubtful luxuries of drink and tobacco, Speke lived close to the land, eating unsparingly of pure, plain food, drinking nothing much stronger than goat's milk or clear mountain water.

He was at last his own master, free from limitations of every sort. Doing what he enjoyed most, it is little wonder that he was supremely happy. Consider this eulogy of Himalayan life written a decade later:

'Without exception, and after having shot over three quarters of the globe, I can safely say, there does not exist any place in the whole wide world which affords such a diversity of sport, or such enchanting scenery, as well as pleasant climate and temperature, as these countries of my first experiences. . . .'[21]

The outstanding quality which distinguished these five years was that of innocence, and with innocence, utter contentment; as Speke devoted himself exclusively to preparing for his African adventure, it never occurred to him that his path might be blocked by refusals, or that he might be overstretching the patience of his commander. The fact that his faith in himself was so amply rewarded must have been a source of continual envy to his fellows. If so, they were probably mollified, if not altogether silenced, by the presents of game and the trophies which he distributed about the mess after each of his expeditions.

The extent of Speke's liberality is comparable with that of a shy and frightened child, who attempts to secure companionship and immunity with sweets; comparable, that is, until one realises that in his patronage there lurked an element of scorn. For was there not nobility in his wanderings, and manliness in his lone encounters with wild beasts? 'To what good account I always turned my leave,' he wrote, 'instead of idling my time away or running into debt . . .' It was indeed 'a simple approach to life'. Another serious aspect of Speke's wanderings has subsequently been diminished for want of a detailed description in his own words. Even Burton was compelled to admit that he had 'an uncommonly good eye for country' and it is therefore not surprising that his maps, all sketched freehand, were remarkably accurate. For example, his complex 'Skeleton Map of Conquered Thibet', now in the archives of the Royal Geographical Society, is beautifully drawn and, according to modern interpretation, relatively precise. It has been examined by Mr. Marco Pallis, author of *Peaks and Lamas*, and Mr. Richard Nicholson, who, travelling together toward Lake Pangong, followed closely the route used by Speke. On this particular map, for some reason, Speke carefully indicated all the mountain passes, but omitted the mountains themselves. When the map was submitted to Norton Shaw in 1859, he excused himself by remarking gaily that 'This much given, anybody understanding physical geography could fill in the mountains. . . .'[22] Unfortunately the dearth of information about this period of Speke's life in general cannot be compensated with such ease; and for this, Speke was himself largely responsible.

Correspondence during 1860 between him and the publisher, John Blackwood, confirms that he wrote numerous letters to his family describing his Himalayan journeys in the form of a loosely-knit travel diary. The introspective nature of these letters, which have since been either lost or destroyed, may explain why, in that year, Speke's grim determination to withhold their contents from the public should have contrasted so sharply with Blackwood's desire to publish them.

Knowing his instinctive dislike of journalism, Blackwood had introduced the subject carefully. On 3rd November 1859, he wrote as follows:

'When we were talking the other day you said that there was at home an immense collection of your letters from Thibet etc., to your mother and other members of the Family. It has frequently occurred to me that something very interesting about Thibet might be made up from these letters. Could you ask your mother to select a few which you might not object to my seeing and send them to me. . . .'[23]

By that time, *Blackwood's Magazine* had published several articles in which Speke summarised his part in the Lake Regions expedition of 1856–9, during which he again travelled under Burton's leadership. In view of the fame, and in certain quarters notoriety, which the articles had generated, Blackwood could immediately foresee in the Indian material a distinct political as well as commercial value, but to his disappointment, and our loss, Speke refused to co-operate:

'. . . I do not think you or anyone else save myself could make head or tail of my letters from Tibet,' he replied, 'for they are not connected nor do they give any likely stories. . . .'[24]

Whatever the reason for his refusal, it is hardly explained by conventional excuses alone, for instance a surfeit of other work, for although at the time of Blackwood's request, Speke was busily organising another expedition to Central Africa, he still found ample leisure for various social engagements, including protracted shooting-parties in the Highlands of Scotland.

It may have been that the broadcasting of essentially private news struck him as insensitive and indecent; for, with the exception of his last book, written at the end of his life,* Speke evinced little taste for self-revelation. Perhaps with his mind already occupied, he simply could not be bothered to cope with the detailed recollection of the past, compared to which the present seemed infinitely more important. Had Speke thought fit to accommodate Blackwood, or had he extended the scope of either of his books to include a preface on his early life, it might have been possible to establish more accurately the origin of his interest in Africa, particularly his attraction to the River Nile.

Burton, who had told him of his meeting with Krapf, and his intention of travelling westwards into Central Africa, where he suspected the 'coy fountains' of the Nile to rise, commented that 'He [Speke] never *thought* in any way of the Nile, and he was astonished at *my* views, which he deemed impracticable.'[25] Speke, however, contradicted this statement in 1864, by writing in *What Led* . . . that his plan (for exploring Africa) 'was made with a view to strike the Nile at its head, and then to sail down that river to Egypt'. While he took care to state that the plan 'was conceived . . . not for geographical interest', he did make it clear that, as early as 1849, he had become aware of the geographical parallel between the White Nile and the Ganges.

His solution to the centuries-old enigma took the form of a simple equation. It was accepted that the Ganges rose in the Himalayas, and was perpetuated by the melting of ice and snow, as well as the seasonal rainfall swelling its many tributaries. It appeared to him obvious that the White Nile, which

* *What led to the Discovery of the Source of the Nile* (Wm. Blackwood, 1864).

rose and fell in regular sequence and never succumbed even to the longest drought, must be fed from a similar source. The Mountains of the Moon from Ptolemy's map and another, highly spurious concoction prepared by Lieutenant Francis Wilford provided him with his answer. It is therefore possible that his apparent rejection of Burton's scheme covered the disappointment of finding his own plan unexpectedly subordinated to another, almost identical; but also there remains the possibility that the dream of discovering the Nile sources derived, not from lonely wanderings through the Himalayas (a delightful, romantic theory), but from the first exciting interview with Burton.

Subsequent events suggest that each premise contains an element of truth, and that while Speke's inspiration may indeed have burst upon him in the high hills, the ultimate reasoning and consolidation most likely developed from the discussions in Aden.

It could not have taken long for Speke to appreciate the delicacy of his position, wherein his only hope of hunting and exploring the region of the Upper Nile lay in confirming his place on Burton's expedition.

The fact that Burton had declared an interest in the river's origin merely intensified his desire to at least share, if not entirely capture, the honour of its discovery. By sending him into the Dulbahanta country, Burton had put the young officer on probation. His old friends Herne and Stroyan were tried and tested; Speke as yet remained an unknown quantity. How then could Burton or Outram have foreseen that, in trying to help him, they had deeply wounded his pride? How could they have comprehended the value which Speke set upon leadership and status, or that his gratitude concealed a greater chagrin at the inferior role to which he had, unwittingly, been relegated? Subsequent events show to what extent he felt slighted, not least among them the fact that, ten years later, in *What Led to the Discovery of the Source of the Nile*, Speke sought to restore the balance, inferring with subtle insistence that he was by virtue of position, capacity and local knowledge, fully the equal of his commander.

In the circumstances, Burton's peeved rejoinder, 'You would now think . . . that he had taken me, not I him'[26] was understandable, but an exaggeration. In fact, by the end of that expedition, it was for Speke to feel, with some justification, that at the hands of Burton, as much as the Somali, he had been made the victim of outrageous condescension, treachery and deceit.

From the start of the Wady Nogal expedition, Speke's progress was hampered and his authority undermined by his inability to communicate directly with his abban, or even clearly by way of the interpreter. Apart from the Somali dialects, the interpreter had only 'a slight smattering' of Hindustani, which meant that Speke, whose grasp of the language was only less limited, was forced to rely heavily upon the integrity of the abban and the honesty of his servants.

The crossing of the Gulf, prolonged by unfavourable winds, took nine days and terminated at the tiny harbour of Bunder Goray, a hamlet situated approximately half-way between Berbera and the most easterly point of the Somali coast. There, a month elapsed while permission to traverse the Warsingali country was sought for and obtained. However, in granting them leave to travel, the Warsingali sultan, Gerad Mohamed Ali, at first refused to allow Speke's party to proceed beyond the border with northern Dulbahanta territory, as the northern and southern Dulbahanta tribes were then embroiled in civil war. In peacetime, to say nothing of war, the northern Dulbahanta were a largely uncontrolled, disorderly and dangerous people, but the sultan assured Speke that even if he succeeded in penetrating their country without serious mishap, his life would be worthless the moment he entered the southern Dulbahanta, travelling from the north.

Nevertheless it was a beginning. The expedition's route led from the barren coastal plain up and over a range of mountains, six thousand seven hundred feet high, running east and west and roughly parallel to the line of the shore. Dropping three thousand feet, it continued across what Speke described as, '. . . a howling blank-looking desert, all hot and arid, and very wretched to look upon'. He commented wryly that

'. . . the Somali had pictured this to me as a land of promise, literally flowing with milk and honey, where, they said, I should

Speke in 1844, by an unknown artist

Mr. and Mrs. John Petherick

see boundless prairies of grass, large roomy trees, beautiful valleys with deep brooks running down them, and cattle, wild animals, and bees in abundance. Perhaps this was true to them, who had seen nothing finer in creation; who thought ponies fine horses, a few weeds grass, and a puny little brook a fine large stream.'[27]

The plateau made a disappointing prospect compared to the coastal range, 'green and fresh in verdure', below which, to the north, there stretched 'the vast waters of the Gulf, all smooth and glassy as a mill-pond'. To the south-west of the desert lay the Yubbé Tug, the river which formed the Warsingali boundary with the Dulbahanta.

For the first part of the journey, Speke was accompanied by the sultan's youngest son, Abdullah, an unhelpful and singularly unpleasant youth, who was joined from time to time by his father, his uncle and his elder brother. In this fashion, the expedition crept up the northern slopes of the mountains as far as the Yafir Pass. Meanwhile Sumunter stayed at his house in Bunder Goray, where, unknown to Speke, he strove to placate a horde of creditors who had followed him from Aden, determined to extract their dues for commercial transactions which the abban had been making there.

In an attempt to clear a portion of his debt, Sumunter deceived Speke into giving him twenty rupees with which to purchase baggage mules; and not only that, he disposed of his employer's supplies of salt and rice, exchanging the latter for a consignment of much inferior quality. Too late, Speke realised the significance of Sumunter's absence and in an effort to get him away from the coast, dispatched his few trustworthy servants to Bunder Goray, thus throwing himself at the mercy of the remainder. The consequence of his action was not long delayed. The Wasingali camel-drivers, supported by a group of local natives, set up an immediate clamour for extra rations of food. Presently Speke found himself surrounded by an ugly mob

'. . . jeering and vociferating in savage delight at the impunity they enjoyed in irritating me when all alone and helpless. However, I stood by the date and rice bags with my gun, and prevented anybody coming near me.'[28]

The rebels instantly retaliated. Catching sight of a native

goatherd and his flock further down the hillside, they seized one
of the animals and killed it. Then, encouraged by the sultan's
youngest son, they commandeered all but one of Speke's water-
bags.

> 'This one', wrote Speke, 'I immediately captured, and requested
> Imam to fill from a spring . . . but the men, thus far outdone,
> rather than allow it, said they would kill him if he dared attempt
> to go now. As Imam showed alarm at their wild threats, I took
> the water-skin myself and walked off to fill it, upon which the
> savages threw themselves out in a line, flourishing their spears and
> bows, and declared they would kill me if I persisted in going.'[29]

The outcome, which might have proved serious, was luckily
forestalled by the intervention of the sultan's eldest boy, who
at that moment had ridden up from Bunder Goray ahead of
his father, Speke's other servants and Sumunter. When the
sultan and Sumunter eventually arrived, Speke persuaded the
sultan to preside over a brief trial in which he himself played
the dual role of prosecutor and claimant. The ensuing fiasco
completely destroyed his faith in Somali justice, for, although
the evidence of the abban's misappropriations and general
negligence was easily established, it was unaccountably ignored
and the culprit vindicated.

Speke's threats of retribution by way of Aden gave his
followers little apparent cause for concern. Thereafter, and for
the duration of the journey, he was powerless; Sumunter and
the interpreter, being of the same tribe, took each other's side
in every dispute. Relations between Sumunter and Speke
rapidly deteriorated until, at the southern Dulbahanta border,
a considerable distance from the main Wady Nogal, it appeared that no alternative remained but to abandon the expedition and return as quickly as possible to the coast.

The men, taking advantage of the divided leadership, grew
more and more uncooperative and apathetic: Sumunter, who
never lacked their support, played Speke like a fish, alternating
meaningless vows of abject servitude with sudden impertinent
assertions of superiority. By January 1855, having threatened
and cajoled his way in the heart of the northern Dulbahanta
country, Speke, who still 'could obtain no satisfactory information' about the Wady Nogal, was fast running short of time and

supplies; he recalled how his patience, too, was wearing thin:

'It was impossible to keep one's temper under such constant provocation ... he [Sumunter] had abused his commission, as well as the Government authorities who had engaged him . . . for his presence simply made my position one of purgatory.'[30]

It is doubtful whether, given an understanding of the Somali tongues and a little insight into local conditions, Speke would have been subjected to such consistently wicked treatment. Yet it says much for his courage that he was able to override the strain of incidents such as the following, which, as the weeks progressed, became a matter of almost daily occurrence:

'I rose early and ordered the men to load, but not a soul would stir. The Abban had ordered otherwise, and they all preferred to stick, like brother villains, to him. And then began a battle-royal; as obstinately as I insisted, so obstinately did he persist; then to show his superior authority, and thinking to touch me on a tender point forbade my shooting any more. This was too much for my now heated blood to stand, so I immediately killed a partridge running on the ground before his face. Seeing this, he wheeled about, preparing his pony, and, mounting it, with his arms agitated and ready for action, said to the people standing by that he would kill me if I dared shoot again. I was all this while standing prepared to shoot, without understanding a word of what was said, when the interpreter rushed towards me pale and trembling, and implored me not to shoot, but to arrange matters quietly ... I of course was ready to do anything I could to help me on the journey, and . . . stated the terms on which I would grant the man a pardon.'[31]

In such moments of dire stress, Speke would go off by himself to soothe his temper by shooting, a habit which, as we shall see, persisted throughout his life. In the hills, he shot hyraxes, small birds, and klip-springer (literally, 'rock-jumper') antelope. Among the rocks he found and collected large numbers of fossil shells and also a new species of snake, *psamophis sibilans*, which was preserved, and afterwards presented by Burton to the Asiatic Society's Museum in Calcutta. On the plains he stalked numerous gazelle and antelope and shot the florikan, partridges and bustard which roamed and flew about in great profusion.

Near the powdering ruins of Kin's City, where an ancient Christian legion had built and abandoned its church, its cemetery and its fort, Speke killed a big spotted hyena in the act of dragging away some leather thongs from the edge of the camp. He later remarked how it had been impossible to determine the creature's sex until it had been cut open, for the hyena is hermaphrodital, the organs of both sexes being present in the male, as well as (in this case) the female.

By contrast with the abban and his men (always excepting Imam and Farhan), the baggage camels did their work uncomplainingly and well. They ambled tirelessly over miles of stony desert and plateau, and when crossing the coastal mountains, Speke noted how '. . . it was very marvellous, with their long spindle-shanks and great splay feet, and the awkward boxes on their backs striking constantly against every little projection in the hill, that they did not tumble headlong over the pathway . . .'.[32] The tenacity and endurance of the camels, like that of the other animals, both domestic and wild, seemed to defy the harsh aridity of their environment.

'It was very remarkable to see the great length of time animals in this country can exist, even under hard work, without drinking water. In an ordinary way, the Somali water camels only twice a month, donkeys four times, sheep every fourth day, and ponies only once in two days, and even object to doing it oftener, when water is plentiful lest the animals should lose their hardihood. I do not think antelopes could possibly get at water for several months together, as every drop of water in the country is guarded by the Somali.'[33]

Watching the tiny humming-birds drinking nectar from the flowers, Speke was continually reminded of the dryness in his own throat.

'Without animal flesh I do not know what I should have done here [writing of the Dulbahanta frontier: A.M.]. The water was so nitrous I could not drink it. To quench my thirst, I threw it in gulps down my throat; and rice, when boiled in it, resembled salts and senna.'[34]

Yet the wild beauty of the tribesmen, particularly the native hunters, evoked a sympathy which had much in common with Speke's feeling for gazelle and other creatures of the desert. Their bravery and cunning soon won his admiration and respect. They hamstrung elephant which were dispatched with spears and arrows; they ran down gazelle, sometimes on foot, sometimes on horseback. The smaller antelope, which to the natives' amazement, Speke shot 'right and left, when running like hares', the hunters would catch after a stiff sprint; the larger animals they exhausted, riding their ponies at the herd leaders, so that they were forced to gallop round and round in circles, until they fell panting to the ground.

Ostriches the natives either baited or shot, or ran to a standstill pursued by a mounted hunter. Knowing that the huge birds cannot see to feed by night, the horseman would keep them moving all day long, resting and feeding himself and his pony after dark; in this way, after a few days, the ostriches weakened rapidly enough for the hunter to ride in and club a whole flock to death.

Speke's admiration for Somali men and boys did not extend, curiously enough, to the women and girls, especially after the latter had married and given birth to a family, when, he wrote,

'all their fair proportions go. After that marked peculiarity of female negroes, they swell about the waist, and have that large development behind, which, in polite language, is called steatopyga.'[35]

The men, on the other hand, were

'. . . tall, slender people, light and agile as deer; slightly darker than, though much the colour of Arabs, with thin lips, and noses rather Grecian when compared with those of blacks, but with woolly heads like the true negroes'.[36]

In Aden, he observed, the Somali were obliged to disarm, so volatile and unpredictable were their natures, and, perhaps, reflecting upon an experience of his own, of which we have yet to hear, Speke commented in his diary that 'There is scarcely a man of them who does not show some scars of wounds . . .

some apparently so deep that it is marvellous how they ever recovered from them.'³⁷

Eight years later, Richard Burton was to echo Speke's view of masculine beauty, by writing in *Abeokuta and the Cameroons Mountains*:

'The male figure here, as all the world over, is notably superior . . . to that of the female. The latter is a system of soft, curved, and rounded lines, graceful, but meaningless and monotonous. The former far excels it in variety of form and sinew. In these lands, where all figures are semi-nude, the exceeding difference between the sexes strikes the eye at once.'³⁸

Not only did the natives contrast delightfully with the sulky manners of the abban, his 'artful and dishonest machinations' and the wearisome insubordination of the camel-men, but the northern Dulbahanta country, as the expedition moved inland, grew more fertile, well watered and abundant in wild life.

'. . . I shot gazelles [Speke wrote], little saltiana antelopes, hares, Egyptian geese, rock-pigeons, ducks and teal, and snipe and partridge, besides a choice collection of small birds . . . The climate was very delightful at this season, and the nights so cold I had to wrap myself well up in flannels. But perhaps that which best illustrates the healthiness of the country and the pleasantness of its atmosphere, is the fact that I, although I had no bedstead, but always slept on the ground, never pitched my tent a single day in the interior, and neither wore a hat or a shoe throughout the journey, save on one or two occasions, when, severely stabbed with thorns, I put on a sandal, I never knew a moment's illness.'³⁹

Despite their initial tolerance of the Wady Nogal expedition, the Dulbahanta regarded it with the same undisguised suspicion which, according to Speke's ultimate report, was also shown by the Warsingali and another tribe, the Habr Girhajis. The suspicions of the Dulbahanta had first been aroused as far back as the coastal range, where itinerant members of the tribe, travelling to Bunder Goray, discovered the paper trails by which Speke had threaded his way about the forests which grew up thickly on the northern side. Word that he must be a

Government spy preceded him to the Dulbahanta frontier, where, stimulated no doubt by the lies and gossip of Sumunter, the rumour soon confirmed the tribesmen in their anxiousness to be rid of him. Every unfamiliar characteristic, no matter how trivial, was picked upon and unfailingly misconstrued. Wrote Speke:

'If I threw date-stones in the fire . . . they looked upon it as sacrilege . . . If I walked up and down the same place to stretch my legs, they formed councils of war on my motives, considering I must have some secret designs upon their country, or I would not do it, as no man in his senses could be guilty of working his legs unnecessarily.'[40]

By Christmas Day 1854, the situation had grown alarming. It appeared that the chieftain by whose leave he had entered the Dulbahanta country was Sumunter's brother-in-law. Not only that, but the violent intimidations of a party of armed warriors (a renegade faction opposed to the expedition's presence), forced Speke to strike camp and flee. He managed to find shelter in a near-by valley, close to a spot where, after a series of especially heated arguments, the abban had been for many days ensconced in a tiny hut, together with his Dulbahanta wife, his children and his wife's two dwarf sisters.

So callous was Sumunter's attitude to Speke's predicament, so frequent were his absences from camp, so infinite was his capacity for quarrelling and deception, and worst of all, so cowardly was his intrigue with the Dulbahanta (which finally determined the failure of the expedition), that his harassed young charge was hard pressed to control a terrible murderous urge, which, on due reflection, made him shudder. He wrote of Sumunter: 'He seemed to me only as an animal in satanical disguise; to have shot him would have given me great relief, for I fairly despaired of ever producing a good effect upon his mind.'[41] The duel had reached its climax: desperate, Sumunter viciously countered Speke's repeated assurances that his financial ruin and severe punishment by Government were inevitable, by asserting publicly that the Aden force was impotent. The challenge was strengthened by his Dulbahanta kinsmen, who swore that their cavalry could easily demolish the Government troops. They scoffed at the East India Company's army, which was 'only efficacious behind walls' and which, they added, although it often threatened violence, never backed its words by action.

But this was the abban's final stand. In a last gesture of contempt he commanded the Warsingali camel-drivers to reinforce his assembled Dulbahanta. Then fully armed and mounted on his war-horse, he invited Speke to negotiate the terms of a truce. Notwithstanding his flamboyance, Sumunter quite clearly feared the consequences of his misdemeanours. He therefore promised Speke safe conduct to the coast, in return for some presents for the Dulbahanta chieftains; a simple request, and one to which Speke with much relief and little hesitation agreed.

Although the movement of the civil war and the difficulty of passing through certain of the tribal areas along the coast forced the party to alter the course of its return journey from due west to north-east, it eventually reached the starting-point, the fort at Bunder Goray, after a further month of tedious marching.

In the mountains, the dryness of the interior was replaced by soft sea breezes and layers of cool cloud bearing the seasonal rains. Here, Sumunter lived in daily dread of Aden's vengeance, hoping that Speke might be persuaded to withdraw his complaints against him and that he might go unchastised. The Somali, who had but lately vowed to murder him, now grovelled miserably at his feet. 'Oh, why did you not whip me when I was at fault?' he whined. 'I could have borne that well, but writing to the English at Aden is more than I can bear.'[42] Speke had by this time received an answer to a letter describing Sumunter's activities, which he had sent to Captain Playfair from the Dulbahanta border so that the abban had indeed just cause for fear. He had also much to lose by his stupidity and wicked conceit; in Aden, he had another wife and children, and the port was the centre and headquarters of his considerable trading interests.

Yet, despite everything he had suffered in Somaliland, Speke had no wish to involve either the abban or himself in a lengthy prosecution, a somewhat unexpected sentiment which reflected no consideration on his part for Sumunter or his dependants, but rather his own desire to put the sorry affair behind him as expeditiously as possible.

On 9th February 1855, Burton returned to Aden from

Harar. When Speke arrived there about a week later, Burton listened with a mixture of sympathy and contempt to the story of his failed mission. To some extent Burton was disgusted by Speke's inability to dominate Sumunter, just as he despised the cowardice implicit in the abban's conduct.

To Speke's doleful assertions that his Arab costume had impaired his chances of success, the older traveller paid no heed. He was, however, quite wrong when he stated in 1872, in his book *Zanzibar*, that Speke 'came back, determined that no such feature as the Wady Nogal existed'.[43] In his own account, published in 1864, Speke wrote that he had received reports of a stream, some six days' march away, in the southern Dulba-hanta country, which he later suspected, having studied Lieu-tenant Cruttenden's map and having made further enquiries, to be the Wady Nogal referred to in Burton's original instruc-tions.

Regarding Sumunter, Burton was adamant, insisting that the man must be tried and punished, for the sake of future travellers in Somaliland. The matter was settled when Burton was in-formed that the abban's record had been a bad one, and that Speke's unfortunate experiences were not unique. 'Against my inclination,' Speke explained, 'I was appointed Sumunter's prosecutor, and with my servants as witnesses, a verdict of guilty was speedily effected against him in the Aden Police Court.'[44] The abban was sentenced to two months' imprison-ment, fined 200 rupees (with the alternative of an additional six months' jail and hard labour should he fail to pay), and after that, to be banished from the colony, with his wife and family, for life. The sentence gave Speke but little satisfaction and, to Burton's everlasting regret, greatly angered the tribal chieftains of the northern Somali.

Nevertheless, the difficulties encountered by Speke and, to a lesser degree, by Herne, prompted Burton to declare in public that, in his opinion, the system of abbanship had outlived its usefulness, and should henceforth be dispensed with for good. When, in the April of that year, Burton's camp at Berbera was ravaged by two hundred tribesmen, Speke felt certain that this speech had contributed to the resulting disaster; the imprison-ment of Sumunter may have supplied a secondary motive.

While Burton chose to make an example of Sumunter, he

subsequently wrote that '. . . though he [Speke] was delayed
. . . and threatened . . . his life was never in real peril. Some
allowance must be made for the people of the country.'[45] Yet
by sending his companions about Somaliland in disguise, how
much allowance had Burton made for native reaction? Of this
and his speech on abbanship, Outram's assistant, Playfair,
later wrote: 'In this Lt. Burton erred; and this was the *termina
causa* of all the mishaps which befell the expedition.' Playfair
continued:

'A traveller who hopes for success in exploring a new country must
accept the institutions he finds in existence; he can hardly hope
by his simple *fiat*, to revolutionise the time-honoured and *most
profitable* institutions of a people, amongst whom precedent is a law
as unchangeable as that of the Medes and Persians.'[46]

In the book *First Footsteps in East Africa*, Burton's final summary of Speke's wanderings among the Somali was, as Mr.
Gordon Waterfield, a recent commentator, has pointed out,
'unnecessarily patronising'. He wrote: '. . . savages cannot
believe that a man wastes his rice and cloth to collect dead beasts
and to ascertain the direction of streams. He was known to be a
Christian; he is ignorant of the Moslem faith; and, most fatal
to his enterprise, he was limited in time.'[47]

Nevertheless, it seems incredible that Burton could have
deliberately ignored the fact that three species obtained by
Speke in Somaliland were quite new to science, that the
mission to explore the Wady Nogal was originated by himself,
that Speke had neither the taste nor flair for disguise, and that
the time available, quite apart from the use he made of it, was
a factor without Speke's control, which had been settled even
before he disembarked at Aden.

To occupy the two months until the break-up of the Berbera
Fair, and to avoid, perhaps, the embarrassment of Burton's
company Speke, immediately after the trial, proposed that he
should return to the Somali coast, to rendezvous as agreed with
Herne and Stroyan, and to help Herne collect the baggage
animals for the Zanzibar expedition.

For this purpose Lieutenant Dansey, Assistant Political Agent in Aden, obtained the services of an excellent abban, Mohamed Gooled, otherwise styled el Balyuz, meaning 'the Ambassador'. The Balyuz's past record had been exemplary and, under his guidance, Speke's experience of Somali travel was utterly transformed. In *What led* . . . we are told how, at the end of the expedition, he parted from the Balyuz 'with pure feelings of affection'. Having failed to secure an escort of trained Somali policemen, Speke himself recruited and drilled 'a dozen men of various races (Egyptians, Nubians, Arabs and Seedis)', whose weapons consisted mainly of sabres and muskets drawn from the pile which he had brought from India.

Because of the Fair, and the inevitable scarcity of livestock, Burton advised him to make for the seacoast village of Kurrum, which lay between Berbera and Bunder Goray. There, thanks to the assistance of the Balyuz and the eagerness of the Kurrum Somal, to trade, the complement of ponies and camels was quickly rounded up. Speke observed that the villagers

> '. . . showed me great deference because I was an Englishman and bought their camels readily, though, of course, they were canny in their mode of dealing, trying to dispose of their worst animals first and asking prices much above the market tariff. For poor animals they asked from four to five and a half dollars, which, though not a third of the price I paid in the Warsingali country, was full price for the finest animals at Berbera.'[48]

But the apparent cheerfulness of the people concealed much troubled minds. Rumours had spread that the British intended to suppress the slave-trade, an action conflicting with Moslem religious belief. There was a fear that the presence of Herne in Berbera indicated the Government's intention to hand the town over to their old ally, Sheikh Shamarkay of Zayla, who although aged, was not a man to lose sight of opportunity and who meditated 'nothing but the conquest of Harar and Berbera'. Most of all they had been startled by Burton's rash bid to destroy the system of abbanship. Nearer Berbera, at the village of Aynterad, a huddle of old men were overheard, as they computed the probable fate of Burton's expedition; it would never, they asserted, reach even the Webbe Shebelli, let alone the Ogaden country.

These danger signals passed among the tribes during the six months from October 1854 until the following April. During that period the suspicions of the natives were given time to consolidate and in consequence the antipathy towards the travellers assumed a more violent and disturbing character. Writing ten years later, in 1864, Speke expressed his conviction that

'Had we gone straight from Aden without any preliminary fuss, and joined the Ogaden caravan at Berbera just as it was starting, I feel convinced that we would have succeeded.'[49]

In this instance, there is little doubt that he was right.

On 3rd April he arrived at Berbera, where he was welcomed by his two companions. Four days later, on the 7th, Burton sailed in on board the Indian Navy's schooner *Mahi*, only a few hours after the arrival of an enormous trading caravan from Harar. The strength and size of the caravan impressed Speke tremendously:

'Down the whole breadth of the plain, like a busy stream of ants, they came in single file, one camel's nose tied to his leader's tail. Immediately on their flanks were Somali, armed with spear and bow, the men who tended them and looked after the loading. Outside them again were occasional detachments of men riding ponies, all armed, and guarding the caravan from sudden surprise or attack. In this caravan alone there were about three thousand people, as many head of cattle, and 500 or more slaves, all driven chained together for sale in the market.'[50]

By contrast, Burton's camp was comparatively small and vulnerable in face of any large-scale onslaught. The tents housing the four Englishmen were pitched in a line, each one twelve yards apart from its neighbour; Stroyan's stood on the landward side, Burton and Herne shared another in the middle, and Speke occupied the third nearest the sea. The rest of the camp included three abbans, commanded by, and including, the Balyuz, and some thirty-three other followers consisting of servants, guards and camel-drivers—'in all about forty souls'. Forty to fifty camels and half a dozen ponies comprised the baggage train.

In order to conserve their energy for the months ahead, Burton had only two sentries to guard the encampment at night. To begin with, one of his companions would inspect the sentries during their watch to make sure they had not fallen asleep, but, as time went by, this slender precaution was dropped, and the men, one at the front and the other at the rear, kept their vigil undisturbed.

'In this isolated position,' wrote Speke, 'we felt no alarm for our safety, as long at least as we remained on the sea-shore, deeming the Somal would never be so imprudent as to attack us in such a vital place to them as Berbera, where their whole interests of life were centred, and where, by the simple process of blockading, we could so easily take retribution in any way we liked.'[51]

Comforted by the illusion, the party organised itself for the journey, each member of Burton's group being assigned to a special duty. Burton of course remained the leader, interesting himself in ethnology and linguistics and, in addition, acting as the expedition's chronicler. Herne assisted Stroyan, who had been appointed surveyor and also undertook the work of geology and photography. Speke 'was to be a Jack-of-all-trades, assisting everybody, looking after the interests of the men, portioning out their rations, setting the guards, and collecting specimens of natural history in all its branches'.[52]

On 9th April, the Ogaden caravan, under whose protection Burton had promised Outram he would travel, left Berbera. Burton, who impatiently awaited the arrival of mail and some equipment from England, imprudently decided to let the caravan go. This final act of procrastination overtaxed the patience of the Somali and brought the force of their wrath full down upon his head and the heads of his friends.

By the 18th, virtually nothing remained of the Fair. That evening, while Burton was entertaining the captain and crew of an Arab buggalow which had brought over a handful of Somali and their wives intent upon marching to their homes, the sharp challenge of the rear guard, followed by the rattle of musketry, broke the peaceful atmosphere of coffee-drinking and conversation. Three strangers were sighted, leading their ponies towards the camp, walking unconcernedly at their heads in face of the gunfire. Speke shouted to the guard to cease firing at once, and, having reprimanded them for wasting ammunition contrary to orders, led the three horsemen across to Burton's tent for interrogation.

Burton soon concluded that their presence did not constitute a threat. Their story was plausible – seeing a strange vessel moored offshore, they had come to investigate. Were there not rumours current that Shamarkay of Zayla wished to possess Berbera? Therefore might not the ship have contained materials brought for the construction of a fort? Even the Balyuz, wrote Burton later, 'with all his acuteness, was deceived'.[53]

The Balyuz's statement was different: 'I did not believe their assertion,' he said, 'and recommended that eight or nine additional men should be set to watch that night.'[54] Be that as it may, the abban managed to recognise two of the spies: one was Dublay of the Ali Ahmed, the other, Mahomed of the Sahil (a sept of the Eesa Moosa); the third rider, a lad of perhaps sixteen, he did not know. The Balyuz was certain that Dublay took part in the events which ensued, and saw him riding near by the following day.

The four travellers retired to sleep at the usual hour. 'Shortly after midnight, probably at one or two a.m.' the silence was shattered by a deluge of yelling, the rushing of many feet, gunshots, and bits of wood and stones being hurled about, some of which fell directly upon Speke's tent. Implying that he was first into the fray, Speke wrote: 'I bounced out of bed, with pistol and dirk in hand, and ran across to the central tent to know what was the matter, and if we were to have any shooting.'[55] Burton, fumbling with his revolver, told him: 'Be sharp, and arm to defend the camp.' Speke, who had stepped out in front of Burton's 'Rowtie', was suddenly hit on the right knee by a stone. Although he had been looking in that direction, he could not see the thrower, so, thinking to get a better view, he quickly dodged back under the fly of the tent. Seeing the move, Burton snapped out: 'Don't step back, or they will think we are retiring.'

Enraged by his commander's rebuke, Speke ran forward into the gloom, firing at three men in rapid succession, dropping two of them. A fourth appeared and then others, who crowded in, surrounding him completely. He thrust the muzzle of his Deane

Adams five-shot* revolver at the chest of the nearest and pulled the trigger, but the weapon's cylinder had jammed. Next moment a tremendous club-stroke on the chest felled him, gasping for breath upon the ground, with a dozen of the Somali on top of him. The seconds which followed were quite hair-raising. Speke later stated, 'whilst I was being pinioned they felt my private parts'[56] – in fact the natives were searching for concealed weapons, but being ignorant of their motive, he lay in fear of imminent castration, knowing how some tribes in the area practised this form of 'unmanly mutilation'.

Presently he was tied with his hands behind his back and led away through the rear of the camp, on the end of a rope. His chest was swollen where the war-club had struck him over the lungs. His wrists were bound so tight that the blood stopped. At each step he nearly collapsed, for he could scarcely draw breath. At length Speke begged his captor to tie his hands in front of him, to relieve the strain on his chest, and to bring him a mouthful of water to quench his thirst. As he lay, dazed and in pain, he was taunted by the Somali, particularly by a raga-muffin donkey-boy, who, like a shade of the 'naughty boy', Prince Abdullah, walked round him, jeering, and assuring him that death was imminent. All night he lay, surrounded by wounded and dying Somali, until, in the dawn light, he could perceive the broken mass of the encampment, the livestock and luggage boxes standing about untouched, but the tents flattened and not one of his companions in sight.

In the dawn twilight Speke's captor, linking arms with two of his comrades, made a victory circuit of the camp, singing in 'deep stentorian voices' a tune which kept pace with their solemn marching. The ritual over, the three singers joined the rest of the tribesmen in plundering the stores, a sickening sight, as Speke aptly described it, '. . . very like that of an Indian poultry-yard, when some entrails are thrown amongst the chickens, and every fowl tries to rob the other'.[57]

While the pillaging continued, Speke was guarded by an-other, more savage-looking Somali, carrying a heavy spear. At one moment three others approached him and amused them-

---

* See F. Wilkinson, *Small Arms*, Ward, Lock & Co., 1965, plates 149, 150. There is a Deane Adams pattern 54-bore revolver displayed in the arms collection at Blair Castle, Blair Atholl, Perthshire.

selves by cutting the air above his face with their sabres, grimacing frightfully, and evidently determined to break his nerve. But he lay quietly watching their every movement, without flinching or uttering a sound.

Suddenly word flashed among the plunderers that another tribe had heard of the attack and was on its way to wrest the spoils from its rivals. Instantly the encampment cleared, the oldest men being first away, 'flying in long jumps' over the plain. Speke's guard, however, did not join them at once, but instead walked back towards his prisoner and raised his spear. What followed is taken from Speke's own account.

'My jailer, who was still holding the string, stepped up close to me, and coolly stabbed me with his spear. I then raised my body a little in defence, when he knocked me down by jabbing his spear violently on my shoulder, almost cutting the jugular arteries. I rose again as he poised his spear, and caught the next prod, which was intended for my heart, on the back of one of my shackled hands; this gouged the flesh up to the bone. The cruel villain now stepped back a pace or two, to get me off my guard, and dashed his spear down to the bone of my left thigh. I seized it violently with both my hands, and would not have relinquished the gripe until he drew a shillelah from his girdle, and gave me such a violent blow on my left arm, I thought the bone was broken, and the spear fell helplessly from my hands. Finding his spear too blunt for running me through by a simple job when standing still, he now dropped the rope-end, walked back a dozen paces, and, rushing on me with savage fury, plunged his spear through the thick part of my right thigh into the ground, passing it between the thigh-bone and the large sinew below.

'With the action of lightning, seeing that death was inevitable if I remained lying there a moment longer, I sprang upon my legs, and gave the miscreant such a sharp back-hander in the face with my double-bound fists that he lost his presence of mind, and gave me a moment's opportunity to run away; which, by the Lord, I lost no time in doing, taking very good care, by holding my hands on one side, not to allow the dangling rope to trip me up. I was almost naked, and quite bare upon the feet, but I ran over the shingly beach towards the sea like wildfire. The man followed me a little way, but, finding I had the foot of him, threw his spear like a javelin, but did not strike me, for I bobbed, and allowed it to pass safely over my head; he then gave up the chase. Still I had at least forty more men to pass through, who were scattered all

Lieutenant Richard Burton in 1854

Speke's African guide, 'Bombay'

about the place, looking for what property they could pick up, before I could get safe away. These men, seeing the chase, all tried to cut off my retreat.

'However, I dodged them all by turns, running fast across them, and bobbing as they threw their spears after me, until I reached the shore when I had the satisfaction of seeing the last man give up the pursuit and leave me to myself. I was now fast fainting from loss of blood, and sat gently on a mound of sand, picked the knots which bound my hands open with my teeth, and exposed my breast to the genial influences of the refreshing sea-breeze, which at sunrise, as this was, is indescribably pleasant.'[58]

Burton, in the Postscript to *First Footsteps*, commented that 'Lieut. Speke's escape was in every way wonderful.' Concluding a description of the adventure, he wrote:

'When pursuit was discontinued . . . he staggered on to the town, where some old women directed him to us. Then pursuing his way, he fell in with the party sent to seek him, and by their aid reached the craft, having walked and run at least three miles, after receiving eleven wounds, two of which had pierced his thighs. A touching lesson how difficult it is to kill a man in sound health!'[59]

Speke, alas, was not the only one to suffer as a result of the Somali attack. Burton received a tremendous spear-thrust in the face which, according to Lady Burton's *Life*, 'carried away four back teeth and part of his palate'. The spear, which stuck fast in his jaw, could not be removed until after he had boarded the buggalow, which was fortunately still moored near the shore. The scar was permanent and can be seen in the famous portrait painted by Lord Leighton. Herne, although beaten up with war-clubs, came the least injured out of the affray. William Stroyan, the favourite of the party, was killed.

Stroyan had been speared through the heart; his head had been gashed and his stomach ripped open by another spear cut. His body which bore the marks of heavy clubbing had even been mutilated after death. The young lieutenant's murder cast a morbid gloom across the future, and left the three survivors feeling depressed and miserable. Speke later wrote of his dead companion: 'For courage, daring, and enterprise, as well as good-fellowship, there never lived a man more worthy of esteem than poor Stroyan.'[60]

SPEKE

With the ruin of his camp, the high hopes held by Burton and his friends for exploring Equatorial Africa were roughly dashed out upon the ground. All prospects of the expedition south had been totally destroyed in the space of a terrible few hours. The dream was replaced instead by feelings of numb grief, shock and bitter anger against the killers of Stroyan.

When, that night, the donkey-boy had glanced down at Speke as he lay trussed and silent upon the sand, and had asked him lightly whither he was bound, Speke, even then, had managed to answer confidently, 'Zanzibar'. Now Zanzibar had become no more to him than a word, an empty name, and was no longer the objective at the end of a long, exciting journey that was to come.

NOTES

1. Richard Francis Burton: *First Footsteps in East Africa*, New Edition edited by Mr. Gordon Waterfield: Routledge & Kegan Paul, Travellers and Explorers series, London 1966. Introduction, pp. 20–1.
2. Letter from Burton to Dr. Norton Shaw, Secretary of the Royal Geographical Society, dated Cairo, 16 November, 1853. Burton MS. collection, R.G.S. archives, London.
3. An MS article on Outram, written by Burton and now in the collection of Mr. Quentin Keynes, describes how Outram and his brother Francis, as the result of a furious dispute that occurred during a tiger hunt, are said to have fired rifle-shots at each other in their anger.
4. J. H. Speke: *What led to the Discovery of the Source of the Nile*, William Blackwood & Sons, Edinburgh and London, 1864, p. 2.
5. Burton: *Zanzibar; City, Island and Coast*, 2 vols., vol. II, London, 1872, pp. 373–4.
6. *The Life of Captain Sir Richard F. Burton, K.C.M.G., F.R.G.S.*, by Lady Isabel Burton, 2 vols., Chapman and Hall, 1893, vol 1, p. 315.
7. Burton: *Zanzibar: City, Island and Coast*. 2 vols., vol II, London, 1872.
8. Speke: *What led . . .*, p. 22.
9. *Ibid.*, p. 23.
10. Capt. William Speke of Jordans, who married Georgina Eliza-

beth Hanning of Dillington in 1824, had tenancy of Orleigh Court from that date until 1844.

11. Letter from Joseph Wolff, vicar of Tole Brewer, Somerset, to Mrs. Colonel Lowe, 8th November 1850. By courtesy of Mr. Quentin Keynes.

12. This fact is recorded in *The Nile Quest* by Sir Harry Johnston, 1903, although no source is given. Mrs. Fawn M. Brodie has observed in her biography of Burton, *The Devil Drives* (1967), that the date of Edward Speke's death corresponds to that of his brother, Hanning, six years later. A wall plaque in the Speke vault at Dowlish Wake church, Somerset, commemorates Edward's death.

13. This information was furnished to the author in consequence of researches made by Mrs. Hugh Hanning of Blackheath, London, S.E.3.

14. Burton: *Zanzibar*, vol. II, p. 373.

15. *Ibid.*, p. 373.

16. Charles St. John: *Wild Sports and Natural History of the Highlands*, John Murray, London, 1846, Introduction, p. 6 (1924 reprint).

17. Burton: *Zanzibar*, vol. II, p. 373. Speke's commander in the Punjab War, Sir Colin Campbell (1792–1863), was born in Glasgow, the son of a carpenter. Like Sir Hugh Gough (1779–1869), under whom Speke served in Multan, Campbell, who later became Lord Clyde, served also in the West Indies, China and the Peninsular War.

18. *Ibid.*, p. 373.

19. Lady Isabel Burton: *Life of Sir Richard F. Burton*, 2 vols., Chapman and Hall, 1893.

20. Speke: *What led . . .*, p. 3.

21. *Ibid.*, p. 3.

22. Letter from Speke to Dr. Norton Shaw, 31 Mount Street, W.1, 30th June 1859.

23. John Blackwood in a letter to Speke dated 3rd November 1859. By courtesy of William Blackwood & Sons, 45 George Street, Edinburgh.

24. Speke to John Blackwood. The letter dated 5th November 1859 was written from Monk's Park, Corsham, Wiltshire, the home of William Speke Esq., J.P., the explorer's elder brother.

25. *The Life of Sir Richard F. Burton*, vol. I, p. 315.

26. *Ibid.*, pp. 315–16.

27. Speke: *What led . . .*, p. 59.

28. *Ibid.*, p. 46.

29. *Ibid.*, p. 47.

30. *Ibid.*, p. 93.

31. *Ibid.*, pp. 64–5.
32. *Ibid.*, p. 58.
33. *Ibid.*, p. 73.
34. *Ibid.*, p. 72.
35. *Ibid.*, p. 15.
36. *Ibid.*, p. 13.
37. *Ibid.*, p. 14.
38. Burton: *Abeokuta and the Cameroons Mountains* (1863), vol. 1, pp. 110–11.
39. Speke: *What led . . .*, pp. 84, 86–7.
40. *Ibid.*, p. 85–6.
41. *Ibid.*, p. 88.
42. *Ibid.*, p. 106.
43. Burton: *Zanzibar,* vol. II, p. 383.
44. Speke: *What led . . .*, p. 109.
45. Burton: referring to Speke's diary, appendix I, *First Footsteps,* 1st edition, 1856, pp. 502, 503.
46. Captain (later Sir Robert) Lambert Playfair. See note in *First Footsteps,* 1966 edition, p. 306, ref. chapter *Burton Attacked in Official Reports.*
47. Burton: *First Footsteps,* 1856, appendix I, pp. 502, 503.
48. Speke: *What led . . .*, p. 115–16.
49. *Ibid.*, p. 144.
50. *Ibid.*, p. 125.
51. *Ibid.*, p. 128.
52. *Ibid.*, p. 126.
53. Burton: the Postscript to *First Footsteps in East Africa,* 1856.
54. *First Footsteps,* 1966 edition. Statement made by Mohamed Gooled, the Balyuz, taken from the official report in the India Office Library and transcribed for the first time by Mr. Gordon Waterfield.
55. Speke: *What led . . .*, p. 131.
56. Speke in his official report, quoted as footnote to *First Footsteps,* 1966, p. 256.
57. Speke: *What led . . .*, p. 137.
58. *Ibid.*, pp. 138–9, 140.
59. Burton: *First Footsteps,* Postscript, new edition (1966), p. 257.
60. Speke: *What led . . .*, p. 142.

❧❦❧❦❧❦❧

CHAPTER 2

WAR, AND AN UNEXPECTED INVITATION

❧❦❧❦❧❦❧

SPEKE, in the company of Burton and Herne, sailed from the Somali coast on 20th April and arrived in Aden two days later. The bronzed young hunter, who had left the port only seven months before aglow with health and high spirits, returned 'a miserable-looking cripple, dreadfully emaciated from loss of blood . . .'. His arms and legs were twisted grotesquely by muscular contractions; his body was a mass of lacerations and purple contusions.

An acquaintance, Lieutenant Dansey, at once set aside a room at his house to which Speke was brought, and there he lay, watched over by Outram's successor, Colonel Coghlan, who sat tearful and anxious at the foot of the bed. The Acting Civil Surgeon, who examined Speke at the hotel to which he first went before being moved to Dansey's, shared the subsequent opinions of several other doctors that only three years' leave and complete rest in England would ensure his recovery. In fact, the fearful spear wounds healed incredibly quickly and Speke was restored to almost perfect health a month or so afterwards![1] His arduous Himalayan apprenticeship, clean living and the continuous hard exercise to which he had been for so long a slave, had now paid dividends by saving his life against odds which would certainly have vanquished any ordinary man.

A wave of criticism and remonstrance was quick to follow. Added to the wails of the timid who, from the beginning, had predicted the expedition's failure came a series of stinging official rebukes, mainly directed at Burton. Far from attracting praise, Burton's swashbuckling character and spirit of reckless adventure provided a convenient target for the many in authority who envied his ability or had perhaps already felt the

43

rough edge of his tongue. The tragedy at Berbera gave these men a marvellous opportunity for venting their pent-up spite and many took immediate advantage of it.[2]

Coghlan, in spite of his concern for Speke's life, spoke out unequivocally against what he believed to be the 'want of caution and vigilance' so marked in Burton's provisions for safeguarding the encampment. While noting that the tragedy made it disagreeable to criticise, he felt that criticism was justified. The attack, he added, had caused a 'serious embarrassment of our already complicated relations with the political range [?] of this Residency'.[3] Coghlan did not believe, as Burton did, that the motive for the attack was solely plunder, nor did he concede that its violence had been occasioned only by resistance. Yet, overall, Coghlan's report was a fair one. In it, he recommended a blockade of the Somali coast, a punishment far more effective than any direct military reprisal, and also a heavy fine of fifteen thousand rupees, which was a matter of twelve hundred rupees, or £120, over and above the total loss sustained by Burton's expedition.

The Governor-General of India, Lord Dalhousie, although he agreed with Coghlan's suggestion of a blockade, considered it a pity that the subject of a fine had ever been mentioned. Surveying the evidence in far-off India, his Lordship thought it a mistake that the conduct of Burton and his friends had not been severely censured. In the light of the material presented to him, Dalhousie concluded by stating that the officers concerned could press no claims whatsoever on Government, for the reimbursement of their losses. In Speke's case the loss of cash and property amounted to £510, a sum almost equal to the combined losses of his three companions. On the other hand, the survivors, Burton, Herne and Speke, were united in the firm belief that there had been no chance of making a better stand against the Somali, who had outnumbered them by five to one. Speke and Burton went further, denouncing the cowardice displayed by the main body of their followers, but, as numbers of these were, in Speke's words, 'raw recruits', they could hardly be blamed for running away.

The collation of new evidence, including the relevant India Office reports, by Mr. Gordon Waterfield, has highlighted certain discrepancies in the various accounts of the attack, and the fact that the views of the members of the party so strongly oppose that of the Government makes it worth while to describe them. Speke's statement, as prepared for the India Office records, began thus:

> 'I was awoke about 3 a.m. [in *What led* . . . he wrote 'probably at one or two A.M.'] on the morning of the 19th by hearing Lieut. Burton crying out to Lieut. Stroyan, "Get up, old fellow"— almost at the same instant I heard the report of three discharges from firearms as if fired in a volley . . . the sound proceeded from the rear of my tent; conceiving it to be nothing but firing to keep off persons supposed to be prowling about the camp, or in other words a false alarm, I remained in my tent.'[4]

In *What led* . . . Speke referred only to sounds of hurried movement and firing, but did not mention that Burton attempted to rouse Stroyan; he went on to say that, on hearing the shooting, after his 'tent shook as if it would come down' when beaten by clubs and sticks, he 'bounced out of bed . . . and ran across to the central tent to know what was the matter'. It is especially difficult to understand why, in the official report, he should have stated that after the sounds of firing he stayed in his tent, thinking it to signify nothing of importance when, only the previous evening, he had lost his temper with the guard for shooting over the heads of the three strangers and had instructed them that, if opposed, they must 'fire into, and not over, their object'.

Why, therefore, should he suddenly have ceased to regard the sound of near-by firing as unworthy of immediate investigation? Burton's version was again slightly different:

> 'Hearing a rush of men like a stormy wind, I sprang up, called for my sabre, and sent Lieut. Herne to ascertain the force of the foray . . . Lieut. Herne . . . rejoining me, declared that the enemy was in great force and the guard nowhere. Meanwhile, I had aroused Lieuts. Stroyan and Speke, who were sleeping in the extreme right and left tents.'[5]

The fact that in *What led* . . . Speke did not mention that Burton roused him may be explained by the bitter animosity which he felt for Burton at the time of writing, 1864. But still unexplained is his slow reaction to the gunfire, especially as in *What led* . . . he confirmed that the appearance of the strangers had made him uneasy and that in spite of their convincing excuses, he 'did not like the cool manner in which the men walked in under fire'.

Discussing the attack in a letter to Lambert Playfair, dated Jordans, Ilminster, 3rd September 1859, Speke referred sarcastically to his leader's role:

'. . . I cannot answer for Burton, all I saw about him . . . was that from the onset until I last saw him he was engaged in loading his pistol *within* his tent. I never for a moment saw him out of it, but that Herne was ready is proved by his having advanced, at Burton's order I believed, to check the advance of the plunderers.'[6]

Apart from the direct imputation of cowardice on the part of Burton, Speke, in the last phrase, supported Burton's view of the motive for the attack. Like Burton, he too was much annoyed by a statement contained in Playfair's book, *A History of Arabia Felix*, published in Bombay in 1859. Playfair wrote:

'During the afternoon of the same day [18 April, 1855], three men visited the camp, *probably as spies*, and, as such, *the officers of the expedition were warned against them by their native attendants*. Heedless of this warning, they retired to rest at night, in the fullest confidence of security, and without taking any extra *or even ordinary measures* to guard against surprise . . . the following morning, the expedition was attacked by a body of from 150 to 200 well-armed Somalis.'

(The italics were later inserted by Burton, when quoting the passage in *The Lake Regions of Central Africa*, 1860.)

Burton dismissed Playfair's criticisms with contempt. 'I received no warning of personal danger,' he wrote in *The Lake Regions* . . . 'The "ordinary measures", that is to say, the posting of two sentinels in front and rear of the camp during the night were taken, and I cannot blame myself because they ran away.'[7]

Although Jami Hasan, Stroyan's former abban, stated that 'Mr. Burton said that if a thousand attacked him he had no fear',[8] Lieutenant George Herne was convinced that the sheer weight of warriors hurled against them had decided the issue. He commented in his report, 'Had any of the guard or Somalis stood, we should have resisted the attack, but under such over-powering numbers we had no chance.'[9] Nor did Speke believe that the ordinary guard had been inadequate; in an answer to the criticisms made by Playfair in his book, he justified its size and disposition.

'I placed only two, because I felt it would only have distressed the guard and have made them discontented without producing any benefit had I put more on. Of this I told Burton, Herne and Stroyan, and all agreed. I still maintain that the guard could not have been better disposed of than it was that night and so far I did my duty. If there was any error at all, except Burton's own confessed upreparedness, it was that no officer was on watch. This we did considerately and with the full belief that we had better reserve ourselves for the interior. . . .'[10]

Yet, while he expressed such confidence in his judgement, he fully agreed with Herne that, for effectual resistance, the odds had proved much too great: '. . . If *all* the guard had been on sentry that night and, if we had *all* been awake, I am certain that we could not have resisted the attack . . .'.[11] The statement made by the Balyuz reinforced Speke's views on the adequacy of the guard. He had been sleeping in the open between the tents occupied by Burton and Stroyan.

'About midnight I heard the sentries – one of whom was posted on either flank . . . call out "Get up! Get up!" They did not come towards me but remained in the position in which they formerly were. As soon as I heard the shout I immediately jumped on my feet and seized my arms and looked about. I saw a crowd approaching; they were about thirty yards off, and appeared to have come from the south, skirting the west . . . they were then all on foot.'[12]

As much as anything, Speke felt bitter at the Government's casual attitude to the expedition's personal losses; he had striven hard to save sufficient money for a private journey and had given of it freely not merely to further his aims by travelling with Burton, but also to assist his commandant in a moment when funds were limited. This, and an upsurge of his rather Old Testament sense of justice, prompted him to write to Playfair on 24th October 1859: 'Nothing would have appeared more just to the Somali . . . than treating them in accordance with their own laws, of taking like for like – blood or money – and they owed us both and should have paid us both . . .'[13] In the same letter, Speke affirmed that he had no intention of allowing the question of compensation to rest: 'When I have done my next journey [meaning the expedition to the Victoria Nyanza with Captain J. A. Grant, A.M.] and have time to get about it, I shall move for an appeal to Government for an investigation into the matter in a more general way.'

But no investigation was every promoted. In October 1855, when Speke and Burton were serving in the Crimea, a letter reached Playfair at Aden during Coghlan's absence on a coastal cruise. The letter, written by the elders of the Ayyal Nuh, a sub-tribe of the Habr Awal, confirmed Somali fears that the presence of the English expeditionaries had revealed the existence of official designs upon their country. With reference to Burton's party and the attack in general, the letter read: '. . . the fault is with the English, not the Ayal Noh, not upon the Habr Awal but upon those who cover the country. . . . We are not to blame, all the blame is with the English gentlemen.'[14] The comment recalled the tribesmen's efforts to persuade Burton to accompany them on his journey south after the termination of the Fair. Playfair was exultant: 'Brigadier Coghlan's original opinions relative to the atrocity are fully borne out by it,' he wrote.[15]

The Ayyal Nuh's letter was backed by a deputation of elders from the Habr Awal, who arrived at Aden to visit Coghlan on 15th October. So skilfully did they negotiate, that Coghlan was moved to report yet again to Lord Dalhousie, this time stating that he had not, until that moment, been in full possession of the facts and explaining that, despite the Governor-General's request, no steps could be taken to apprehend the murderers of Lieutenant Stroyan. To do so, even assisted by the Habr Awal, was likely to bring about a full-scale war, and so for the time being the men, known to be members of the Eesa Moosa tribe, must go free.

When Dalhousie challenged Coghlan's submission that at the

request of the Habr Awal the coastal blockade should be lifted, the Resident replied, restating his case, and assuring Dalhousie that previous Somali evidence had been sadly wanting in accuracy and overflowing with contradictions. Thus no fair retribution was exacted for Stroyan's death or for the appalling injuries inflicted upon Speke and Burton. The Government, apparently satisfied that it had fulfilled its obligations to the letter (an opinion shared by the Aden authorities), paid not a penny of compensation. In fact, as Speke pointed out, the Government possibly gained by the Berbera affair:

'. . . taking advantage of the disruption, [the Government] turned everything to their own advantage: by making the robbery of our kit by the Somali a penalty on them to stop their slave trade, and so the Government enhanced their own requirements to the detriment of us, the prime losers'.

Of his own position, Speke harboured no illusions: he told Playfair: 'I am a great loser by reputation as well as by pocket in consequence of the failure and feel very sour about it as you may suppose . . .'.[16] Perhaps better than any other the concluding paragraph of a letter written by Speke to Playfair on 3rd September 1859 summed up the outcome of his catastrophic sojourn in the Somali country. Reflecting on its faults and dangers, he wrote:

'Burton's defying danger and bragging, as well as the Somalis' intimidating speeches (although so much remarked upon), I regard as only so much clap-trap and not deserving of any notice. If a man is to be frightened by men who live by lying and tricking everybody they can, travelling amongst them should cease. The matter rests on this: either we were equal to penetrating the country or we were not, for we could not always have been dependent on any supporting caravans. Again if we were not to hazard anything, we could not expect to gain anything and therefore, if the Government were not prepared to risk on this occasion as they would have done in any case of war, they should not have promoted the project at all . . .'[17]

By the time Speke returned to England in June 1855, the war raging in the Crimea had come through its first terrible winter;

cholera, malaria, malnutrition and the awful penetrating cold had claimed many thousands of victims, while a series of grossly mismanaged actions had buried thousands more. With recruitment at its height, Speke, who by then felt fit and unattracted by the prospect of further convalescence, wrote immediately to a certain Major Graham who had been appointed by the Horse Guards to sign on officers for General Vivian's contingent.

Giving him a fortnight to collect his kit and take leave of his family, Graham arranged that Speke should sail out to Constantinople and there join one of the Turkish regiments. He was upgraded to the rank of captain and made second in command under a Major Greene. Greene's regiment, which had been stationed in Buyukdere, soon afterwards took ship for Kertch in the Crimea and there remained throughout the closing stages of the war. The captaincy must have appealed to Speke who in India, like Burton, had never risen above the level of lieutenant. One suspects that, obliging as his Indian commanders had been, they had soon perceived, in spite of his distinguished record, that soldiering was by no means Speke's first love.

Once more we find that Speke kept no written account of this interlude between his explorations; there is no indication as to how his plans were developing, no revelation of his hopes, save for one scant but important reference contained in Philip Henderson's biography of Laurence Oliphant. Oliphant recalled that both he and his father had met Speke briefly in Constantinople, where he had spoken of his ambition to revisit Africa and discover the sources of the White Nile.[18] Clearly his friendship with Burton had altered the emphasis on his motives for African travel, and the settlement of one of geography's greatest enigmas had to a large extent superseded the hitherto uncomplicated desire to shoot and accumulate interesting trophies. Speke's curiosity may well have been stimulated by the rumours which he had heard of a huge inland lake, or sea while living in Kurrum the previous March: 'The Somali', he wrote, 'described its dimensions as equal in extent to the Gulf of Aden, and further alluded to its being navigated by white men. None of the men present had been there to see it, though it was currently known as a positive fact amongst them.'[19] Yet, despite its fascinating similarity to the story told by Krapf and relayed to him by Burton, Speke had apparently paid as little heed to this as he had to the other. He continued: 'I did not believe this story in the light they expressed it, supposing they confounded an inland sea with the Western or Atlantic Ocean.'

But if indeed Speke had cherished the hope that after the war he might resume his original plans for exploring Central Africa, it seems that as the campaign progressed he grew more and more pessimistic about carrying them out. In *What led . . .*, he stated openly his fear that 'there would be no further chance of . . . being able to return to Africa . . .' To compensate, he set about organising a hunting expedition to the Caucasus Mountains with a friend, Edmund Smyth, of Welwyn, Hertfordshire, whom he laughingly described as 'an old and notorious Himalayan sportsman'. In the villages dwelled strange tribes of skilled wild horsemen, whilst in the Caucasian forests and upon the hills there lived a profusion of bears, wolves, chamois and mountain sheep.* By the time the war ended, Speke had purchased most of his equipment, including guns and rifles, thereby showing that his purpose was fixed.[20]

With Smyth he wrote to the Secretary of the Royal Geographical Society, asking for assistance in obtaining the passports required to cross over into Russian territory. A few weeks later Shaw's reply arrived stating bleakly that, because of the war, passports were almost impossible to procure and that, the moment for such a venture being ill-chosen, it would be wise to abandon it altogether.

However, Shaw's letter added that another expedition to explore the unknown heart of Central Africa was at that very instant being organised by Captain Richard Burton, and strongly advised Speke to join it. The same mail brought an invitation from Burton himself, stating that the enterprise had the support of the Home as well as the Indian Government and stressing that, unlike the Somali affair, no expenses would be incurred by his acceptance.

If Speke felt a momentary pang of pity for poor Smyth, it was

---

* Excellent descriptions of the life and environment of the Caucasus are contained in two works by the late Agube Gudsow, a native of Vladicavcas. These are: *The Princess Biaslantt* (Heinemann, 1926) and *The Unknown Land* (an unpublished MS. at present in the possession of the author, c. 1940).

quickly swamped by his elation at the unbelievable prospect of returning so soon to Africa; if, in view of the outcome of Berbera and the Wady Nogal mission, he paused to consider why Burton had selected him for a second expedition, he hurriedly dismissed his doubts. Bidding farewell to his companion, who evidently accepted the disappointment like a gentleman, Speke hastened back to England, travelling night and day until he reached London. There he went at once to call on Burton, from whom he received the general outlines of the proposed journey.

At the offices of the Royal Geographical Society in Whitehall Place Speke saw, displayed on one of the walls, a map which the German missionaries Erhardt and Rebmann had compiled and sent to the Society in 1855. This map, together with its accompanying memoir on hydrography, had sparked off the support for Burton's proposals and with it, a howling controversy; it depicted an enormous lake eight hundred miles in length by three hundred miles in breadth, stretching from the equator to the fourteenth degree of south latitude. Its shape was ugly, like that of some 'gigantic slug' or salamander, and its appearance so extraordinary, so incredible, that, as Speke remarked '. . . everybody who looked at it . . . laughed and shook his head'.[21]

Admiral Sir George Back, famed for his Arctic journey to the Fish River, rightly insisted that the authenticity of the map could only be proved or discounted by a practical investigation. He therefore recommended that Burton's scheme of marching inland from Zanzibar should be accepted. The President of the Royal Geographical Society, Sir Roderick Murchison, used his personal influence at the Treasury to secure a grant of £1,000 for the expedition, but unfortunately a similar sum which had been promised by Colonel W. H. Sykes, Chairman of the Court of Directors of the East India Company, was later cancelled and Burton's officer's pay substituted as the Company's contribution. Without doubt the Berbera affair and Burton's stinging report were responsible for this withdrawal, as a result of which the expedition fell critically short of money.

At this point, Speke decided to back out. For one thing, he did not wish to obligate himself to Burton financially; for another, he had already spent and lost an appreciable amount on the Somali expedition. On the other hand, Erhardt and Rebmann, Dr. John Steinhaeuser and Corporal Church of West Africa, all of whom Burton had invited to accompany him, were either unable to accept or else refused, as in the case of Rebmann, for personal reasons. In the end, Speke alone remained to share the ordeal of the Lake Regions expedition and to help Burton overcome the serious deficiency in its funds. It was largely Murchison's assurance of certain repayment coupled with his enthusiastic encouragement that finally determined Speke yet again to sink private resources into one of Burton's projects and go with him. It seems probable that the recurring fear that Burton might beat him to the discovery of the Nile sources may also have influenced his decision, but without definite proof this is mere supposition. Nor did money prove to be the only hurdle.

In 1856 the Indian Government had begun to strengthen its Indo-European forces in general, and in particular its complement of European officers. An order had been issued forbidding any extension of overseas leave and confining the location of officers' duty to India. Thus India House, while privately favouring Speke's request to join Burton, felt obliged to withhold its permission. Here was a calamity. Having abandoned his plans for hunting in the Caucasus, having steeled himself to the heavy expenditure of exploring Africa anew, the opportunity so nearly within his grasp had in the end eluded him.

But relinquish his hold upon it he would not. Accompanied by Burton, Speke travelled to Bombay to explain his predicament in person to the Governor, Lord Elphinstone. Elphinstone, a generous, far-sighted individual, at once appreciated the importance of the expedition and petitioned the Government. The petition was successful, and Anderson, the Government Secretary, agreed that the circumstances being exceptional, Speke should forthwith be released from ordinary duty.

After a week in Bombay spent collecting scientific instruments and equipment, the two men embarked in the Indian Navy's sloop *Elphinstone*, which at Burton's suggestion had been placed at their disposal. This political gesture was designed to ensure the local support of the Sultan of Zanzibar, Sultan Majid, by demonstrating that both Governments had guaranteed the venture. In this, it contrasted markedly with the pitiful shilly-shallying which had preceded and indeed paved the way for the disaster at Berbera.

Most significant of all, however, was the contrast of personalities between the travellers themselves. Each man had his own private reasons for going again to Africa, just as each proffered numerous and plausible excuses for taking the other as a companion. Burton respected Speke's unusual strength and bravery. He felt compassionate towards him, having lost so much hard-won capital in Somaliland and for the dreadful injuries he had received there. He knew him for a capable hunter and an eager, if occasionally moody, accomplice. In short, Burton considered it right that Speke should have a second chance, and for this reason he chose to overlook the failure of the Wady Nogal mission. Speke regarded Burton, who was six years older than himself, with a curious mixture of contempt and awe. He despised Burton's indifference to sport and slightly feared his intellectual capacity. Although he could hardly have failed to admire, perhaps secretly envy, his leader's facility in languages and extensive knowledge of tribal and national customs of the East, Speke's admiration was already somewhat diluted with mistrust, and feelings of suppressed anger at the consequences of the Somali expedition.

Burton had quite unfairly commandeered the specimens which Speke had so industriously sought for and obtained, an important collection comprising twenty mammals, thirty-six bird specimens, three reptiles, one fish, one scorpion and three specimens of *Coleoptera*. All these he had sent off under his own name to the zoologist, Edward Blyth, in Calcutta who identified them and published the results in volume XXIV of the *Journal of the Royal Asiatic Society of Bengal*. Blyth's learned sixteen-page report which was subsequently reprinted in London, in 1860, by N. Trübner and Co., contained only a few brief commentaries on the game-animals written by Speke. Not only that, Burton had taken possession of Speke's Somali diary, which he had slashed from 24,000 to 13,000 words in length, thereafter publishing it, rewritten in the third person, as an apparent afterthought tucked away at the end of his own book, *First Footsteps in East Africa*.[22]

In the same book Burton recorded his admonition, 'Don't step back or they will think we are retiring', the slighting remark which had so angered Speke during the Eesa Moosa's attack on the encampment, causing him to rush headlong at the approaching tribesmen. At the time, Speke had not retaliated, but had instead brooded over what he believed to be a deliberate insult; that Burton had seen fit to publish the episode in 1856 mystified and upset him even more. This remark, and the misappropriation of his diary and specimens, created a germ of bitter feeling between the younger and the older man, which did not die with the passing of time, but gradually expanded, growing steadily more malignant, until some four years later it flared up into the notorious quarrel generally associated with the Nile.

NOTES

1. Speke: *What led . . .*, p. 148. 'They literally closed as wounds do in an India rubber ball after prickings with a penknife.' In *First Footsteps*, 1966 edition, Mr. Gordon Waterfield has written on p. 260: 'Speke's wounds were so severe that it was surprising that he lived; his arms and legs were "contracted into indescribable positions", and he began to suffer from partial blindness.'
2. *First Footsteps*, 1966, pp. 260–76; *ibid.*, p. 1, ' "The human head once struck off does not regrow like the rose." '
3. *Ibid.*, p. 263.
4. *Ibid.*, p. 281.
5. Burton: Postscript to *First Footsteps*, new edition, 1966, p. 253.
6. Letter obtained from and published by courtesy of Sir Edward Playfair, who has given the author much generous assistance.
7. Burton: *The Lake Regions of Central Africa*, 2 vols., London, 1860, Vol. 1, p. 68 n.
8. *First Footsteps*, 1966, appendix 1, p. 278.
9. *Ibid.*, p. 281.
10. Letter from Speke to Captain R. L. Playfair, dated 24th October 1859. By courtesy of Sir Edward Playfair.
11. *Ibid.*
12. *First Footsteps*, 1966, p. 279.
13. Letter written from Jordans, Somerset. By courtesy of Sir Edward Playfair.
14. *First Footsteps*, 1966, pp. 267, 268.

15. *Ibid.*, p. 268.
16. Speke to Playfair, 24th October 1859. Letter made available by courtesy of Sir Edward Playfair.
17. Letter from Speke to Playfair, *First Footsteps*, 1966, p. 284.
18. Philip Henderson: *The Life of Laurence Oliphant*, London 1956, p. 52.
19. Speke: *What led* . . ., p. 116.
20. Having decided to make a journey Speke always first assured himself with a number of suitable weapons. A letter to John Blackwood written in August 1864 confirms this custom. Speke's chosen companion, Smyth, lived, when in England, at 'The Grange', Welwyn, Herts.
21. Speke: *What led* . . ., p. 156.
22. *First Footsteps*, 1966, p. 246 and fn.

✿✿✿✿✿✿✿✿✿

CHAPTER 3

LAKE TANGANYIKA AND BEYOND
1856–9

✿✿✿✿✿✿✿✿✿

AFTER a pleasant voyage lasting eighteen days, the *Elphinstone*, carrying Speke and Burton, hove in sight of Zanzibar. To Burton, the island seemed to pulsate with a femininity that was sensual and exotic: '. . . it showed no trace of mountain or crag, but was all voluptuous with gentle swellings, with the rounded contours of the girl-negress, and the brown-red tintage of its warm skin showed through its gauzy attire of green.'[1] As they drew closer, the nostrils of the travellers were assailed by a delicious, heavy perfume wafted towards them on the off-shore breeze. Describing the experience in his delightful volume *The White Nile*, Mr. Alan Moorehead has written:

'Their first view of the island cannot have been so very different from the scene one sees at the present time. Then, as now, a whiff of cloves and tropical spices came out to greet the traveller from the shore, and on the shore itself a slow, oily sea of marvellous blue washed up on to white coral beaches. The jungle that began at the water's edge was green with a hectic greenness, and although occasional rainstorms and even tornadoes swept the island it was oppressed throughout the year by a deep soporific heat.'

On the island itself, in Speke's day, all was not beauty, nor was its brilliant seashore undefiled. 'Rubbish of every kind floated by . . . and it was not unusual for a dead body to be seen among the debris.' Mr. Moorehead continues his description:

'There was worse to come when they got ashore. The population of Zanzibar Island was about 100,000 at this time, and most of the people were living in the town itself. In the crooked, dirty streets, barely 20 feet wide, a teeming procession went by of half-naked negroes, Arabs, Indians, Persians, Swahilis and many others.

Cattle and donkeys thrust their way into the crowd. Merchants, sitting cross-legged in holes in the walls, called out their wares, beggars reached up their hands to the passers-by, and over all in the stifling air hung the devastating smell of copra and decaying fish.'

But there amidst the noisy jumble of animals, merchandise and men, existed a phenomenon so stark and terrible as to draw an indelible line of demarcation which separates the present scene from that which Speke and Burton observed a century ago. The phenomenon was the slave.

'They roamed through every street, men, women and children, those who had been domesticated by years of captivity, and those who had just arrived from the interior and who were half mad and half dead through hunger and maltreatment . . .'.[2]

From the stinking holds of the slave ships that plied along the coast, the sick and dying were often thrown overboard to cut the duty payable on the human cargo. The sight of curs devouring their flesh upon the beaches was not uncommon. In 1860, Speke participated in the capture of a slaver carrying five hundred starving wretches, half its usual load, in 'ferret-box' conditions. He later wrote how even 'old women, stark naked',[3] were forced to lie tightly packed below the reeking decks.

Upon their arrival, on 20th December, Speke and his leader were met by the British Consul, a genial, hospitable Irishman called Atkins Hamerton, who had then been resident in Zanzibar for fifteen years. In spite of illness, Lieutenant-Colonel Hamerton possessed a seemingly unlimited fund of energy and high spirits. His house was the focus of all activity on the island and his word, even to the Sultan Majid himself, virtually law. Yet in a sense, the Consul's merriment and enthusiasm were contrived; although he was no more than fifty, sickness and boredom had bleached his hair pure white and had drained every vestige of colour from his face. He pined for his native Ireland, yet found it impossible to summon the drive required to pack his boxes and quit a climate which every day brought him nearer and nearer to death. The advent of Speke and Burton provided no more than a temporary release from the supine existence which eventually killed him. Hamerton nevertheless did everything in his power to help the expedition on its way. Only in one respect, the settlement of porters' pay, did he take less care to define the terms as accurately as he would have normally, and thus contributed to a subsequent dispute which his successor, Captain Rigby, was unable to resolve except on paper.

The journey into the interior did not commence until six months later. A series of unforeseen setbacks nibbled away the precious weeks. Dr. John Steinhaeuser, whose final permission to leave India and join the expedition had been delayed for months, eventually became ill and dropped out, while the fact that Speke and Burton had arrived at the height of the dry season, which that year had grown particularly arid, made serious travel inland an impossibility.

Meanwhile, Burton amassed careful notes covering almost every facet of life in Zanzibar, ranging from government and climate to the commerce of the brothel and the bazaar. The results, which litter the pages of his classic two-volume works, *The Lake Regions* and *Zanzibar*, can only be described as brilliant.

Speke, equally fascinated, wandered the streets, scribbling and observing, but his published account was a mere summary of Burton's, and lacked the subtlety, insight and penetration of the more experienced man. For Speke, many hours were devoted simply to organisation: 'Taking advantage of the time, especially the evenings, I spent most of them in rating the chronometers and getting all the surveying instruments into working order. . . . Captain Burton, besides book-making, busied himself in making all the other arrangements for the journey . . .'.[4]

At the mission run by Johann Rebmann near Kilwa, the travellers gained much information about Mount Kilimanjaro, which Rebmann had visited with Dr. Krapf in 1848. From Rebmann they learned that because of the drought, which had killed several hundreds of Masai cattle, the warrior-pastoralists had begun flighting down to the coast, raiding the Wanyika herds and spearing the herdsmen. In Zanzibar, Hamerton later reinforced the missionary's opinion that the direct route over the Masai plains, which Burton had intended to take, would be much too dangerous and that he should instead follow the circuitous, but infinitely safer, caravan route, established thirty years before, which passed through the Arab settlement of Kazeh (nowadays known as Tabora).

Had the expedition taken the Masai route from Mombasa, it would almost certainly have struck the Victoria Nyanza and possibly the Nile, whilst preceding by over twenty years the famous journey made by Joseph Thomson,* who, aged twenty-six, crossed the Masai plains and reached the eastern shore of the lake in December 1883.

Speke looked upon his leader's decision with evident disgust, declaring stoutly 'I thought we could easily have walked round the Masai . . .' and noting that Burton '. . . complained of the shock his nerves had received since the Somali encounter'.[5] Strange therefore that still in Zanzibar, Speke himself admitted to an unfamiliar nervousness or unease which he attributed to the sultry, storm-laden climate: '. . . I experienced a nervous sensibility I never knew before, of being startled at any sudden accident. A pen dropping from the table even would make me jump.'[6] Burton's attempts to persuade Rebmann to accompany the main expedition met with no success. The missionary knew the country along the coast and was familiar with the coast tribes and their languages; the Church Missionary Society had agreed to his absence for 'a specified time, say, 3, 4, or 6 months';[7] but, as Alan Moorehead has suggested, Rebmann turned the offer down because Burton refused to allow him to convert the natives along the route to Christianity.

In the course of an exploratory cruise southwards from Mombasa, Burton examined some Portuguese ruins contemporary with Vasco da Gama at the mouth of the Pangani river, and pored over fascinating Persian inscriptions at Tangata. Speke's interest in such activities was negligible and thus on a par with Burton's disdain for his 'flirtations with the hippopotami' at Tanga, further north. Wearily Burton noted that, at Tanga, 'sundry excursions delayed us six days'.

After a brief journey up the Pangani river, followed by a rapid march to the hills of Fuga, Speke, annoyed by the needlessly gruelling pace,† the daily storms which heralded the

* *Through Masailand* by Joseph Thomson, 1885.
† It will be noted that Speke employed a similar tactic when approaching the source of the Nile in July 1863.

approach of the rainy season, and above all Burton's refusal to indulge his zest for killing, wrote moodily in his journal that 'Captain Burton, being no sportsman, would not stop for shooting. . . .' On the journey to Fuga, both men contracted 'a violent, bilious fever', which, to Speke's undisguised relief, put paid to Burton's plans for visiting Mount Kilimanjaro and forced them to return at once to Zanzibar. At Pangani, Speke was barely able to stagger to the ship which Hamerton had sent down for them, whilst Burton, to his chagrin, had to be carried on board in a litter.

The Fuga 'flying trip' had two important consequences: firstly, among the men supplied as guides and porters by a little Beluchi garrison at Chogue, was the freed slave destined to become Speke's staunch companion throughout two major African expeditions, the celebrated Seedy Mubarak Bombay. Bombay was a delightful character, 'thoroughly honest and conscientious . . . added to which his generosity was unbounded'. Speaking reasonably fluent Hindustani he proved an easy conversationalist and knowledgeable on the habits of Indian and African game. He made an immediately favourable impression upon his new master by undertaking with him a thirty-mile-return walk in search of a valuable surveying compass which had been left behind at the site of the first overnight camp. Speke fondly recollected the incident in *What led* . . .

> 'Cheerily did we trip along, for Bombay – astonished at my oddities or peculiarities, as he thought them, when I picked up a river shell, or dilated much on the antelopes and birds we sometimes saw – broke into a series of yarns about his former life, and of the wild animals with which he was familiar in his fatherland.'

Continuing in praise of Bombay's unusual powers of endurance, Speke added: 'He seemed to me a surprisingly indefatigable walker, for he joked and talked and walked as briskly at the end of thirty miles as he did starting.'[8] Burton shared Speke's high opinion of the new recruit, a view contrasting with the utter contempt in which he held the average native African, the common 'jungly nigger', who was alike despised and avoided by Bombay; Burton went so far as to call him 'the gem of the party', praise indeed from one whose usual custom was to criticise.

The second aspect of the journey was, however, less fortunate. Some unpleasant exchanges took place between Speke and Burton over the fate of the Somali expedition, in particular the use to which Speke's diary and specimens had been put. In an angry letter, written on 20th June 1860, Speke reminded Burton of this and his generally tactless behaviour: 'You then added Gall to it by saying, that you considered such appropriation legitimate and that anybody similarly circumstanced would do the same. . . . After that confession I felt to make any more collections and especially remarks about them labour in vain.'⁹

The argument gave both men cause to fear the outcome of two years living cheek by jowl in the wilderness, under the strain of what threatened to be an unsympathetic relationship. With genuine concern Burton wrote how 'Even at the beginning of our long absence from civilised life I could not but perceive that his [Speke's] former alacrity had vanished: he was habitually discontented with what was done; he left to me the whole work of management, and then he complained of not being consulted.'¹⁰

The instructions issued to Burton by his sponsors, the Royal Geographical Society, were quite specific regarding the starting point and the ultimate objectives:

'The great object of the expedition is to penetrate inland from Kilwa or some other place on the east coast of Africa, and make the best of way to the reputed Lake of Nyassa: to determine the position and limits of that lake; to ascertain the depth and nature of its waters and tributaries; to explore the country around it etc. Having obtained all the information you require in that quarter, you are to proceed northwards towards the range of mountains marked upon our maps as containing the probable sources of the Bahr el Abiad, which will be your next great object to discover.'¹¹

These instructions were echoed in a letter dated Bombay, 30th November 1856, which Burton had brought to Colonel Hamerton as an introduction from Lord Elphinstone: 'He [Burton] has now undertaken to explore the great inland sea of Niassa [sic], and to reach if possible the sources of the Nile from the Southward. . . .'

Escorted by the dying Hamerton, Burton and Speke crossed

the straits from Zanzibar to Kaole, or Wale Point, in the corvette *Artemise* on 16th June 1857. The expedition left from Bagamoyo, a village eighty-four miles north of Kaole, whose beaches are decorated with scarlet flamboyants and whispering coconut palms. The caravan led by an Arab *cafila bashi*, Sheikh Said bin Salim, included eight Beluchies from the Sultan's personal guard; Valentine and Gaetano, two Goanese servants who had been specially brought from India; Bombay, who eventually replaced Sheikh Said, and two gunbearers. Burton had estimated that 170 porters would be required, but could muster only 132; thirty baggage mules purchased to supplement the porters were all dead within six months.

Some loads, including the parts of a heavy iron boat, could not be carried, but had to be left to follow behind the expedition. Soon after leaving Bagamoyo, both leaders began to suffer desperately from fever. The fever affected Burton continuously throughout the journey, while it struck Speke down in bouts of terrible violence. The effect of one of these attacks resembled severe sun-stroke, causing spasms of fainting in addition to a burning temperature.

Illness, desertions among the men, incessant wranglings and delays incurred by suspicious chiefs and indolent, inhospitable tribes along the route, slowed progress to a steady crawl. In spite of the comparatively easy going of the first stage up to Zungomero, when the expedition reached the Arab settlement of Kazeh on 7th November, the rate of advance had dropped to less than six miles a day. Desertions, which near the villages had to be allowed for, continued even though each porter had been paid at the coast, guaranteed a daily wage and promised a bonus for honest service at the end of the journey. This is partly explained by the reaction to the news of Hamerton's death which, according to Speke, 'struck a blow on the minds of Sheikh Said and the Beluches [*sic*] for they, naturally, thought their security was gone'. Later, Burton succeeded in transferring the mule-loads to the shoulders of the slaves accompanying the caravan, offering payment out of the expedition's dwindling funds. Scandalised, Speke wrote that

'... on my saying we should find it difficult to keep faith with them, [Burton] mildly replied, "Arabs made promises in that way, but never kept them; and, moreover, slaves of this sort never expected to be paid." I grew angry at this declaration – for I had seen Tibet ruined by officers not keeping faith with their porters – and argued the matter, but without effect.'[12]

Indeed, so great was Speke's concern at the alarming daily expenditure, which threatened to exhaust their resources before they could reach the Lake, that he persuaded Burton to send back from Zungomero to the coast for more money. '. . . I could not brook the idea of failure,' he reflected, 'even though we might have to pay future travelling expenses out of our own pockets.'[13] Such anxiety contrasted with Speke's total indifference to personal comfort. He worked and slept unceasingly in 'the reeking, miry tent', even when, at Kiruru, a dry hut and a warm fire had been placed at his disposal. Admiringly, Burton described how 'Night after night, at the end of the burning march, he sat for hours in the chilling dews, practising lunars and timing chronometers.'[14] Meanwhile, as the coast receded further and further away, the hardships and difficulties of the march grew more pronounced. The country through which they passed sometimes sprawled beneath a blazing sun, sometimes cowered, lashed by showers of torrential rain which pulped the earth to a sea of clinging mud. How different was this weary trekking from the peaceful cruise to the Pangani river which had presented the travellers with 'one continuous undeviating scene of tropical beauty'.

Like Speke's journey to the Wady Nogal, the march to Kazeh was characterised by extreme loneliness. He found himself unable to converse directly with anyone save Burton or Bombay, nor did he find many opportunities for shooting which, in Somaliland, had helped to relieve the tension. His cryptic references covering the 600-mile march highlight the austerity of day to day existence during the period. Burton, on the other hand, indulged himself in pages of description decrying the squalor of the villages, the apathy of the inhabitants, the agonies of fever, the discomforts of the rainy season; yet for all that he could praise the beautiful country, especially that of the Usagara Mountains, where after sunset

'. . . the soothing murmurs of the stream . . . mingled with the faint rustling of the breeze, which at times, broken by the scream of the night-heron, the bellow of the bull-frog in his swamp home, the cynhaena's whimper, and the fox's whining bark, sounded through the silence most musical, most melancholy'.[15]

But even in this distant paradise lurked disease, worst of all the horrifying smallpox which left the pitted shells of its victims strewn about the expedition's path. Speke, who all his life had practised a kind of body-worship and detested illness, avoided giving any description of the smallpox dead. Burton, who for little thanks had nursed his companion with almost motherly devotion when fever and delirium had overcome him, later observed that 'Unaccustomed to sickness, he could not endure it in himself nor feel for it in others; and he seemed to enjoy pleasure in saying unpleasant things. . . .' The latter criticism, which Burton defined as 'an Anglo-Indian peculiarity', is common to many who extol the human form and was a characteristic admitted to by the poet, Rupert Brooke, whose physical perfection is now a legend.[16]

In a well-documented account of the expedition, Mrs. Fawn M. Brodie, author of the latest Burton biography, *The Devil Drives*, has stated that 'Speke . . . held the African in contempt, and would write of his "obstinate fatalism" and "mulish temperament" and insist that "he has as great an antipathy to work as a mad dog has to water" '. Despite Burton's more intimate involvement with the African, studying his sexual habits, measuring his genitals, sampling his liquor and possibly consorting freely with his women, an attitude of 'contempt' is more applicable to him, for he had scarcely any respect for the native whose life he so persistently investigated. It is true that Speke, for all his appreciation of the male splendour of the Somali, thought many of the Central African tribesmen 'hideously black and ugly', deplored their idleness and pictured them lying '. . . about their huts like swine, with little more animation on a warm day than the pig has when basking in a summer's sun'.[17]

The tone of Speke's criticism contrasts notably with the more sympathetic observations of his contemporary Captain (later Sir Alfred) W. Drayson. Although such a comparison is not quite fair, as Drayson's book *Sporting Scenes among the Kaffirs* (1858) described South Africa, where the environment was

65

different and relations between the white settlers and the tribes had by then acquired a degree of 'familiarity'.

Yet for the slaves, the women in particular, Speke felt an undeniable sympathy, as much on account of their denigration and loss of human dignity as for the sufferings which they were forced to endure. At Zanzibar, in 1857, he was greatly moved and incensed by

'. . . the way in which some licentious-looking men began a cool deliberate inspection of a certain divorced culprit who had been sent back to the market for inconstancy to her husband. She had learnt a sense of decency during her conjugal life, and the blushes on her face now clearly showed how her heart was mortified at this unseemly exposure, made worse because she could not help it.'[18]

This passage is of interest in that it displays a sensitivity towards womankind which elsewhere Speke either deliberately or instinctively suppressed. Most of his dealings with women and girls reveal an awkwardness, an inability to comprehend the female mind. He had no close relationship with any apart from his mother and sisters. So far as is known he never fell in love nor courted any girl in England, nor did he ever marry. Instead he courted India and Africa, dedicating himself to exploration and travel as a priest or monk dedicates his life to the service of God. Perhaps inherent in his celibacy was a need to subjugate the flesh and its desires, a paradoxical consequence of body-worship which developed as Speke tuned himself to physical perfection in the Himalayas.

There is however ample evidence of Speke's deep attachment to his mother, a powerful maternal image, Mrs. Brodie tells us, sometimes confused in his dreams with Queen Victoria and latterly expressed in his naming of the Nyanza Lake. In Africa, where his inhibitions were gradually relaxed, Speke was destined to measure a naked fat princess, give piggy-back rides to Kabaka Mutesa's wives and, during his stay at the court of Buganda in 1862, flirt mildly with various young Baganda women whilst carrying on a complex intrigue with the Queen mother. But unlike Burton, he firmly resisted every opportunity for physical sexual experience and even confessed to being 'staggered' when the Queen Mother of Buganda offered him two of her daughters as mistresses.[19] The apparent want of maternal feeling, apart from the sexual implications of the offer, disturbed him greatly, for, as early as 1858, he had noted that

> 'The mothers of these savage people have infinitely less affection than many savage beasts of my acquaintance. I have seen a mother bear, galled by frequent shots, obstinately meet her death, by repeatedly returning under fire whilst attempting to rescue her young from the grasp of intruding men. But here, for a simple loin-cloth or two, human mothers eagerly exchanged their little offspring, delivering them into perpetual bondage to my Beluch soldiers.'[20]

It is however possible that Speke's growing conviction that Burton was 'going to the devil', because of a too close liaison with the African and his culture, stemmed from frustration and envy of his companion's liberal code as much as a sincere, if slightly prudish, concern for his health and morals.

When, on the 134th day from the coast, the expedition reached Kazeh, both Speke and Burton were tattered and gaunt, weak from the effects of fever and the painful ocular complaint, trachoma, which had seriously impaired their eyesight. Supplies of food had fallen low and the game on the plains of Ugogo was scarce and very wild. For many weeks Speke had been too ill to hunt intensively; indeed one feverish attack had so unhinged his mind that Burton had felt obliged to remove his weapons lest he injure himself or murder one of the porters. His tongue loosened by delirium, Speke poured forth a stream of pent-up grievances against his maltreatment in Somaliland: outbursts which Burton claimed took him completely by surprise. Yet had not Burton paved the way for this at Fuga? Although he never described the outbursts precisely, beyond specifying certain charges, the revelation of this unstirred pool of torment and bitterness must have caused Burton to consider his relationship with the younger man in a new perspective, if not tremble a little for his safety. Nevertheless, Burton continued to behave considerately toward Speke, sharing with him the meagre contents of his library, correcting his field-notes – on one occasion even insisting that he should use the last of the riding mules, while he himself stumbled blindly along beside it, stopping every half-hour to rest and regain his breath.

At Kazeh, the two men recuperated for five weeks in clean, comfortable surroundings amidst the enfolding hospitality of the Arab community. Assisted by its ageing yet still imposing chief, Sheikh Snay bin Amir, they replaced deserters and replenished the emaciated caravan. Meanwhile Sheikh Snay delighted Burton with a wealth of excellent conversation and gave unsparingly of his time and knowledge, his victuals and the conveniences of his household. Burton, himself a colourful exponent of Arabic, reciprocated by provoking lengthy discussions on religion and Arab history, by telling stories which demonstrated his fund of Arab folklore and by sowing innumerable questions whose fruits he plucked and stored away in notebooks. Thus he and Speke (who pecked disconsolately at the grains of information Burton threw him) gained an insight into the customs of the region, its economics and geography, leading up to the enigma of Erhardt and Rebmann's map and the probable location of the Nile sources.

In this respect Speke's first sojourn at Kazeh was less satisfactory than Burton's. Unable to participate in any of the conversation, he spent the evenings in shadow withdrawn and alone, while Burton and Snay occupied the centre of the firelight. Though Burton later stated that illness and the want of Arabic made Speke 'a little sour', or, as Alan Moorehead puts it, caused him to be left 'a little in the cold', Speke wrote of Kazeh and the Arabs without any trace of pique, but emphasising the importance of his role there while modifying that of Burton. In *What led* . . . he explained that while '. . . Captain Burton got desperately ill . . . I picked up all the information I could gather from the Arabs, with Bombay as an interpreter'. As if to equalise his position with that of the older traveller, Speke added in a footnote: 'To save repetition, I may as well mention the fact that neither Captain Burton nor myself were able to converse in any African language until we were close to the coast on the return journey.'

Finally, a few triumphant strokes of the pen reversed completely the roles of commander and subordinate, thus fulfilling in 1864 what was Speke's dearest wish as he sat in silence by Sheikh Snay's fire in December 1857. '. . . I thought Captain Burton would die if we did not make a move, so I begged him to allow me to assume the command *pro tem*. . . . Accordingly, as he agreed, I made arrangements with Snay . . .'²¹ Thereafter, according to his account, Speke organised the expedition's departure from Kazeh. When Ramji's escort of armed slaves refused to march with them, it was he who pacified them by paying over the extra wages promised by Burton. And it was he who later insisted upon their discharge, in order to conserve the expedition's money and rations. Yet, curiously enough, the route westward from Kazeh was selected by Burton on the advice of Sheikh Snay and in direct opposition to Speke's wish to advance northwards to the Ukerewe lake. From Snay they had learned that the huge lake delineated by the missionaries was not in fact one mass of water, but three. The Sea of Ujiji, or Lake Tanganyika, lay immediately to the west of Kazeh; to the southward stretched the great Nyassa, 'Livingstone's lake', and to the north the Ukerewe, a lake 'much larger than the Ujiji', of whose existence Speke had first heard at Kurrum on the Somali coast.

But four decades of Arab slave and ivory dealers had never yet mapped the area, nor could Snay confirm or deny that the principal units of the lake system were linked by rivers. He tended to affirm the Somali information, hinting that 'vessels frequented some waters to the northward of the equator', yet successfully dissuaded Burton from proceeding north by warning him of hostile, avaricious tribes and instead bade him go to the westward 'if our only motive in coming here was to look at a large piece of water'.

Leaving Kazeh on 14th December, Speke and Burton spent Christmas at the Swahili outpost of Msene, where for nearly a fortnight the porters were permitted to relax, 'giving themselves up to dancing, pombe-drinking and related pleasures'. During this time, to Speke's consternation, 'even Bombay became so *love-sick* we could hardly tear him away'. In January 1858, at Kanjanjeri, Burton was brought down by a dreadful attack of malaria which paralysed his legs, so that for the remainder of that year he had to be carried everywhere on a *machila* supported by eight strong bearers. Speke, for his part, suffered desperately from trachoma, his blood having grown thin and impoverished from inadequate and insufficient feeding, and his chronic ophthalmia aggravated by recurring bouts of fever. Now he went forward as if through a brilliant fog, his eyes inflamed and sore, seeming to be filled with particles of hot, sandy grit. Burton and Valentine, one of the Goanese servants, also suffered from the complaint, but far less acutely than Speke who was so nearly blinded that he and his riding-mule had to be escorted by a native.

The caravan slowly traversed the Unyamwezi country, crossing with some difficulty the rivers Ruguvu and Unguwwe and lastly, by canoe, the crocodile-infested Malagarazi, until, on 13th February, at the summit of a steep, rocky hill, its leaders stood overlooking a daub of glittering light that shone below them through the trees. Gradually, as they moved forward, Lake Tanganyika unfolded itself to Burton in all its beauty, but the first sight of the discovery was denied to Speke, before whom every object appeared 'enclouded as by a misty veil'. On the way to the hilltop Speke's mule had dropped dead beneath him from sheer exhaustion, so that again (with the mysterious regularity that persisted throughout his life), the death of an animal had been timed to expatiate disappointment, just as it marked success or celebrated victory.

At the village of Ujiji, on the eastern shore of the lake, Speke wandered about the market place, 'protected by an umbrella and fortified with stained-glass spectacles . . . beads in hand, to purchase daily supplies'.[22] After a fortnight spent resting, bathing in the azure water and living off a balanced diet of fowls, fruit and fresh vegetables from the market, his eyesight improved and he began rapidly to regain his former strength. The side-effects of fever and debilitation gradually disappeared, including a 'peculiar distortion of face, which made him chew, sideways, like a ruminant'.

As no boats of sufficient size for a serious exploration of the lake could be obtained locally, Burton, whose progress lagged far behind that of his companion, decided to send him across to the island of Kasenge, near the opposite shore, to bargain with the Sheikh, Hamed bin Sulayim, for the hire of his sea-going dhow. Speke, already 'longing for a change', and no doubt tired of waiting for Burton to recover, wrote determinedly 'I proposed to go myself'. His leader did not immediately agree to the plan, as only crude native dug-outs were available, which he feared might sink in rough weather. But Speke, his mind set on the voyage to Kasenge, applied the same persuasion to Burton that had weakened the 'Bayard of India' and a succession of resolute commanders in the Bengal Army, in view of which the prostrate invalid 'finally gave in'.

The dug-out carrying Speke, Bombay, Gaetano, two of the Beluchies, a *nakhoda** and a crew of 'twenty-six stark-naked savage sailors' was tossed by flying waves and driven at the mercy of incessant gales until, five days out, it was dragged ashore at Kivera island in the early hours of 8th March.

'This day', Speke wrote, 'passed in rest and idleness, recruiting from our late exertions. At night a violent storm of rain and wind beat on my tent with such fury that its nether parts were torn away from the pegs, and the tent itself was only kept upright by sheer force. On the wind's abating, a candle was lighted to rearrange the kit, and in a moment, as though by magic, the whole interior became covered with a host of small black beetles, evidently attracted by the glimmer of the candle. They were so annoyingly determined in their choice of place for peregrinating, that it seemed hopeless my trying to brush them off the clothes or bedding, for as one was knocked aside another came on, and then another; till at last, worn out, I extinguished the candle, and with difficulty – trying to overcome the tickling annoyance occasioned by these intruders crawling up my sleeves and into my hair, or down my back and legs – fell off to sleep.'

The worst, however, was yet to come. Speke awoke just too late to prevent one of the insects entering the exposed orifice of his ear.

'He went his course, struggling up the narrow channel, until he got arrested for want of passage-room. This impediment evidently enraged him, for he began with exceeding vigour, like a rabbit at a hole, to dig violently away at my tympanum. The queer sensation this amusing *measure* excited in me is past description. I felt inclined

* Captain

to act as our donkeys once did, when beset by a swarm of bees, who buzzed about their ears and stung their heads and eyes until they were so irritated and confused that they galloped about in the most distracted order, trying to knock them off by treading on their heads, or by rushing under bushes, into houses, or through any jungle they could find. Indeed I do not know which was worst off. The bees killed some of them, and this beetle nearly did for me. What to do I knew not. Neither tobacco, oil, nor salt could be found: I therefore tried melted butter; that failing, I applied the point of a penknife to his back, which did more harm than good; for though a few thrusts quieted him, the point also wounded my ear so badly, that inflammation set in, severe suppuration took place, and all the facial glands extending from that point down to the point of the shoulder became contorted and drawn aside, and a string of boils decorated the whole length of that region. It was the most painful thing I ever remember to have endured; but, more annoying still, I could not masticate for several days, and had to feed on broth alone. *For many months the tumour made me almost deaf,* and ate a hole between the ear and the nose, so that when I blew it, my ear whistled so audibly that those who heard it laughed. Six or seven months after this accident happened, bits of the beetle – a leg, a wing, or parts of its body – came away in the wax.'[23]

Contrary to the implications of Speke's remark, the resulting deafness was never *completely* cured, although the irritation caused by the beetle reduced the blinding inflammation in his eyes. However, the pain from his swollen ear and twisted jaw had scarcely lessened when on 31st March he returned to Burton's camp at Ujiji. Both he and his equipment had suffered so badly from the weather that, appalled, Burton wrote, 'I never saw a man so thoroughly moist and mildewed; he justified even the French phrase "wet to the bone" . . . his guns were grained with rust, and his fire-proof powder-magazine had admitted the monsoon-rain.'[24]

For all Speke's pitiful appearance, Burton found it difficult at the time, and impossible later, to refrain from bitter comment on the negative results of the twenty-seven-day excursion. Sheikh Hamed had detained Speke almost a fortnight, showering him with surpassing hospitality, from time to time reviving his offer of the loan of the dhow, but never once alluding to payment or the actual release of the craft. In the end, when even a frantic offer of £100 had failed to procure its services, Speke wisely concluded that to spend more time in bargaining was futile.

For the second time under Burton's leadership he had volunteered for special duty only to return having 'done literally nothing'. Yet now, as before, Burton's immediate outward reaction had been sympathetic, he writing afterwards how he 'consoled him and myself as best I could'. Admittedly the journey did not accomplish its main task, the hire of Sheikh Hamed's dhow, but this did not give Burton sufficient reason for condemning it as entirely useless. On the eastern side of Lake Tanganyika, on the shore of a tiny inlet called Luguvu Khambi, Speke made a discovery which he described almost diffidently in *What led* . . .: 'Here I picked up four varieties of shells – two univalves and two bivalves – all very interesting from being quite unknown in the conchological world.' As if to further suppress the importance of the find, he added, 'There were numbers of them lying on the pebbly beach.' The shells, and many others, were later identified by Mr. Woodward of the British Museum and included in an exhibition of specimens held at the Zoological Society of London when Speke lectured there in June 1859.[25]

The fact that he succeeded in finding the shells suggests that the trachoma had by then cleared sufficiently for him to distinguish quite small objects close at hand. Indeed, the following morning he managed to identify fresh elephant spoor, although he had difficulty in locating a herd of buffalo which his servants pointed out to him.

From Sheikh Hamed Speke received a detailed description of the hydrography of Lake Tanganyika:

'He said he had visited both ends of it, and found the southern portion both longer and broader than the northern. "There are no islands in the middle of the sea, but near the shores there are several in various places, situated much in the same way as those we are amongst; they are mere projections, divided from the mainland by shoals or narrow channels. A large river, called the Marungu, supplies the lake at its southern extremity; and in a visit to the northern end, I saw one which was very much larger . . . and which I am certain flowed out of the lake; for although I did not venture on it, in consequence of its banks being occupied by desperately savage negroes, inimical to all strangers, I went so near its outlet that I could see and feel the outward drift of the water." '26

Hopeful that the northern river might prove to be the Nile, Burton obtained two enormous dug-out canoes at great expense from a local chief, Kannina, in which, accompanied by Speke, he paddled up the lake as far as Uvira. Here three Arabs who had actually seen the river (the Ruzizi) explained to a disappointed Burton that it was a feeder and not an effluent of Lake Tanganyika; and when cross-examined, Bombay ingenuously confirmed that Speke must have misinterpreted Sheikh Hamed's information which tallied with that of the Uvira Arabs.

Speke apparently took the abortive journey less to heart than his companion. While he did not acknowledge his initial misunderstanding of the Sheikh's account in so many words, he qualified his report in *What led . . .*:

'My retrospective opinion of this story [he wrote] – for everyone tells stories in this country – is that Hamed's Marungu river more likely runs out of the Tanganyika and into the Nyassa, forming a chain of lakes, drained by the Shire river into the Zambeze; but I did not, unfortunately, argue it out with him. I feel convinced also that he was romancing when talking of the northern river's flow, not only because the northern end of the lake is encircled by high hills . . . but because the lake's altitude is so much less than that of the surrounding plateau.'27

Apart from the fact that both travellers underestimated the true altitude of Lake Tanganyika by approximately seven hundred feet, due to their thermometers being inaccurate, Speke subsequently published his map of the region describing the 'high hills' as the Mountains of the Moon. Had it not been for Burton's condition which was so weak that 'anybody seeing him attempt to go would have despaired of his ever returning', the fast-failing supplies and lastly the Arabs' denial of Sheikh Hamed's story, they would have explored the Ruzizi and also the hills. As it was, Speke's hasty portrayal of the Mountains of the Moon became an irritation and an embarrassment, for Burton could neither positively accept nor reject it, just as neither man could choose for certain between the conflicting accounts of the Ruzizi river.

At Uvira, where Speke and Burton enjoyed the compensation of 'good grub', they communicated little. Speke lived alone in a ragged tent which gave almost no protection from the daily onslaught of wind and heavy rain. Remarkable as it seems, this did not hinder a marked improvement in his health, particularly his eyesight, although the weather could hardly have relieved the strain of knowing that his journey to Kasenge had failed conspicuously in its two most important objectives.*

Burton's recovery was a slower process. Nevertheless, his ulcerated palate (which for a period had rendered him mute) began to heal and his strength gradually returned, so that by the time they again reached Ujiji, both he and Speke were physically fitter. Their spirits, which for the last month had, like the clouds of the monsoon, lain low and heavy, were further dampened by the discovery that the *cafila bashi*, Sheikh Said, had disposed of practically all the caravan's supplies imagining that the leaders must perish on the stormy waters of Lake Tanganyika. More depressing still, when on 22nd May, amid a great outbreak of shouting and gunfire, the remainder of the expedition's stores arrived with porters from the coast, it was found that most of the loads contained nothing but worthless trash, scarcely any food, and bullets which to Speke's disgust did not fit their rifles.

Faced with such meagre resources, Burton was forced to abandon his plans for completing the survey of Lake Tanganyika, and thereafter heading back to Zanzibar by way of Lake Nyassa and Kilwa. Instead the expedition returned to Kazeh, where Burton proposed to refit, with the help of Sheikh Snay, before continuing on to the coast. At this point, unlike Speke, Burton considered that enough had been accomplished. They had partly solved the enigma of the missionaries' inland sea, added to which Burton could claim for himself the discovery of Lake Tanganyika; furthermore, he had gathered almost all the information he required to write his book, *The Lake Regions of Central Africa*. Now he felt tired and weakened from constant illness, but, perhaps most important of all, inwardly downcast

---

* Speke, *What led . . .*, p. 252, stated that he also swam in the lake and that the exercise helped him.

and bitter at having failed to connect his Tanganyika with the source of the White Nile.

Speke, for his part, brooded upon his recent blunders, yet sought to re-establish himself in the eyes of his commander, at the same time securing some of the personal success which, until then, had tended to favour Burton. On the way to Kazeh he suggested that together they should travel north from there to explore the Ukerewe lake, 'described by the Arabs to be both broader and longer than the Tanganyika'. When Burton proved to be unenthusiastic, Speke as usual persisted, declaring somewhat ruthlessly:

'If you are not well enough when we reach Kaze I will go by myself, and you can employ the time in taking notes from the travelled Arabs of all the countries round.'[28]

If, on the other hand, one accepts Mrs. Brodie's argument contained in *The Devil Drives*, it is more likely that Burton used this reasoning for remaining at Kazeh with Sheikh Snay and his friends. According to Burton, Speke had so antagonised the Arabs by a relentless display of 'Anglo-Indian' superiority, that this as much as his desire to find the Ukerewe lake hastened Burton's decision to let him go – as he later wrote, 'To get rid of him!'[29] Although both Burton and Speke afterwards described the brief parting at Kazeh in discreet and unrevealing terms, Speke's letter to Dr. Norton Shaw, dated 2nd July 1858, reflected the growing tension created by the conflict of interests and personalities. He wrote, 'Burton has always been ill; he won't sit out in the dew, and has a decided objection to the sun . . .' Whilst avoiding a wholly personal attack, Speke continued, expressing his boredom and misery by criticising the country, the people and the absence of game:

'This is a shocking country for sport, there appears to be literally nothing but Elephants, and they from constant hunting are driven clean away from the highways; all I have succeeded in shooting have been a few antelopes and guinea fowls besides hippopotamus near the coast . . . There is literally nothing to write about in this uninteresting country. Nothing could surpass these tracts, jungles, plains for dull sameness, the people are the same everywhere in fact the country is one vast senseless map of sameness. . . .'

Then, with unmistakable relief: 'I am off to the Ukerewe Lake to see if the accounts of it are true. . . .'[30] Speke's letter clearly inferred that he considered his journey to the northern lake an undertaking of infinitely greater consequence than his commander's relatively domestic pursuits in Kazeh. He wrote: 'Burton meanwhile stays here to get things in order for our journey seawards, a good arrangement for rest seems to do him a power of good.'[31]

On the other hand, Burton had little reason to suppose that Speke's latest endeavour would turn out to be more successful than its predecessors. Yet on this occasion, by underestimating the younger man's true capacity and talent, by disregarding his invitation to visit the Ukerewe, Burton tragically erred and in so doing denied his expedition *and himself* the benefits of what became its greatest achievement. Likewise, by choosing to remain at Kazeh, Burton finally defined his role as a traveller and an ethnologist, while Speke, by responding to the challenge of the unknown, confirmed his as an explorer.[32]

NOTES

1. Burton: *Zanzibar*, vol. 1, pp. 28–9.
2. Alan Moorehead: *The White Nile*, London, 1960, pp. 10, 11.
3. Speke: *The Journal of the Discovery of the Source of the Nile*, William Blackwood & Sons, 1863, p. 8.
4. Speke: *What led . . .*, p. 189.
5. *Ibid.*, p. 166.
6. *Ibid.*, p. 188.
7. Alan Moorehead: *The White Nile*, p. 25.
8. Speke: *What led . . .*, p. 178.
9. Letter made available by courtesy of Mr. Quentin Keynes.
10. Burton: *Zanzibar*, vol. 2, p. 388.
11. Speke: *What led . . .*, p. 191.
12. *Ibid.*, p. 197.
13. *Ibid.*, p. 196.
14. Burton: *Zanzibar*, vol. 2, p. 388.
15. Burton: *The Lake Regions*, vol. 1, pp. 162–3, R.G.S. 541B.
16. Extensions of this argument including that referred to by John Maynard Keynes as 'comprehensive irrelevance', are to be

found in the late Christopher Hassall's *Rupert Brooke*, London, 1964, pp. 155–6, 429.

17. Speke: *What led* . . ., p. 234.
18. *Ibid.*, p. 190.
19. Speke: *The Journal of the Discovery of the Source of the Nile*, William Blackwood & Sons, 1863, p. 361. Mrs. Brodie uses this information in *The Devil Drives* in a paragraph which begins, 'Speke at thirty-three was inhibited and prudish', pp. 152, 153.
20. Speke: *What led* . . ., p. 235.
21. *Ibid.*, p. 200.
22. *Ibid.*, p. 207.
23. *Ibid.*, pp. 324–5.
24. Burton: *The Lake Regions*, vol. II, p. 90.
25. A great number of Speke's shells were used to decorate a grotto built close to a lake in the grounds of Jordans. In addition to shells, the walls are finished with a frieze of coloured coral and the floor is made up of sheeps' knuckle-bones set on end in cement and arranged in concentric circles. The Jordans' grotto is quite possibly the only one of its kind in the British Isles.
26. Speke: *What led* . . ., pp. 230–1.
27. *Ibid.*, p. 231–2.
28. *Ibid.*, p. 251.
29. Burton's comment was written in the margin of p. 265 of his own copy of *What led* . . ., which is now part of the Royal Anthropological Institute's collection in Bedford Square, London, W.C.1.
30. Letter contained in the MSS collection of the R.G.S., London, S.W.7.
31. *Ibid.*
32. On p. 161 of *The Devil Drives*, Mrs. Brodie has written, 'So Burton was betrayed into the greatest mistake of his life . . . betrayed by the fact that he was an ethnologist first and only secondarily an explorer.'

≈≈≈≈≈≈≈

CHAPTER 4

THE EFFECTS OF INSPIRATION

≈≈≈≈≈≈≈

IN its initial stages, Speke's twenty-five-day journey to the Ukerewe lake had much in common with his expedition to the Wady Nogal. The twenty porters accompanied by a guard of ten Beluchies left Kazeh on 9th June, 1858, trudging sullenly in the wake of their leader and his swaying mule. The men did not relish this latest prospect of entering unfamiliar and possibly dangerous country, and besides feeling homesick they put only a wavering faith in Speke's authority, especially as he had not succeeded in persuading Sheikh Said to join the party. This picture drawn by Speke in *What led . . .* contrasted with a somewhat more buoyant account written in a letter to Hamerton's successor, Captain C. P. Rigby, during 1860.* In fact, Burton stated that he himself was 'not over-anxious' in influencing Sheikh Said, reflecting no doubt upon his companion's earlier difficulties with the Somali abban, Sumunter, and more recently with Sheikh Hamed and the Arab community at Kazeh. In the circumstances, he concluded that the presence of the crafty Sheikh might prove to be more of a hindrance than a help. Even the faithful Bombay's '. . . Seedi nature came over him, and he would not move a yard [without] a month's wages in cloth upon the spot'. To make matters worse, the porters took immediate advantage of Speke's inability to exercise direct control over them, for want of communication, and once beyond Kazeh spent the first night and the whole of the second day immersed in drink and dancing at a nearby village. 'Fortunately', wrote Speke, 'tempers like butterflies soon change state.'[1] Having had their fling, the porters re-assembled on the 11th, and, marching briskly, rapidly drew away from

* See *General Rigby, Zanzibar and the Slave Trade* by Mrs. Charles E. B. Russell, 1935, pp. 235–8, and Speke to Rigby, Kazeh, 10th March 1861.

Kazeh heading northwards over the Unyanyembe plains. That same afternoon, the caravan, which had strung out Indian file in the traditional manner, came into literally head-on collision with a troop of Wasukuma carrying ivory. Neither one of the opposing kirangozis, or leaders walking ahead of his men, would step aside and, closing in, lowered their heads 'like rams preparing for a fight', charged each other and 'butted continuously till one gave way'. The joust and the pandemonium which followed seemed so realistic and so earnest that Speke 'hastened to the front with [his] knobbed stick, and began reflecting where [he] could make best use of it in dividing the combatants . . .'. Only then did his natives pause to explain that the proceedings were perfectly amicable and occurred whenever two parties met face to face in the bush, using the same track.

Unyambewa, the region into which Speke now advanced, was characterised by series of 'low straggling hills' and 'open, waving well-cultivated ground'. Its novelty lay in the fact that Sultana Ungugu was an elderly woman possessed of great charm, but with a decidedly undistinguished appearance. With typical bluntness, Speke described her as '. . . a short stump old dame, who had seen at least some sixty summers. Her nose was short, squat, and flabby at the end, and her eyes were bald of brows or lashes. . . .' If Speke had been curious to see the Sultana, she in turn expressed even greater curiosity about him:

'Squatting by my side, the sultana at once shook hands. Her nimble fingers first manipulated my shoes (the first point of notice in these barefooted climes), then my overalls, then my waistcoat, more particularly the buttons, and then my coat—this latter article being so much admired, that she wished I would present it to her, to wear upon her own fair person. Next my hands and fingers were mumbled, and declared to be as soft as a child's, and my hair was likened to a lion's mane.'[2]

Leaving the Unyambewa district, the caravan proceeded without incident until on 18th June it arrived at the village of Ukuni where Speke recorded seeing two albino native women. In contrast to some treacherous country near Kazeh through which he had stumbled, 'grasping at darkness to preserve his

equilibrium', the going became easier by the day and the landscape greener and more fertile, in consequence of which Speke
had frequent opportunities for contemplation. While crossing
the Salawe plains, a chance encounter with a child caused him
to reconsider the sensitive and nowadays highly topical question of differences separating the Negro peoples from the white,
in particular the African from the European. On page 293 of
What led . . . he wrote:

'As nothing proves better the real feelings and natural propensities
of a nation than the impulsive actions of the children, I will give
a striking instance, as it occurred to me today. On seeing a child
approach me, I offered him a handful of beads, upon which the
greedy little urchin snatched them from my hand with all the
excited eagerness of a monkey. He clenched tight hold of them in
his little fists, and, without the slightest show of any emotions of
gratitude, retired, carrying his well-earned prize away with a self-
satisfied and perfectly contented air, not even showing the beads
to his parents or playmates. I called Bombay's attention to this
transaction, and contrasted it with the joyful grateful manner in
which an English child would involuntarily act if suddenly
become possessed of so much wealth, by hurrying off to his mamma
and showing what fine things the kind gentleman had given him.'

Speke's demonstration of righteous pity for the child, although the stereotype of respectable nineteenth-century opinion, has suffered less change in many quarters of society than
we might imagine; and this in spite of a liberal system of education and the protests of our more enlightened countrymen. Not
that Speke intended to be scathing. His comments on the little
boy's behaviour were but a natural reaction to the facts of life
in Africa as he saw them and his conclusion, while it may in
modern eyes seem narrow and unsympathetic, was inevitably a
reflection of his former experiences in Somaliland and of the
grasping chieftains he had met on the way from Zanzibar. Nor
should one forget Speke's liking for the native hunters[3] or confuse this attitude with his equally definite opinions on the slave-
trade which, on the whole, were tempered with a great compassion for the African.

Most important of all, however, would be the subtle change
which took place during the expedition with J. A. Grant, when,

as a result of closer contact with the ordinary native, but more especially with two African rulers, Kabaka Mutesa and King Rumanika, Speke's rigid morality became in a sense infused with a drop of the negro's spirit, thus affording him deeper understanding of a people which hitherto had often seemed incomprehensible and bizarre.

On 30th July, the day when Speke first sighted the Ukerewe lake, the caravan broke camp at 6 a.m. It is touching to observe that as the climax of the march came nearer, the earlier Speke roused his men each morning as though he grudged every second given to sleep and must appease the mysterious power which drew him towards his target. After a short walk through tilled fields and villages, Speke, looking over to his left, 'could discern a sheet of water, about four miles from [him], which ultimately proved to be a creek, and the most southern point of the N'yanza, which . . . the Arabs described to us as the Ukerewe Sea'. In a footnote, he added emphatically, 'This I maintain, was *the* discovery of the source of the Nile.'⁴ The party carefully picked its way down the grassy, bush-covered slopes of the creek, forded it with some difficulty and then, as it was nearly dark, put up at a village on the other side.

During the next day and the next, Speke led his expedition down the course of the creek until, from being a dirty, insignificant little stream, it suddenly broadened into a vast archipelago, the sight of which reminded him of a cruise he had once made in the Greek islands sometime presumably in the course of his Crimean service. From the back of his mule Speke peered at the shimmering panorama through French-grey tinted spectacles. The glasses had never failed to fascinate the natives, who annoyed him by stooping and staring under the brim of his wideawake, so that eventually when he could stand their curiosity no longer he pocketed them, preferring the glare to the endless gaze of the passers-by.

Having attained the southern extremity of the lake, Speke celebrated the event in the customary fashion. As he trotted along, his '. . . trusty Blissett made a florikan pay the penalty of death for his temerity in attempting a flight across the track'.

It is as if the brooding spirit with whom Speke held intensely private communion demanded a sacrifice of blood in return for its favours, if not to compensate some transgression. In this and other similar killings there is evidence of a primitive submission to ritual, for their pattern is constant and clearly-defined. They relate to specific moments of uplift or upheaval and may also have explained Speke's quite eccentric preference (indicated on p. 356 of *What led . . .*) for the foetus-meat of pregnant game. The previous day he had merely chosen to 'amuse' himself by shooting partridges in the jungles along the creek, but a profoundly different quality distinguished the killing of the florikan, whose death represented a gesture of thankfulness, an instinctive expulsion of primitive feeling.

On 3rd August 1858, Speke ascended to the top of a long, low hill from which he saw for the first time the huge expanse of the Ukerewe Sea, receding pale and placidly into the far distance. This for Speke was the greatest moment of the journey and perhaps the greatest moment of his life. The discovery of Lake Tanganyika had been exciting, but was essentially Burton's triumph. Now Burton lay three weeks' march away in Kazeh and, save for his African companions, the thrill and satisfaction of the hour was concentrated upon Speke alone. It was in this moment of inexpressible perfection that the inspiration struck him, so clearly henceforward he could never be in doubt, that here, stretching out before him, was the lake which formed the great reservoir of the White Nile.

From that moment on, the whole pattern of Speke's life and the lives of many others would be bound inextricably to the vast area of water which lay outstretched at his feet. It is unlikely that he could as easily have guessed the extent of the strife, the heartache or the severed friendships destined to follow as a consequence, not so much of the discovery, but of the vision it inspired. Indeed, we are told that the beauty and romance of the experience did not linger long upon Speke's practical mind. Putting such matters rapidly aside, he wrote 'the pleasure of the mere view vanished in the presence of these more intense and exciting emotions . . . called up by the consideration of the commercial and geographical importance of the prospect before me'.[5]

Speke took considerable pride in the fact that his Ukerewe, which he afterwards named the Victoria Nyanza, had proved to be enormous, thus fulfilling the Arabs' forecast 'to the letter'. 'This is a far more extensive lake than the Tanganyika,' he remarked, 'so broad you could not see across it, and so long that nobody knew its length.'[6]

The naming of the creek which had led them to the Nyanza, the hill from which Speke had made his discovery and, lastly, the lake itself, gave the explorer little trouble. The hill he named Somerset after the county of his boyhood; the creek he described as Jordans Nullah in memory of his home (not, as suggested in 1953 by Mr. E. A. Loftus, after the River Jordan), and the lake itself he of course named after Queen Victoria, 'our gracious sovereign'. (Yet, if we reflect upon the dreams mentioned in the previous chapter, it will be apparent that the naming of the lake was in reality a supreme compliment paid to his own mother.) Last of all, it would be pleasant to imagine that when describing the creek Speke used the Hindustani word 'nullah', meaning a seasonal water-course, in acknowledgement of the preparatory years in India which had laid the foundation for his moment of brief glory.

Speke felt extremely pleased with the accuracy of Sheikh Snay's information, as indeed he had reason to feel pleased with himself. There was a particular satisfaction in knowing that the map constructed at Kazeh from Arab reports and which had been sent off to the Royal Geographical Society before he left for the north, was now shown to be so exact that 'in general outlines [he] had nothing whatever to alter'.

Thus ended the great flying trip to the Victoria Nyanza. Its progress had been curiously slow, although the travelling conditions were mostly easy, and the marching average – two hundred and twenty-six miles in twenty-five days – barely exceeded nine miles a day. On 4th August Speke climbed Observatory Hill, close to Somerset Hill, and took careful bearings of all the main topographical features. A local chieftain, Mansur bin Salim, had provided him with a much-travelled guide to lead him about and, through the medium of Bombay, to answer questions concerning the Nyanza. When asked for an estimate of the lake's breadth, the guide indicated a distance of some eighty to one hundred miles, but of its length he could give no approximation. It represented a distance so tremendous that he could only stand throwing forward his right hand and cracking the fingers in a series of despairing gestures as he tried to define an immensity that far exceeded his powers of imagination and expression. Pathetically he told Speke that 'nobody knew, but . . . it probably extended to the end of the world'.[7]

A visit to Mansur's neighbour, the gentle mysterious Sultan Mahiya, proved to be equally frustrating; no boats were readily available and on account of the lakeside tribes, 'so savage and inhospitable to travellers', neither Mahiya nor Mansur would assist Speke to explore even the isthmus known as Ukerewe Island. The only helpful member of the Sultan's household was his wife, whom Speke ungratefully described as 'a pretty crummy little creature'. She had formerly lived further north along the lakeshore and knew the names of many districts near the Nyanza. But of the extreme north end of the lake, she herself knew nothing, while of its circumnavigation she replied with truly African acceptance that 'if any way of going round it did exist, she would certainly have known of it'.

In English geographical circles, the country beyond the Nyanza was reckoned to be flat, probably marshy and intersected with a dense network of streams and watercourses. No mountains rose above the lake. At latitude 5°N. the known level of the Nile lay almost two thousand feet below the level of the Nyanza, which itself, according to Speke's thermometers, lay nineteen hundred and fifty feet above Lake Tanganyika. From these statistics Speke correctly assumed that the inevitably violent cataracts produced by a sharp fall of six hundred yards over a mere three hundred miles (together with the Sudd), must have created so impenetrable a barrier to river transport that no expedition coming up the Nile from Egypt could possibly have negotiated them.* This was subsequently verified.

In *The Devil Drives*, Mrs. Brodie writes: 'After only three days Speke left the lake and rushed back, jubilant and triumphant, to tell Burton of his discovery. One cannot help wondering exactly how he expected Burton to react to the news that he had snatched "the greatest geographical prize since the discovery of America" from his grasp.'[8]

* It should be noted, however, that the presence of 'sudd' (see H. E. Hurst, *The Nile*, 1952, pp. 116–17) created the main hazard to explorations by the river route. Sudd means, literally, a 'stopper'.

The implication of thoughtless haste, while perhaps unintended, is nevertheless so apparent that the passage should be expanded a little.

In fact, Speke realised fully the need for definite proof of his inspiration while still at the Nyanza, and bemoaned the lack of time and supplies which precluded further serious exploration in the area. As Mrs. Brodie goes on to say, 'There were barely enough supplies to get them safely back to Zanzibar; the monsoon was beginning, and they were nearing the end of their army leave.' It was only these considerations and the nagging burden of Burton's indifferent health, that forced Speke to quit the Nyanza (prematurely). Writing later of his dilemma, he commented: 'Had I had but a little more time, and a few loads of beads, I could with ease have crossed the Line and settled every question which we had come all this distance to ascertain.'[9]

Recalling his feelings in 1864, Speke wrote that his 'reluctance to return may be easier imagined than described. I felt as much tantalised as the unhappy Tantalus must have been when unsuccessful in his bobbings for cherries in the cherry-orchard, and as much grieved as any mother would be at losing her firstborn, and resolved and planned forthwith to do everything that lay in my power to visit the lake again.' Thinking ahead, Speke's laudable determination could hardly fail to have been mixed with other more depressing feelings of trepidation and, indeed, of anticlimax. The excitement having attained its height, the journey south became routine, 'without anything to excite the mind'.

On the return, unlike the journey to the lake, Speke slept well every night, untroubled as he had been previously by ticks or by 'the anxiety to catch stars between the constantly-fleeting clouds'. Rest was denied to him only at Salawe, where the natives, ruthless in their desire to see the white man, would persistently enter Speke's hut and even, as in the case of one old man, try to waken him by tugging at his pillow. Speke bore these intrusions only for a time and at last, 'out of patience, sent [his] boots whirling' at the greybeard's head.

By 20th August the marching speed of the caravan had

Landscape drawn by Speke, Unyanyembe, 1858

Ingenge Mehamba i e Elephant Busch 2t Sept 1858 (jotho)

Landscape watercolour, by Speke, 1858

almost doubled. On 24th, Speke noted that over the four previous days a distance of fifty-eight miles had been covered; by then Kazeh was only eighteen miles away, so close that neither he nor his men could resist making a final sprint. Starting out at 1 a.m., they raced over the last leg and reached the main camp at Kazeh in the morning of 26th, their arrival heralded as usual by raucous yelling and bursts of musket-fire.

Burton heard these familiar sounds with feelings of genuine relief. He had spent the six weeks of his companion's absence very profitably, as the brimming pages of *The Lake Regions* testify, but having finished his notes and having sent off another parcel of field-books, letters and reports to the Royal Geographical Society, he had begun to feel bored and perhaps a trifle lonely. Like Speke, Burton needed constant activity and an atmosphere of perpetual challenge, without which life grew meaningless and dull. When Speke arrived he had just begun to organise a small expedition to K'hokoro, south of Kazeh, to pass the time, but instead he met his young friend, full of the concern he had borne for his safety and the rumours of civil war in the north, which for weeks had been circulating in Kazeh. Upon hearing the news that Speke had discovered the Nyanza, Burton was delighted, especially delighted that Speke had 'At length . . . been successful'. What a change overtook him, therefore, when Speke announced quite coolly and evidently seriously, that not only had he discovered the Ukerewe Sea, but that he was completely convinced that it represented the principal feeder of the White Nile.

Burton was startled and confused. He did not know whether to laugh in his companion's face, or be sarcastic or angry. That the claim was true he very much doubted, yet what a bitter blow if it were, for compared to himself, what right had Speke by virtue of knowledge, qualifications or experience, to make so tremendous an assertion and with such authority? It seemed an outrageous impertinence, worthy only of scorn, and a blemish on all the remaining geographical results of Speke's journey which Burton found stimulating and acceptable.

Yet, in describing his inspiration, there must have shone in Speke's eyes such a certainty, like the light of God in a martyr's face, that Burton for all his logic felt a wincing doubt. As time passed so the measure of doubt increased, until Speke began to suspect that his commander's sharp denunciation was no more than a bluff behind which lay insecurity and fear. Despite the inadequacy of his reasoning and the quite shattering impact of his claim, Speke felt surprisingly piqued that Burton had chosen to reject it; that he was utterly sincere, yet had failed to impress the older man, was perhaps what hurt him most. Burton, on the other hand, placed little faith in inspiration and wrote defensively that Speke's '. . . reasons were weak, were of the category alluded to by the damsel Lucetta, when justifying her penchant in favour of the "lovely gentleman", Sir Proteus – "I have no other but a woman's reason – I think him so because I think him so".'[10] Heated arguments followed the first discussion, until, after several days, the subject was dropped by mutual agreement. Wearily, Burton wrote: 'Jack changed his manners to me from this date. . . . After a few days it became evident to me that not a word could be uttered upon the subject of the lake, the Nile, and his *trouvaille* generally without offence.'[11]

Speke suffered his disappointment in silence, retreating further and further into himself, nursing his discovery protectively, solicitously like a mother. The recurring image of the mother-and-child relationship was at this time more than ever firmly entrenched in his mind. Only the state of maternal serenity which followed in the wake of his intuitive flash had been disturbed, so that while Speke believed implicitly in his inspiration, yet recognised the precariousness of his position, he could at the same moment ridicule what he called 'the effect of supernatural impression on the uncultivated mind'.

A boyhood recollection served to illustrate the point.

'. . . my old nurse used to tell me with great earnestness of a wonderful abortion shown about the fairs of England – a child born with a pig's head; and as solemnly declared that this freak of nature was attributable to the child's mother having taken fright at a pig when in the interesting stage. The case I met in this country was still more far-fetched, for the abortion was supposed to be producible by indirect influence on the wife of the husband taking fright.'[12]

One wonders if the fact that Burton shied away from Speke's belief in the Nile source induced a peculiar sexual schizophrenia that drew from Speke maternal feelings almost as strong as his driving current of masculinity; if perhaps Speke's ridicule of the gawping peasantry was a defence against the fear that his 'child', the discovery conceived of inspiration, might, like the fair-child,* turn out to be a freak and an object of common curiosity and derision. Thus may be explained the sudden passion for self-preservation, the desperate need to thrust the discovery into the arms of men more influential than Burton, that transformed the quiet satisfaction Speke had felt returning from the lake into a sense of bitter urgency. Anxious as he had been to venture inland with Burton, he could now hardly wait to get away from him and from Africa. That Burton's illness and the phase of boredom with Kazeh might have contributed to his intolerance for Speke's claim mattered nothing, for by now the thirty-one-year-old explorer had been alienated, painfully slighted by his commander, and had himself become secretly but very definitely angry.

When at breakfast on 26th August, Speke had proposed that they return together to explore the Nyanza fully, he may not yet have realised the extent of Burton's interest in the Nile. On this latter journey he saw Burton's role as subordinate to his own, and required his presence only to confirm his theory. Burton refused, pleading age and illness, but suggested they should 'go home, recruit our health, report what we have done, get some more money, return together, and finish our whole journey'. Immediately Speke suspected Burton's desire to claim the discovery of the Nile sources for himself and therefore agreed, while privately intent upon reaching England first.

In this atmosphere of strained cordiality and mutual distrust the companions left Kazeh for Zanzibar on 6th September 1858, accompanied by a hundred and thirty-two porters (some new, others recruited from the old deserters), and several Arabs. On the first day out, the caravan was beset by bitter, cold winds which bloodshot one of Speke's eyes and aggravated the damaged ear which was still swollen and painful. To add to these irritations a stabbing pain roved ceaselessly about his body, forewarning of an agonising fever that days later nearly

* Speke's boyhood experience suggests a comparison with the grotesque main feature of Messrs. Erhardt and Rebmann's map.

killed him. Sympathetically, Burton observed his companion's misery, noted the development of his sickness in minute detail and included a full account of it in *The Lake Regions*, writing that the pain

'began with a burning sensation, as by a branding-iron, above the right breast, and then extended to the heart with sharp twinges. After ranging round the spleen, it attacked the upper part of the right lung, and finally it settled in the region of the liver. On the 10th October, suddenly waking about dawn from a horrible dream, in which a close pack of tigers, leopards, and other beasts, harnessed with a network of iron hooks, were dragging him like the rush of a whirlwind over the ground, he found himself sitting up on the side of his bedding, forcibly clasping both sides with his hands. Half-stupefied by pain, he called Bombay, who having formerly suffered from the "Kichyoma-chyoma" – the "little irons" – raised his master's right arm, placed him in a sitting position, as lying down was impossible, and directed him to hold the left ear behind the head, thus relieving the excruciating and torturing twinges, by lifting the lung from the liver. The next spasm was less severe, but the sufferer's mind had begun to wander, and he again clasped his sides, a proceeding with which Bombay interfered.'

The following morning, Speke suffered a prolonged epileptic attack which, Burton said, bore a disturbing resemblance to hydrophobia. 'He was once more haunted by a crowd of hideous devils, giants, and lion-headed demons, who were wrenching with super-human force, and stripping the sinews and tendons of his legs down to the ankles.' At the climax of the fit

'. . . sitting, or rather, lying upon the chair, with limbs racked by cramps, features drawn and ghastly, frame fixed and rigid, eyes glazed and glassy, he [Speke] began to utter a barking noise, and a peculiar chopping motion of the mouth and tongue, with lips protruding – the effect of difficulty of breathing – which so altered his appearance that he was hardly recognisable. . . .'[13]

Presently the spasm ceased and Speke grew calm; like Burton, he felt that death must only be a matter of time, and calling for pen and paper, he composed with difficulty a shaky, quite incoherent letter of farewell to his mother and the family. By a miracle, the letter was never needed. It is clear that Speke possessed an abnormally strong heart, but in those last moments when everyone crouched near him, hushed, afraid, waiting for him to die, it could only have been his sheer determination to live that overcame the worst of the 'little irons'. Gradually the pain lessened. Exhausted, the sick man feebly voiced his gratitude, whispering 'the knives are sheathed'.[14] Burton immediately sent back to Kazeh for supplies of medicine; however the Arab poultice of myrrh mixed with egg-yoke proved useless, as did the treatment prescribed by a local witch-doctor, who strung two slivers of wood dipped in goat's fat round Speke's waist. Speke ripped off the contraption almost at once, for it rubbed against the most tender part of his body, just above the liver.

But fresh air, food and ample rest succeeded where the patent medicines had so spectacularly failed. Three days after the crisis, the caravan moved away from the 'dirty cow-village' of Hanga, with Speke carried shoulder-high upon a hammock. Only two weeks later he pronounced himself sufficiently recovered to take once more to riding on a donkey. At last, on 2nd February 1859, the delighted yells of the porters, the familiar sight of mangoes, coconut palms and pineapple trees, and then in the distance, the glittering streak of the Indian Ocean stretching taut 'between earth and air', told Burton and Speke that the long months of wandering were over. A winding road, on either side of which white skulls stared down from poles stuck into the ground, led the caravan into Konduchi village, where a hut was instantly provided for the two leaders. Girls giggled at them, men, women and children surrounded them in waves of joyful, uninhibited curiosity; Speke wrote in his diary that by nightfall everyone in the little seaside village had 'stared and laughed until they could stare and laugh no more'.

The same day, a boat bound for Zanzibar took off the Jemadar of the Beluchies and Kidogo, a particular *bête noir* of Burton's, who caused endless trouble throughout the expedition. Burton also sent a note to Captain Rigby, Hamerton's successor at the Consulate, asking for a coasting vessel and some provisions so that a brief exploration could be made of the

Rufiji river and its delta. This hitherto unexplored river lay two hundred miles south of Konduchi, opposite the island of Mafia, and by visiting the area Burton meant to finish his expedition in style, as well as providing a sop for the boredom of the past four months. Six days of idleness slipped peacefully by, like the dhows on the warm, slippery sea, until on 9th February the boat arrived, and on the 10th Burton and Speke left their paradise for the Rufiji.

Again bad luck assailed them. A plague of cholera raging along the coast swept the ship's crew like wildfire; hardly a man escaped and no other sailors would venture near. Over the Rufiji itself, low clouds poured floods of torrential rain into the delta, while further inland the river burst its banks, flooding the countryside for miles. Sadly but wisely, Burton concluded that the time for travelling was finished, turned the vessel about, and headed up the coast to Zanzibar. One may imagine that Speke, in his mounting impatience and apprehension, blessed the rain, perhaps even the cholera, and eagerly approved his commander's decision to retire.

Speke's impatience to reach Zanzibar was not entirely shared by Burton. The new Consul, Captain Christopher Palmer Rigby, was an old acquaintance from the Indian Army, intelligent and self-opiniated, a brilliant scholar and linguist, but a man inclined to professional jealousy, who had been, it was rumoured, most unpopular at Addiscombe, the Indian Army officers' training establishment in England. Burton had narrowly beaten Rigby in a Guzerati interpreter's examination while both were still in India, a considerable feat, and one which Rigby did not easily forget. At the same time, Rigby possessed a certain quality of charm and with it a talent for persuasion. From their first meeting he and Speke fell on each other's necks like Greeks, but, for Burton, who grew to dislike Rigby intensely, the sojourn at the Consulate was a period of strangeness, unease and crushing anticlimax.

Soon after their return, there arose the question of final payments to the caravaneers. Sheikh Said, the *cafila bashi*, visited the Consulate daily, stressing his claims with what seemed to Burton an unwarranted and aggravating persistence. The extra expenses of the journey, when calculated, exceeded the Government's grant by nearly two thousand pounds, of which Burton agreed to pay fourteen hundred from his own pocket, leaving the remainder, six hundred pounds, owing from Speke; but he stoutly refused Sheikh Said further payment on the grounds that he had deceived him at Ujiji by squandering valuable stores and by a general lack of co-operation throughout the expedition. In *The Lake Regions* Burton stated that, when consulted, Rigby agreed that in the circumstances Hamerton's advance to the Sheikh had been adequate. Nor did Burton consider that any extra reward had been merited by the Beluchi guard.

Speke disagreed. Although Burton would subsequently recall the violent quarrels which had flared up between Speke and the Beluchies on the journey inland, especially with the Jemadar following a remark which, had not Burton intervened, Speke 'would have noticed with a sword-cut', by 1859 Speke's attitude had radically altered. In 1864, describing the discovery of the Victoria Nyanza, Speke wrote: 'Further, the Beluchies, by their exemplary conduct, proved themselves a most efficient, willing, and trustworthy guard, and are deserving of the highest encomiums; they, with Bombay, were the life and success of everything, and I sincerely hope they may not be forgotten.'[15]

Burton had returned to Zanzibar, confident that Speke supported his views on payment, but, as he wrote in *Zanzibar* (1872), once arrived upon the island Speke 'fell into bad hands' – meaning of course Rigby. Thereafter Speke held that Burton's refusal to meet the claims would prevent any future travellers from obtaining either porters or servants; that news of the affair would quickly spread through the interior and anyone attempting a similar journey would find the difficulties increased and all efforts to obtain bearers frustrated. Not only that, the good name of Britain had been sullied for want of a few pounds.

Later that year, both Speke and Rigby confirmed these views in letters written to the Government of India. Burton countered fiercely, declaring that the name of Britain could hardly suffer where common sense – in this case the refusal to distribute undeserved rewards – prevailed over simple open-handedness, which no one could respect. The Government, however, found

93

Burton's explanation unsatisfactory, as was shown by the lengthy correspondence, most of which will be included and discussed in a forthcoming edited volume of Speke's letters.*

It was a miserable conclusion to the otherwise successful Lake Regions expedition, but a mere precursor of still more sinister intrigue. On 22nd March the cargo vessel, *Dragon of Salem*, carried an eager Speke and a somewhat subdued and thoughtful Burton away from Zanzibar. Rigby did not come aboard to say good-bye. 'His place, however,' wrote Burton, 'was well filled up by Seedy Mubarak Bombay, whose honest face appeared at that moment, by contrast, peculiarly attractive.'[16] The slim, receding line of the palm-fringed shore and the faint, nostalgic scent of cloves gradually faded on the breeze.

At Aden, where the *Dragon of Salem* berthed on 16th April, Speke changed ships in such haste that he left himself no time even to bid farewell to Burton's friend, Dr. John Steinhaeuser, who had generously offered the travellers accommodation at his house. Despite their outward pose of amity, Steinhaeuser, conscious of Speke's extraordinary agitation, soon perceived that 'all was not right' and confided his fears to Burton. It is therefore significant that in their brief adieus, neither Burton nor Speke betrayed the least suspicion of declining confidence in each other and that, on the contrary, Burton's last words were full of optimism while Speke spontaneously offered his hand in friendship and reassurance. Said Burton, 'I shall hurry up, Jack, as soon as I can.' To which Speke answered, 'Goodbye, old fellow; you may be quite sure I shall not go up to the Royal Geographical Society until you come to the fore and we appear together. Make your mind quite easy about that.'[17]

Leaving Burton at Aden to convalesce from the prolonged effects of fever, Speke took a passage to England aboard H.M.S. *Furious*, commanded by Captain Sherard Osborne, which included among its passengers Lord Elgin and Elgin's chronicler and private secretary, Laurence Oliphant. From Cairo, he wrote Burton an almost too solicitous letter, urging him to care

* *The Nile Diary of 1863 and Selected Letters* edited with an introduction by Alexander Maitland.

for his health, reminding him of the promise that together, and only together, they would visit the Royal Geographical Society, entreating him to rest well in Aden and not to consider returning until his recovery was complete.

Let us assume for a moment that the letter was sincere, that Speke's promise was made in good faith; that being himself so careless of sickness and infection, he had felt a sudden remorse for his unsympathetic attitude to Burton during the expedition. It would appear that between the writing of this letter and the arrival of the *Furious* at Southampton, some mysterious influence caused him temporarily to lay aside all moral precepts and abandon the code of gentlemanly conduct by which, until that moment, he had tried to live. Fear lay at the root of this disturbing change of character. In Speke, fear was an emotion previously dormant, an experience scarcely known; yet when skilfully induced and manipulated by the eloquent sophisticate Laurence Oliphant, it drastically altered the course of the young man's thinking, and played around the core of his belief in the Nile sources like fire about the roots of a tender plant. In spite of Burton's kindness to him in Africa, in spite of the openly good terms on which they had so recently parted, Speke was encouraged to see his commander as a thief who, having once stolen from him in Somaliland, would surely steal again. Oliphant's clever insinuations, his stirring up of bitter memories, his sadistic passion for breaking open old wounds and sundering ties of friendship (in this instance admittedly fragile), were never more effective nor used upon more perfectly prepared ground than that provided by Speke.[18]

As a result, the standing promise made in Aden and reinforced in Cairo became Speke's defence, giving him time to plan; it was probably Oliphant's suggestion that he should immediately confront the Royal Geographical Society and thereafter the whole country with the story of his discoveries. In this way he would accumulate such strength, that, by the time Burton reached England, he would be too late to do anything about it. On the other hand, it is possible that while agreeing to refrain from independent meetings with the Royal Geographical Society, Speke had considered a prior discussion with members of the Home Government. With their support he would have faced the Royal Geographical Society, as promised, with Burton; when the facts of the Lake Regions expedition had been reported, he would then, either publicly or at a private session, have proclaimed the theory behind his discovery of the Victoria Nyanza. Speke would almost certainly have asked the Royal Geographical Society for official recognition of his proposed confirmatory expedition, but would have relied directly, through family contacts, upon the Government for political and financial support. Such may have been the reason for Speke's agitation, his obsessive haste in reaching London and the uncharacteristic, barely adequate farewells to his friends at Aden.

Oliphant, directly he had been taken into Speke's confidence, possibly advised him that there would be insufficient time before Burton's return to seek out and establish the financial support he needed. In any case, Burton was even then drafting a letter to the Secretary of the Royal Geographical Society which, if Speke had delayed an instant longer, might have seen him yet again in command of an African expedition, this time directed unequivocally at the Nile. Against which event, the only possible insurance was a meeting with Sir Roderick Murchison, President of the Royal Geographical Society, to whom the 'discovery' and every piece of relevant information must be disclosed.

Speke was not the guilty 'cad'[19] that several writers and commentators would have us believe. Rather, he was trusting, easily swayed by charm, and possessed of that comb of vanity which, if stroked gently and often, would so deprive him of all good judgement that he would temporarily forsake the path of reason for others alien and even quite disastrous. Oliphant was certainly efficient, although his motive is at first somewhat obscure.

Left to himself, Speke would not have deliberately misled Burton, but would have faced him fair and square. Only the fear of losing his discovery of the principal Nile source which was so important to him, so personal, so precious, hastened on the dark error of judgement which, although it directed the course of his last five years to Africa, finally and completely destroyed his relationship with Burton. Speke, for this sad mistake, is more deserving of our pity than our censure.

NOTES

1. Speke: *What led* . . ., p. 270.
2. *Ibid.*, p. 277.
3. See *What led* . . ., p. 13.
4. Speke: *What led* . . ., p. 298 fn.
5. *Ibid.*, p. 307.
6. *Ibid.*, p. 307.
7. *Ibid.*, pp. 311–12.
8. Brodie: *The Devil Drives*, p. 162.
9. Speke: *What led* . . ., p. 326.
10. Burton: *The Lake Regions*, vol. II, p. 204.
11. *Ibid.*, vol. II, p. 209.
12. Speke: *What led* . . ., p. 356. (Also note on pregnant waterbuck.)
13. Burton: *The Lake Regions*, pp. 233–5.
14. *Ibid.*, p. 235.
15. Speke: *What led* . . ., pp. 370, 371.
16. Burton: *The Lake Regions*, vol. II, p. 383.
17. *The Life of Sir Richard Burton*, 1893, vol. 1, p. 327.
18. Mrs. Brodie makes an important reference to Oliphant's influence on Speke on p. 167 of her biography and cites further Burton references to the incident, e.g. *The Life*, 1893, vol. 1, p. 328, and *Zanzibar*, vol. II, p. 390.
19. Byron Farwell: *Burton*, 1963, p. 178. On p. 305 of *Tanganyika Notes and Records* No. 49, December 1957, Professor Kenneth Ingham writes: 'There can be no doubt, however, that something of the self-righteousness of his generation must have moved Speke to act as he did, putting what he believed to be justice before generosity. If this was indeed the case he was to pay a big price for it.'

CHAPTER 5

THE WRANGLERS PART

THE *Furious* reached England on 8th May. From Hatchett's Hotel in Piccadilly Speke wrote to Dr. Norton Shaw: 'I believe most firmly that the Nyanza is one source of the Nile if not the principal one.'

Although he did not then know it, his letter had been preceded and to an extent confirmed by one from Burton written three days after Speke left Aden. Having explained that he would be delayed, Burton continued: 'Captain Speke, however, will lay before you his map observations and two papers...' Referring to Speke's report on the Victoria Nyanza, Burton added:

'To this I would respectfully direct the serious attention of the Committee as there are now reasons for believing it to be the source or the principal feeder of the White Nile.'[1]

Mr. Gordon Waterfield, editor of a recent edition of Burton's *First Footsteps in East Africa*, has stated that while it was 'a generous letter' and 'gave Speke the benefit of the doubt with regard to his theories about the Nile', Burton afterwards erred by determinedly contradicting him, thus 'robbing his own expedition of one of its greatest achievements'.

Had Speke remained silent, it may be that Burton, working upon his established reputation with the Royal Geographical Society, would have claimed the Nile for himself, commanded the return expedition, and left the true discoverer utterly drained of credit and recognition. As it was, by 9th May Speke had contacted Murchison and was at his London house discussing the discovery of the Nyanza and its implications, whilst pressing hard his hopes of an immediate return to Africa to settle the Nile 'by actual inspection'. The interview was exceptionally successful. Proudly, Speke wrote: 'Sir Roderick, I need only say, at once accepted my views . . .' Furthermore, Murchison instantly 'seized the enlightened view that such a discovery should not be lost to the glory of England and the society of which he was president'. Warming quickly to the infectious enthusiasm of his eager young visitor, he declared, 'Speke, we must send you there again.'[2]

It may have been that the lion-haired soldier, so touchingly simple in his manner, so boyish, so attractively enthusiastic, perhaps struck Murchison as a man more fitted to represent Britain at the source of the Nile than the wilder, less predictable Richard Burton, notwithstanding Burton's vast experience, capacity and achievement.

Twelve days later, Burton arrived in London to find 'that everything had been done for, or rather against [him]'. 'My companion,' he added sourly, 'now stood forth in his true colours, an angry rival.' Years afterwards he would still reflect with sadness that 'These were the days when the Society in question could not afford to lack its annual lion, whose roar was chiefly to please the ladies and to push the institution.'[3]

Although quite understandable, Burton's attitude was scarcely a fair one. In spite of Speke's premature announcement, in spite of Murchison's apparent predilection for Speke, Burton continued to be in the running for some time, and was only turned down in favour of Speke at a subsequent Council meeting of the Royal Geographical Society. Before that meeting both men were given ample opportunity to prepare their schemes for the confirmatory expedition and both received a fair and impartial hearing. It is, however, likely that Burton's duel with the Indian Government over the Berbera episode and the current feeling that, despite his assertions to the contrary, he might have acted unwisely, counted against him. That, and the more recent argument over porters' pay, bred concern, even outright hostility, among members of the Royal Geographical Society Council.[4]

Sir Roderick Murchison's confidence in Speke appeared un-bounded. In his presidential address to the Anniversary Meeting of the Royal Geographical Society on 23rd May, he spoke as follows:

'Seeing that this vast sheet of water extends due northwards . . . and knowing that its meridian was nearly that of the main course of the White Nile, Captain Speke naturally concludes that his Nyanza may be the chief source of that mighty stream on the origin of which speculation has been so rife.'

Going on, Murchison urged support for a new expedition:

'Let us hope that when re-invigorated by a year's rest, the un-daunted Speke may receive every encouragement to proceed from Zanzibar to his old station and there carry out to demonstration the view which he now maintains, that the Lake Nyanza is the main source of the Nile.'

Concluding his speech, he confidently observed that the source of the White Nile was 'a problem . . . which . . . by the last discovery of Captain Speke, seems now to approach nearly to a satisfactory conclusion'.[5]

How positive were Sir Roderick's words, but how woefully misdirected. . . .

At a Royal Geographical Society Council meeting convened to determine his probable route, Speke rejected the river approach from Egypt and instead favoured his commander's previous choice, but, strange to say, he neglected the route across the Masai plains. For the proposed three-year-long expedition, Speke, painfully aware of the former venture's lack of money, asked the Council to sponsor his request to Government for a grant of £5,000. On the Council's advice, however, the figure was modified to half that sum.

By 19th May, Speke had confirmed in a letter to Norton Shaw that he would gladly prepare a paper dealing with the geography of the Lake Regions for the thirteenth meeting of the Society to be held on 13th June at Burlington House. During the interval he wrote twice more to Shaw: on 7th June, to make arrangements for his family and friends who were to be present; on 9th June, to say that the papers had run to three in number, totalling fourteen pages, that he could not make them shorter and hoped they would do.

The meeting itself was significant, representing as it did an important development in the Nile controversy. Murchison, while commending Burton's work, claimed that Speke, as much as he, deserved the Society's Gold Medal in recognition of his share in it. Not everyone present felt so strongly. A friend of Burton's, the geographer James McQueen, who was later to become a bitter enemy of Speke, rose to his feet, 'with great reluctance, to express an opinion contrary to the views propounded by Captain Speke as to the sources of the Nile. He did so with hesitation . . .', for he otherwise considered Speke's papers interesting and valuable. McQueen then asked Speke whether or not the vegetation on the southern Nyanza was tropical, for he frankly doubted the accuracy of the latitudes quoted and wanted further evidence. Speke replied evasively that because he had only visited the lake during the dry season, the vegetation was mostly burned off, upon which, silenced but far from satisfied, McQueen resumed his seat.

Despite Sir Roderick Murchison's hope that Speke would be awarded the Gold Medal jointly with Burton, only Burton in the end received the coveted honour. Not only was Murchison displeased, but his displeasure was shared equally by the newly-appointed Secretary of State for India, Sir Charles Wood, and Speke's old ally, Lord Elphinstone, the Governor of Bombay. Whatever his own feelings, Speke correctly and very commendably kept his opinion of the decision to himself.

Burton received his Medal with dignity and, in the speech which followed the presentation, praised the work of his erstwhile companion with a warmth which Speke must have found disconcerting.

'To Captain Speke are due those geographical results to which you have alluded in such flattering terms. While I undertook the history and ethnography, the languages, and the peculiarity of the people to Captain Speke fell the onerous task of delineating an exact topography, and of laying down our positions by astronomical observations, a labour which, at times, even the undaunted Livingstone found himself unequal.'[6]

This generous appraisal of Speke's efforts may have been a last attempt on Burton's part to retrieve the broken friendship – who can say? Perhaps even then, the widening rift between the two might have been closed. But Laurence Oliphant, still intent on mischief, took decisive steps to prevent any possible *rapprochement*. Having read Speke's expedition diaries during the voyage from Aden, Oliphant, a correspondent of *The Times* and *Blackwood's Magazine*, now encouraged him to write to John Blackwood, asking that they might be considered for publication. Although he liked the idea, Speke, who had never imagined himself as a writer, was at first hesitant. Then, after a London publisher had approached him for a book in an unpleasantly commercial manner, he decided to take the plunge and wrote to Blackwood from Jordans on 10th July:

> 'I have just returned from Central Africa having mapped the whole of these regions and discovered what I consider . . . the true source of the Nile, and I have fixed the true Mountains of the Moon. I made two independent trips one across a large lake called Tanganyika . . . the other to the Nyanza Lake, or as I've just said the source of the White Nile.'[7]

Speke informed Blackwood that he had travelled under the leadership of 'Captain Burton a correspondent of yours', and that both Burton and Oliphant had read his diaries which they 'declare[d] to be interesting'. He continued, 'I'm desirous that I should write a book at once and bring it out before Captain Burton.' These diaries, Speke hoped, could be printed 'before or during the coming Autumn'. Yet, impatient as he was, he could not suppress a natural instinct for fair play. In the next letter to Blackwood, dated 12th June, he wrote, 'it has struck me that Captain B. may have some work with you. If so kindly let me know for I would on no consideration be in opposition to him.'

Blackwood, who had been away from his office on business, did not reply to either letter for over a week. Meanwhile Speke,

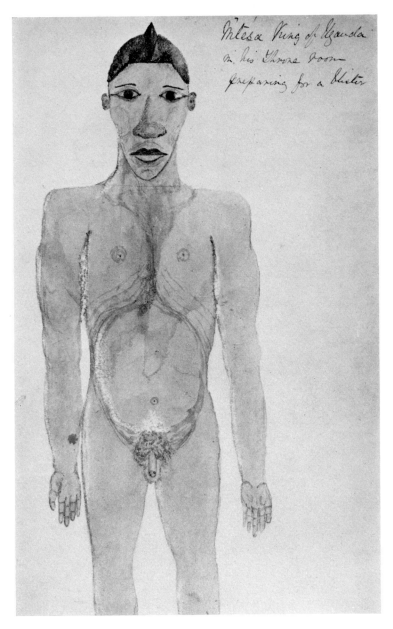

Mutesa in his Throne Room preparing for a blister

Mutesa I, Kabaka of Buganda, watercolour by Speke, 1862

Mutesa's sister, drawn by Speke, 1862

hearing nothing, began to fear that Burton might have intercepted him, and on 15th wrote once again to Edinburgh:
'Captain Burton, I am aware, for he consulted me about it, was
thinking of publishing our journey to Fuga in book form. . . .
Though I agreed to add my opinions to his on the subject of the
country there I have not heard from him again.'

Blackwood's reply, written three days later, was encouraging:

'You had better send your MS at once. If my brother thinks it
suitable for the Mag. there is little fear of anything that has passed
between Capt. Burton and ourselves preventing its acceptance.
My brother referred to him in writing to you and to let you know
that we had been in communication with him, and that therefore
as a matter of courtesy you should mention your MS to Captain
Burton.

Signed W. Blackwood for John Blackwood.'

After a lapse of four days Speke, much relieved, wrote again
from Jordans answering Blackwood's advice with regard to
Burton: '. . . I have omitted to mention Capt. Burton's name
as far as possible; this is because I have not communicated with
him about it and also because . . . I was at the time of keeping
these journals, *nominally* under his command and therefore any
reflections about him by myself would be out of place.'

The summer of 1859 was unusually hot. Speke little relished
the prospect of having to spend so much of it indoors, especially
engaged on work which still seemed slightly distasteful to him.
The weather had been so stifling, even in the open countryside
of Somerset that, writing to Shaw on 18th July, he commented
wryly, 'People say that the heat of London far surpass[es]
Africa. The thermo shows more here than I ever saw it in
Africa if that's any criterion.' At the beginning of August Speke
again returned to London where he stayed at his club, the East
India and United Services, in St. James's Square. On the 3rd
he wrote to Blackwood, enclosing 'a specimen of my diary for
your inspection', and asking for criticism and information
about the formalities of publishing; if somewhat unenthusiastic,
Speke was none the less thorough, and quite incapable of being
otherwise. This time Blackwood's reply came almost by return
of post. It spared the fledgling author nothing in its criticisms
and prompted Speke to answer 'I'm not surprised that you have

found my composition wanting. . . . My fort[e] being in the field and not in the cabinet.' Almost certainly a growing impatience with the Government underlay this last remark; for, in spite of his willingness to spend a year in England arranging details of the Nile expedition, it had as yet neither confirmed Speke's position as commander, nor reached any decision regarding the finances. Lord Ripon, Murchison's successor, had officially approached the Foreign Office for a grant of £2,000 (with a further £500 for the collection of natural history specimens), but the recently appointed Foreign Secretary, Lord John Russell, made no application to the Treasury until November 1859 – a delay of nearly six months.

The Royal Geographical Society was now in its summer recess, and Ripon, involved with the responsibilities of his political life and two earldoms he had but lately inherited, had little opportunity of expediting Speke's affairs. Besides, Speke longed to escape from the claustrophobia of the south, and on 10th July had written, '. . . I am scribbling out my diaries before the grouse come in when please God I shall go to Scotland.' For the time being, however, the less amenable occupation of writing had to take precedence over the opening of the season on the 12th August. Thus on 8th August, he told John Blackwood, 'I have put off shooting till Monday 15th to have a few days to arrange matters as you propose.'

Although critical of its style, Blackwood found Speke's manuscript intriguing, and asked him to send more. His confidence somewhat restored, Speke responded quickly to the request, exclaiming, 'I am glad that you think the 1st part of the journal interesting, for if that is so, the rest must be. . . .' Now that the initial hurdle had been cleared and he was free to leave London for the Highlands, Speke travelled north to Argyllshire, where he had been invited to begin the shooting season at Callton Môr near Lochgilphead. By contrast with the English heat, the weather north of the border was damp and dour. In a note dashed off to Blackwood on 17th August Speke complained: 'Yesterday I went out shooting and killed my first Roebuck and got wet through. Today I shot my first grouse and blackcock with a few snipe.' On the 19th, he wrote to Shaw, 'The weather has been so bad that I have not killed much game.'

In the literary field developments were more encouraging. Blackwood had become so enthusiastic about the Nyanza diaries that publication had been definitely agreed upon and progress rapidly made toward that end. So overjoyed was Speke that he wrote Shaw a rather premature letter from Scotland announcing that the articles would be appearing 'this month' (August). During the last three days of his stay at Callton Môr, he wrote two more letters to Blackwood: on 24th August he asked for the address of his old friend J. A. Grant, a matter in which Blackwood was apparently able to help; and on the 26th repeated the request, writing that he was anxious to renew his acquaintance with Grant and to meet his wife. He also referred to Lord Elgin's sister, and spoke of his desire to see her, presumably hoping that she would influence Elgin, a confidant of the Queen, in supporting his choice of the name 'Victoria' for the Nyanza lake. In a subsequent letter it transpired that Speke had not actually christened the lake at the moment of its discovery, for, as he said, 'If I had thought of doing it when at the Nyanza, I could have written a pretty speech about it.'[8] Having conceived the idea later, he felt anxious about its reception by her Majesty, and wrote, '. . . I don't know how to name the lake after the Queen. I don't think Livingstone mentions his having called the Victoria Falls after her.' But the problem was readily solved, and on 26th August Speke could confirm that Lord Elgin 'thinks I have done right in calling my Nyanza – Victoria. He says that arrangements are being made for my expedition.'

On this happy note, Speke left Argyllshire that same day for the Inchbrae estate, near Garve, in Ross-shire. From here the correspondence to Blackwood continued with a request for copies of the 'Maga' in which Burton's recent article on Fuga had appeared. 'I wrote to Burton,' he said, 'and told him that I hoped my journals would be of use to him in his writings. He wrote a nice reply and asked for information about the animal kingdom as regards Africa: this I have furnished him with.'

With considerable satisfaction he recalled a triumphant excursion on to the Ross-shire hills. 'The first day after arrival here the largest stag that has been killed . . . in this Forest fell victim to my rifle.' The letter concluded with a fascinating reference to Roualeyn Gordon Cumming of Altyre, the famous

lion-hunter, whose travelling menagerie Speke visited at Fort
Augustus. He recorded that the Highland audience, while
quietly impressed with Cumming's collection of caged wild
beasts, which included a lion, felt cheated that, having paid the
stiff entrance fee of a shilling, no lecture accompanied the
show.[9]

However, it was not sport alone that brought Speke to the
north of Scotland in 1859, for he had also been invited to read a
paper describing his African discoveries to Section 'E' of the
British Association's annual meeting, which that year took
place in Aberdeen. Among those present at the meeting was
Laurence Oliphant, whose biographer, Philip Henderson
(1956), mentions that he and Speke met there during their
stay.[9A] Writing in *The Uganda Journal* (1962), Dr. R. C. Bridges
has pointed out that Section 'E', for years directed by Sir
Roderick Murchison and organised and convened by officers
of the Royal Geographical Society, had virtually become the
summer meeting of the Society. This explains a reference in a
letter Speke sent to Blackwood from the Royal Hotel, enclosing
some papers: 'The one marked RGS contains a portion of what
I read out to the geographers. These letters by Mr. Petermann
[Dr. August Heinrich Petermann, editor of the *Mittheilungen*]
are the most authentic memos I've been able to collect of the
explorers . . . up the Nile.'[10] In this connection it should be
noted that after neither the 1856–9 expedition to Central Africa
nor that of 1860–3 did Speke first hand over his journals to the
Royal Geographical Society for publication. This unorthodox
procedure ran directly opposed to the official policy of the
Society, but was less serious in 1859 as Burton had prepared a
detailed account of unprecedented length, which filled an entire issue of the Royal Geographical Society's *Journal*. Oliphant's
advice, as much as his rivalry with Burton, dissuaded Speke
from making a similar contribution and, furthermore, the responsibility for such a report fell more properly to Burton as
commander of the Lake Regions expedition.

The Society was therefore content to accept Speke's observations in the form of lectures, especially as interest in him centred
about the alleged discovery of the source of the Nile, which,

since his return, had become noticeably separated from the remaining mass of the expedition's achievement.

With the publication of the Blackwood articles in September, October and November 1859, the Royal Geographical Society was forced to reconsider its allegiance to the independent, outspoken explorer. In *The Lake Regions* (1860) Burton openly attacked what he considered to be Speke's inaccurate data, insubstantial and hastily gathered evidence and outrageous speculations, maintaining that these hindered rather than encouraged geographical progress. Had it wished, the Society could easily have quashed Burton's opposition at that stage and reaffirmed its powerful support of Speke, but the Council had begun to feel that, after all, Speke had behaved ungenerously by withholding his material from the *Journal* and seeking instead the wider, more profitable recognition of the public.

On the way back from Aberdeen, Speke stayed a night with John Blackwood and his family at St. Andrews. For the benefit of Stewart, one of the younger members of the household, he had written from Inchbrae, '[I] stipulate that you do not let him eat all the oil and macaroni before I come . . .' The favourite dish, which plainly became a great joke between Speke and the little boy, appeared again in a letter from the Royal Hotel, Aberdeen, in which Speke referred to himself as the 'Late Bengal Macaroni', a remark quite typical of his sense of humour.[11]

In Edinburgh, where he visited Blackwood's offices at 45 George Street, Speke was shown a map of the southern Sudan composed by John Petherick, 'the discoverer of the large lake Ghazal', to whom he had already been introduced by Sir Roderick Murchison. From York, where he had spent two days, Speke described the visit and the map in a letter to John Blackwood: 'I saw Mr. Petherick's map of the Upper Nile . . . *a most valuable production* . . . I told the Major I would again correspond with Petherick . . . and *again* would ask him to write something about his experiences in Africa illustrating it with this said map.' Speke concluded, '. . . he is without doubt the greatest traveller in that part of Africa'.[12]

Petherick, who had explored a vast area of the Bahr-el-Ghazal to the west of the Nile, had been a mining engineer in his native Wales until, in 1845, according to the late Sir Harry

Johnston, he came to Egypt to prospect for coal on behalf of Mehemet Ali.* His researches having proved unsuccessful, Petherick thereafter took up ivory-trading in the Sudan and after a time was appointed British Vice-Consul in Khartoum. He was a big, strong, hearty fellow with long curly hair and beard; his movements were gigantic, according to Speke 'like a rampant hippopotamus',[13] his voice voluminous and rich. He already possessed a wife whose patience, charm and courage quite matched the expansiveness of her husband's personality.

At Jordans, Speke continued to work hard correcting proof-sheets and re-writing the original diaries. He never ceased to be grateful for 'another chance of rectifying errors', and appreciated Blackwood's efforts to present the African diaries at their best. 'You have really assisted me materially,' he wrote, 'and I feel extremely obliged to you for it.'

In November 1859, the horizon suddenly darkened as the quarrel with Burton came to a head. As a consequence of his part in the Zanzibar pay dispute, Burton had received a severe reprimand from India, with the result that, thoroughly chagrined, he wrote to Norton Shaw at the Royal Geographical Society telling him, 'I don't wish to have any further private or direct communication with Speke.' From then on, it was arranged that all personal messages passing between Burton and Speke would come via Shaw as mediator. Since parting at Aden, their letters to each other had grown increasingly formal, Burton's greetings descending through 'Dear Jack', 'Dear Speke', finally to 'Sir'. While disturbed by what she calls his 'insensitivity in measuring the effect of his own behaviour on Burton', Mrs. Brodie has noted that it was with 'genuine in-comprehension' that Speke wrote to Burton on 1st February 1860, beginning, 'Dear *Sir*, Since you appear *desirous* of shun-ning me.' The letter explained that, as the Indian Government had decided to grant Speke full pay and allowances from 2nd December 1856 to 14th May 1859, 'I shall be prepared to pay you the half of the excess of expenditure which accrued on the expedition.' He insisted, however, that Burton should formally request a refund from the Government on their behalf, after which the debt, six hundred pounds, would be paid.

* Sir Harry Johnston, *The Nile Quest*, 1903.

Bitterly Speke added that the passage money from England to Zanzibar would have to be included in his payment, and that he would never have joined the expedition had he known that, yet again, he would be liable for a private contribution to help eke out inadequate funds provided by the Treasury.

Burton instantly retaliated, writing, 'I am not desirous of shunning you.'[14] The debt, he continued, was one which Speke had contracted unconditionally in Africa; he flatly refused to accept Speke's terms, which he considered impertinent, and moreover complained that he had been grossly deceived: 'Had I known you then as well as I do now I should have required receipts for what was left as a debt of *honour*. I must be content to pay the penalty of ignorance.' Confirming the view expressed in an earlier letter to Norton Shaw, Burton went on, '. . . any direct correspondence between us cannot be productive of any good and might lead to unmanly disputes which in the cause of Geog. and Science it is most desirable to avoid'.[15]

The disagreement, however, did not end there, nor was Burton's suggestion of avoiding correspondence adhered to by Speke. En route for East Africa, on 17th June 1860, Speke wrote a long letter enumerating his bitter memories of the Somali journey and urging Burton to apply to the Government of India for reimbursement as he had previously suggested. He apologised for raking up the past but pointed out that it had now become an 'L.S.D. affair'. Even then Speke feared that he had perhaps overstated his case. On 20th June he wrote again to Burton, apologising for his references to Somaliland, in particular the complaint (that he now withdrew) that Burton had not offered him so much as half returns on his book *First Footsteps* which contained the abridged version of Speke's diary.

It appeared that Burton had recently sent a flurry of letters demanding that the debt be settled immediately, and that these demands had placed Speke in an acutely embarrassing position. His arrears of pay for 1856–9 had not been met and he wrote begging Burton to stay his request until the money arrived. Could it have been that Speke did not have as much capital at his disposal as many commentators have tended to assume? This being so, it is unlikely that he would have approached his father for assistance; more probably his mother, who had considerable private means, volunteered, thereby still more effectively undermining his independence.*

On 21st August 1860, Speke's brother Benjamin wrote to Shaw: 'I have paid my brother's (Capt: Speke) debt to Burton – 600*l*; and consequently hope there will be no more said about it. I hear from my mother that there was much talk about it in London, rather derogatory to my brother's honour. . . .'[16] Benjamin, a clergyman, was for years both spiritual and temporal counsellor to his family, but there can be little doubt that it was Georgina Speke who, with her favourite son abroad and powerless to object, paid over the money and closed the affair for good.

Payment of money had eventually stilled Burton's tongue on the subject of the expedition debt, but nothing much short of a public retraction could have subdued his attacks on the content of the Blackwood articles. He criticised their geography and objected to alterations in the material extracted from the fieldbooks. Hurt and angry, Speke wrote on 3rd November 1859 from Lypiatt Park, Stroud, the home of his sister, Lady Dorington,[17] 'You used to read and extract from my M.S.S. and there is nothing in them than what I believe you have read.'

The second of the three articles, cautiously entitled by Blackwood *'Captain Speke's Discovery of the Victoria Nyanza Lake, the supposed source of the Nile'*, was unfortunately somewhat incautiously composed. It is true that had Speke shown less confidence, or even invited Burton to return with him to Africa, history might have treated him with more respect. In 1860, his position as an explorer and geographer would have gone unchallenged in professional circles, just as it had been established in London society; but then we would not have been discussing the consequences of inspiration, that mystical phenomenon beyond compromise which, having experienced, Speke upheld at such great personal cost.

Retraction of his claim was impossible, not because of dignity, but because to have done so would have been a contradiction

* This aggravating situation may explain further Speke's anxiety to 'clear out' of England. See his letter to Blackwood dated 25th April 1860, N.L.S., MS. 4154.

of the truth as he saw it. To seek the company of Burton on the return journey would have been equally unthinkable, for Burton had become, in Speke's eyes, a most dangerous, most approximate rival, who, despite all assertions to the contrary, believed his companion's theory.

Besides, although Burton had frequently been kind, Speke had found him, generally, difficult to travel with, and resented his interference with the hunting and collecting of specimens. Worst of all, as he confided to Shaw, Burton was 'one of those men who never *can* be wrong' and with whom, after a time, 'talking becomes more of a bore than a pleasure'.[18]

Following the announcement of Speke's forthcoming expedition, several applications had been made to the Royal Geographical Society by adventurers wishing to accompany him. Speke had himself selected Edmund Smyth, the sportsman with whom he had originally intended to explore the Caucasus, '. . . a chap who won't go to the devil, full of pluck and straight-head foremost . . . a man of precisely my habits, and one entirely after my own heart.' After such a eulogy it may seem surprising that once again Smyth was dropped; Speke, showing little sympathy for the unlucky man, justified his decision in a letter to Shaw: 'Smyth is feverishly inclined,' he wrote, 'I won't have him with me . . . I am as hard as bricks.'[19]

Through John Blackwood, he had managed to contact another old friend, J. A. Grant, who had returned from India to Scotland, and was living close to Dingwall in Ross-shire. Having invited him to join the expedition, Speke was delighted when Grant immediately accepted. On 30th June 1859 Speke, writing from 31 Mount Street, London, W., conveyed Grant's acceptance to Norton Shaw:

'. . . a friend of mine, Captain James Grant of the Bengal Army has volunteered to place his services at my disposal . . . I know him to be a good soldier and sportsman. In the latter capacity we have worked together and know well how to appreciate one another. I can confidently say there is no one who could go with me, in whom I should place more reliance, for his conciliatory manner with colored-men [*sic*], for general good temper and patience, and for physical ability in locomotion than I would do in Grant.'

The members of the Royal Geographical Society Council shared Speke's opinion as did his mother when, in early April the following year, Grant and Petherick stayed with her at Jordans. On 15th April, Speke sent an enthusiastic report of the visit to Shaw: 'Mother thinks no end of Grant and is immensely pleased with the idea of my having such a good companion.' As for Petherick, his impact on the usually quiet household was meteorically successful. Speke's sisters all liked him, laughed openly at his clumsiness and adored him for bringing relief, however transient, from the peaceful monotony of their sober lives. Often the cause of their merriment would be innocent in the extreme, like the instance quoted in a note to Blackwood, Speke writing 'Petherick much to the amusement of the girls could not find his place in the books at church today.'[20] During a more serious visit in December 1859, Petherick had spent hours discussing with Speke what the latter described, in a favourite, though somewhat bloodthirsty, 'hunter's' idiom, as their plan for 'ripping open Africa together'.*

In this ambitious enterprise, for which Speke had enlisted Murchison's support, it was proposed that Petherick should ascend the Nile from Khartoum trading ivory as he went, mapping, and making observations for the Royal Geographical Society. At Gondokoro,[21] a tiny Austrian mission on the Upper Nile, Petherick would leave boats and supplies which Speke and his companion would collect on their way north from the Victoria Nyanza, Petherick meanwhile attempting to reach the lake by travelling south along the old Egyptian route.

Unlike Grant, who had wasted little time considering Speke's invitation, Petherick approached this latest scheme with caution. He estimated that to fufil his part of the plan he would require at least two thousand pounds, and applied through the Royal Geographical Society for Government support. The Society, which had only succeeded in procuring Speke's £2,500 from the Treasury as the result of a personal application from Murchison to his friend, Lord John Russell, rightly feared that Petherick's petition would not be welcomed. Instead, to meet the extra expenses of his journey, they recommended that

* Note Speke's frequent use of these idioms, e.g. 'hitting the Nile on the head'.

his Consular salary be raised to three hundred pounds a year.[22]

Having watched David Livingstone depart for Lake Nyassa with a grant of £5,000 and Speke prepare to revisit the Victoria Nyanza with half that amount, the Permanent Under-Secretary to the Treasury, Edmund Hammond, did not regard the suggestion with much enthusiasm. 'I must say,' he grumbled, 'the Geographical Society draw largely on us.' The proposal was rejected out of hand.

The recent scandal over the porters' pay had impressed on Speke the absolute necessity of re-entering Zanzibar with some display, preferably aboard a man-of-war; but warships, as he soon discovered, were no easier to come by than Government money. At length, Sir Charles Wood, on behalf of the India Office, promised that an Indian Navy vessel, similar to that in which Speke and Burton had sailed to East Africa in 1856, would be withdrawn from service at Aden to convey the expedition to its destination. Unfortunately, because of the war in China, no such vessels were available, nor any of the American trading schooners which Speke had suggested as an alternative. In desperation Shaw applied directly to the Admiralty and, his request being duly granted, a passage to Zanzibar was arranged for Speke and Grant on the 'new steam-frigate' H.M.S. *Forte*, via Brazil and the Cape of Good Hope.

The laborious organisation of the expedition still left Speke sufficient time to prepare a further series of articles for Blackwood which appeared in the issues covering May, June and July 1860, titled 'Captain Speke's adventures in Somaliland'. Even more than the series dealing with the Nile, the Somali articles were a personal statement, a therapeutic exercise which released some of the fierce tensions built up in the author over the previous six years. References to Burton were scant, but compensated in outbursts of exaggerated violence describing the roguishness of Sumunter, the obstructive devices of the sultans and the harshness of the desert. To Blackwood Speke wrote, '[I] feel happy at the relief their absence gives me.'[23]

Playfair, despite Speke's critical assessment of his book, contributed some photographs of Somali virgins and married women, 'a little got up for swell occasions', for which Speke, though he considered them untypical, thanked him generously;

'they are admirable photos,' he wrote, 'and I am very proud to have them'.[24]

Contrary to John Blackwood, Speke evinced little concern for the probable shock-effect on Victorian readers, women in particular, of his descriptions of mutilation and the horrible practice of slitting open pregnant mothers. Defending his frank treatment of these subjects in his first draft, he suggested that Blackwood might 'dodge with Latin or even Greek those *parts* too difficult to handle in simple English . . .'

Having thus provided his publisher with a solution, he proceeded to reassure him, 'Depend upon it, all those who would take the trouble to unravel the mystery concealed in a Foreign language would enjoy it all the more for the bother it occasioned them . . . one lady would translate it for another who could not.'[25]

Already the wary Blackwood had felt the need to modify Speke's 'rather specific description of the extreme nudity' of certain African tribes, but on the whole dealt leniently with the Somali manuscript. Remarking on this in a letter dated 27th March 1860, Blackwood wrote: 'I have not done it so carefully as I ought as constantly when I get interested I forget to note whether you are writing good or bad English. It is a most quaint and interesting narrative. There is a reality about your escape from the Somali which is better than the finest writing.' The letter concluded with a word of warning: 'Be sure you are right as to the exact point where Burton bolted from the camp after the attack, in case he should reclaim while you are away, which you will be when the description is published.'[26]

In fact, Speke was more concerned about leaving England without first having had sight of Burton's eight-hundred page, two-volumed *Lake Regions of Central Africa*, which was published in the early summer of the same year. 'I wish it was already out,' he sighed, 'for although I might be in his way, he could not run foul of me.'[27]

The remainder of the spring was devoted to correspondence and preparation: his letters to Norton Shaw were mainly technical, and concerned such matters as the supply of instruments, carbines for the caravan (about which he badgered poor Shaw unmercifully), the finalising of official Royal Geographical Society instructions and the straggling remnants of the pay-dispute correspondence. Despite his attention to these details, Speke eventually had to sail unencumbered with instructions of any kind from the Society, but when three and a half months later he reached Zanzibar, the council had pulled itself together and the instructions were ready and waiting at the Consulate.

Between himself and Burton, the breach had widened so as to be quite irreparable. In a conversation with Burton's wife, Isabel Arundell, Speke is reported as having said: 'I'm so sorry, and I don't know how it all came about. Dick was so kind to me; nursed me like a woman, taught me such a lot, and I used to be so fond of him; but it would be too difficult for me to go back now.'[28]

Whether or not this actually happened, a letter in the Quentin Keynes collection reflects a quite different attitude. To the end, it seems, Speke sought for a *rapprochement*; from Jordans, on 16th April 1860, two days before he left his home to return again to Africa, he wrote with an emphasis both touching and sincere: 'My dear Burton, I cannot leave England addressing you so coldly as you have hitherto been corresponding . . .'

Whatever his true feelings may have been, Burton's wounded pride forbade in his reply the smallest concession towards Speke's extended palm of friendship: 'Sir . . . I cannot . . . accept your offer concerning me corresponding less coldly – any other tone would be extremely distasteful to me.'[29]

In this way, all communication between the two men concluded, and the curtain fell, though not yet for the last time, upon the seldom happy, often tempestuous association.

Travelling by train from Taunton to Plymouth Speke and Grant arrived on 19th April at the Thomas Hotel, 31 Fore Street, Devonport, where they were obliged to wait for almost a week while repairs were carried out at Portsmouth upon the *Forte*. To Speke's disgust the *'wise* heads of the Admiralty' answered his telegraphed enquiry for advice by telling him to remain where he was; no surprise therefore that, a day or two later, Norton Shaw received a sarcastic little note which read, 'I am come to anchor again, the "Forte" has got a hole in her bottom, and has gone to the Doctor's to be plugged up.'[30]

The intervening days Speke divided between writing letters, correcting and enlarging the proofs of his Somali articles and reading snatches from a large parcel of books sent to him by John Blackwood. Approvingly, he remarked of the latter: 'Mill on the Floss seems very amusing . . . the Naval ones will do well for the ship.'[31]

In another note asking Blackwood to forward the 'Maga' every month to Africa, Speke defined his tastes in literature more precisely:

'I like political statistical or scientific reading better than any other and these your Mag. generally furnishes. Frivolous reading (novels) are refreshing when they come accidentally.'[32]

The damage to the *Forte*'s hull was quickly mended, and on the 25th (having meanwhile apparently joined the ship at Portsmouth Docks) he could write:

'I am now destined to clear out of England in 2 or 3 days at the most . . .'

The *Forte*, under the command of Captain E. W. Turnour, sailed from Portsmouth on 27th April 1860, carrying aboard her Speke and Grant accompanied by Sir George Grey, Governor of the Cape Colony, and the Commander of British Naval Headquarters at the Cape, Admiral Sir Henry Keppel.

Messages of goodwill showered the two explorers on their departure, including a personal letter from H.M. Prince Albert, the Prince Consort, wishing them 'God Speed'. The Prince's message, and the news that the French R.G.S. had decided to award Speke its Gold Medal,[33] came as indisputable signs of national and international recognition for his discoveries. In this respect they were perfectly timed and felt extremely gratifying.

His affairs, literary and financial, he left in the capable hands of his 'padre brother', Benjamin, and the only unfinished business concerned Petherick, and the means by which he might raise funds sufficient for his 'succour' expedition to Gondokoro and beyond.

NOTES

1. Burton to Norton Shaw, 19th April 1859. Archives of the R.G.S.
2. Speke: *Journal of the Discovery of the Source of the Nile,* Blackwood, 1863, p. 2. The *Journal* was published in America by Harper Brothers in the following year, and also appeared in a French edition in 1869.
3. Burton: *Zanzibar,* vol. II, pp. 390–1.
4. The proposals for a subsequent investigation of the reputed Victoria Nyanza were submitted and considered jointly at a special sub-committee meeting of the R.G.S. held on 20th June 1859. Both the proposals made by Speke and Burton were at first accepted, but ill-health prevented Burton from pursuing his romantic approach to the lake, by way of the Juba desert, in disguise. Burton, furthermore, was unable to fix a definite date for his departure and on 27th June the committee recommended to Council that Speke should receive the sum of £2,500 and command of the Nile expedition.
5. *Proceedings of the R.G.S.,* 1859, vol. 29, pp. clxxxii-vi.
6. *Ibid.,* vol. 29 (1859), p. xcvii.
7. Speke to John Blackwood: 10th July 1859. National Library of Scotland, Edinburgh, Blackwood collection, MS. 4143.
8. Speke to Blackwood, Sunday —? 1859, Inverness, N.L.S., Blackwood collection, MS. 4143.
9. Speke to Blackwood, 2nd September 1859, Inchbrae, Garve, Ross-shire, N.L.S., Blackwood collection, MS. 4143.
9A. Henderson, *The Life of Laurence Oliphant,* p. 91.
10. Speke to Blackwood, no date, 1859. Room 31, The Royal Hotel, Aberdeen. N.L.S., MS 4143. Dr. August Heinrich Petermann, editor of the *Mittheilungen,* author of official works dealing with Central Africa, the Arctic, etc.; including two works on Sir John Franklin, one the *Historical Summary of the Five Years' Search . . .* (London n.d.). Also *Reissen im Orient* (Leipzig 1860–1) and *Inner Afrika, nach dem Stande der geographischen Kennt in Jahre 1861 . . .* (Gotha, 1862) etc., etc. The famous *Mittheilungen* is a continuous current series comprising papers on every geographical topic, including reports on expeditions. It appeared first in 1855.
11. Another letter from the Royal Hotel, 1859, headed 'Tuesday', but giving no date. Speke to Blackwood, N.L.S., MS. 4143.
12. Speke to Blackwood, Sunday, no date, 1859, N.L.S., MS. 4143.
13. Speke to Blackwood, Jordans 11th April 1869, N.L.S., Blackwood collection, MS, 4154.

14. This and preceding extracts are published by courtesy of Mr. Quentin Keynes. See also Brodie: *The Devil Drives*, p. 170.
15. Burton to Shaw, undated draft on lined jotter paper, Quentin Keynes collection.
16. Benjamin Speke to Shaw 21st August 1860, Quentin Keynes collection.
17. In a letter from Speke to Blackwood, 11th April 1860, N.L.S., MS. 4154, Speke wrote: 'There is nothing in these papers but the honest truth and in no way do they show Burton in a false light.' Letter of 3rd November 1859, by courtesy of Mr. Quentin Keynes.
18. Speke to Norton Shaw, Archives of the R.G.S., London.
19. Speke to Shaw: 26th October 1859, archives of the R.G.S.
20. Speke to Blackwood: Jordans 18th April 1860, postscript, N.L.S., MS. 4154.
21. Gondokoro. See Speke, *Journal*, p. 4. J. A. Grant: *A Walk across Africa*, 1864, pp. 369, 370.
22. Dr. R. C. Bridges, Speke and the Royal Geographical Society, *The Uganda Journal*, March 1962, p. 33, ref. F.O. 2/36, *Memo* on R.G.S. to F.O., 30th January 1860.
23. Speke to Blackwood.
24. Speke to Playfair, Jordans 16th April 1860, N.L.S., Blackwood collection, MS. 4154.
25. Speke to Blackwood, 17th March 1860, E.I.U.S. Club, St. James's Square, London, S.W.1., N.L.S., MS. 4154.
26. Copy from the letterbook kept at William Blackwood and Sons, 45 George Street, Edinburgh.
27. Speke to Blackwood, 27th March 1860, N.L.S., MS. 4154.
28. Lady Isabel Burton: *The Life of Sir Richard Burton*, 1893, vol. I, p. 331.
29. Burton to Speke, from 14 St. James's Square, S.W., undated. Quentin Keynes collection.
30. Speke to Shaw, R.G.S. archives.
31. Speke to Blackwood, Thomas Hotel, 31 Fore Street, Devonport, 17th? April 1860, N.L.S., MS. 4154. Letter apparently misdated for sequence of correspondence suggests that the correct date should have been April 19th.
32. Speke to Blackwood, H.M.S. *Forte*, Plymouth, 30th April 1860, N.L.S., MS. 4154.
33. Speke to Blackwood, H.M.S. Frigate *Forte*, Portsmouth, 25th April 1860, N.L.S., MS. 4154.

CHAPTER 6

THE SECOND JOURNEY TO THE LAKES
1860-3

THE voyage from Portsmouth to Zanzibar lasted 108 days. From Madeira, Speke wrote twice to Shaw, the letters light-hearted and serious by turn. In the first of these, written on 9th May, Speke explained why his original freehand map, sent to the Royal Geographical Society from Africa, differed from the map subsequently published in *Blackwood's Magazine* in that it showed the Kivira river (supposed by Speke to be the Nile) flowing *into* the Victoria Nyanza and not *out* of it. Speke insisted that, as it had been said to flow in the opposite direction to two other rivers, the Kitangule and Katonga, and as further investigation had shown these to be *feeders* of the lake, the Kivira must therefore be an *effluent*. He had never seen the Kivira; his chief informant had been a slave; these geographical complexities had reached him through relays of interpreters of varying efficiency. Yet he felt confident.

Regarding an Arab merchant Abdullah's story of navigators on the northern waters of the Nyanza, he firmly asserted, 'I did not believe it to be any more than a traveller's tale'; and of the three rivers so critically important to the substantiation of his theory, wrote with airy unconcern, 'As I changed one, I changed all.'[1] This note of abandon had its echoes the following day when, in a vivid description of the previous night's *fiesta*, he confided, 'I was dancing away with the belle dames of this place until I nearly melted. There are some wondrous girls here, chummy, sweet and good natured – Don't you envy me.'[2]

After touching at Rio de Janeiro, the ship swung away south-east across the Atlantic and on 4th July sailed into Simon's Bay at the Cape. Here, Sir George Grey confirmed his 'lively interest' in the expedition by approaching representatives of the Cape Parliament, and Lieutenant-General Wynyard, Commander-in-Chief of the Cape Mounted Rifles, as a result of which the former donated £300 for the purchase of twelve baggage mules, and the latter provided Speke with ten Hottentot volunteers.

Speke meanwhile made arrangements with the firm of Saul Solomon & Company for the printing of a nineteen-page pamphlet called *My Second Expedition to Eastern Intertropical Africa,* which he forwarded to Blackwood through one of his sisters (probably Lady Dorington). This exceedingly rare document, a bound copy of which is now in the possession of Mr. Quentin Keynes, is a condensed version of pages 155–99 of *What led . . .* and was, at the time of printing, 'about the 5th part' of the journal which Speke hoped to publish as a book 'in the winter or next spring season', 1860–1;[3] 'by that time [he wrote] Burton's writings will have had a fair start of me – But a book I must have to do justice to those who accompanied me on that expedition'.

From Cape Town, Speke and Grant were taken north along the coast by one of the British Navy's slave-hunting corvettes, H.M.S. *Brisk*. The voyage was mainly uneventful, yet the travellers did not lack for occupation or amusement: there was 'shooting, band-playing, rubbers at whist . . . the various dogs, – Tawny, a clever collie: Ossian, a deerhound: and Lumpus, a retriever, etc., – sketching and photographing, drying botanical specimens, and picking up daily instruction in nautical observation'. Near the island of Mauritius, they encountered and disposed of an itinerant slaver; and, a fortnight later, on 17th August, the shoreline of Zanzibar, familiar to Speke, to Grant strange and exciting, swept into view. Grant much admired the bay in which the *Brisk* dropped anchor, but unlike his predecessor, Burton, was unimpressed by his first sight of the town; he wrote 'the streets . . . are too narrow for a wheeled carriage, and the supply of water deficient'.[4]

Christopher Rigby, having received them 'with true Indian hospitality' at the Consulate, arranged a meeting with the sultan of Zanzibar, Sultan Majid, to whom Speke handed over the India Office's present of a gold watch. While obviously pleased to renew Speke's acquaintance, the sultan did not hide his amazement that the old caravan route from Bagamoyo had again been chosen in preference to the shorter, more direct route over the Masai plains, but Speke explained (apparently satisfactorily) that he and Grant wished to explore thoroughly the west side of the Nyanza and visit the kingdom of Karagwe of which he had heard interesting reports.

Gradually Grant acclimatised to the township and its torpid way of life. He found the shopkeepers clean and respectful, delighted in the endless variety of the bazaar, and observed with Presbyterian solemnity the collections of slaves chained or guarded by swordsmen, 'saying to you with their eyes, "Buy me from the yoke of slavery"'. Thanks to Rigby's zeal in searching out and emancipating the slaves owned by Indian merchants, the practice had been to an extent controlled, and Zanzibar under his strong hand reposed 'in a state of great tranquillity'.

By contrast, the interior was a turmoil of bloody clashes between the Arab ivory-traders and the natives. After Speke's departure in 1859, a German missionary, Dr. Roscher, had been killed by tribesmen while travelling close to Lake Nyassa,[5] and it happened, by chance, that Grant participated in the execution of Roscher's murderers when Speke was away at Kusiki, shooting hippos with Admiral Keppel. The mood of the spectators gathered in front of the old fort was casual and cold-blooded. After several delays Grant, being one of the most important representatives of the sultan present, was asked to sanction the execution, to which, with characteristic deliberation, he replied, 'Yes, certainly; proceed.'

The sword fell twice; the decapitated natives 'appeared as if in a sweet sleep; two chickens hopped on the still quivering bodies, and the cows in the open space lay undisturbed'.

A further month saw the completion of all preparations for the expedition. Sheikh Said, anxious to redeem his good name, was once more appointed leader of the caravan. Although, to Speke's regret, the Hottentots had displaced the eager Beluchies, the hierarchy of native helpers included his trusted personal assistant Bombay, and Mabruki, Bombay's brother; at Bombay's suggestion Speke hired as servants three Hindi-speaking sailors formerly employed by the Consulate, Frij, Rahan and one other, named Baraka, of whom we shall presently hear more.

The remainder of the porters, one hundred and fifteen in number, were drawn from the ranks of the island's emancipated slaves and hired for a year's pay in advance, the balance to be paid on completion of the journey. With the unfortunate confusion caused by Hamerton still fresh in his mind, Rigby carefully entered all pay agreements in the Consulate's official ledgers, as a permanent, indisputable record. Eleven mules carried twenty thousand rounds of ball-cartridges, three score and four Seedies carried barter and equipment; for the convenience of the men, three or four women followed demurely behind the heavily loaded line.

Meanwhile, Speke and Grant tested thermometers, sextants, watches and compasses, checked guns and rifles, including fifty artillery-pattern carbines presented by the India Office, counted ammunition, purchased supplies of beads, brass wire and cloth, and supervised the dividing up of these and the rest of the stores into approximately equal individual loads. At the beginning of August, following Speke's instructions, Rigby had sent the first batch of barter goods ahead to Kazeh.

Once more the head of his own expedition, Speke was in his element, and certain that it would accomplish its objectives. A degree of recognition and honour had preceded the venture, but nothing to what would follow should it succeed; nor could his old friend 'Jim' Grant have made a better companion. Sympathetic to Speke's surges of boyish high spirits, acquiescent with his bouts of infuriating egotism and intolerance, Grant was able to share Speke's obsession with big-game shooting and preserving specimens, yet somehow still find time to collect wild flowers and plant-life from the wayside. He managed both, just as he managed to find time for encouragement, sympathy, conversation and advice and to be willing always to suppress his own wishes and follow, blindly if necessary, in the restless, inspired footsteps of his leader.

On 25th September, the third anniversary of Havelock's entry into Lucknow, the two explorers, escorted by Rigby, sailed across the narrow straits in the sultan's corvette, *Secundrah Shah*, to Bagamoyo, from where on 2nd October their straggling caravan started inland toward Kazeh. Speke took with him the belated instructions provided by the Royal Geographical Society, which stated that the expedition should go round the

Victoria Nyanza, find the source of the Nile, and thereafter trace its course to the mission-post at Gondokoro. Documentation should include all bearings necessary to establish the exact route on maps and sufficient notes to give a general, but accurate, description of the country through which they would pass. Lastly, and perhaps for Speke's particular benefit, came the reminder that the Society reserved for itself first rights to the publication of the expedition's report. It fell to Grant to record the journey by means of photographs and drawings; upon Speke the task of procuring the zoological collection.

The instructions stressed that the two men should endeavour to reach Gondokoro by December 1861, by which date it was assumed that Petherick would have arrived, bringing boats and further supplies. But how was Petherick going to achieve this? Following his initial proposals to the Society in the autumn of 1859, it had been assumed that the Treasury would provide the necessary finance, but by the time Speke and Grant left England it had become obvious that the only hope of raising the money was by public subscription.

Sir Roderick Murchison lent his powerful shoulder to the fund. He threw in twenty pounds from his own pocket; he persuaded the Royal Geographical Society Council to depart from its non-contributory traditions and give £100; he mustered further support from wealthy and influential members of the Society, and even succeeded in prising £100 out of the hitherto unwilling Foreign Office. Even so, the final total stood at only £1,200, eight hundred pounds short of what Petherick had estimated to be the absolute working minimum.

While the 'well seasoned Hercules' was struggling to launch his expedition, another venture, independently conceived and privately financed, was being planned by Samuel White Baker.* Baker had returned to England after a profitable sojourn in Europe and Asia Minor, where he had divided his time between big-game hunting and the construction of the Danube railway. It had been rumoured that, while still engaged upon the latter project, Baker purchased his second wife, a beautiful fair-haired Hungarian, at a slave auction in

---

* Sir Samuel White Baker (1821–1893), author of *The Rifle and Hound in Ceylon*, 1854; *Wild Beasts and Their Ways*, 1890; *The Albert N'Yanza*, 1866; *Ismailia*, 1874, etc.

Budapest; incredible though it may sound, the story is historically possible, and may explain why Lady Baker, as she afterwards became, was never received at court by the cognisant and scandalised Queen Victoria.

Baker himself was strong, fearless and determined, and like Speke, he thirsted after the thrill of exploration and discovery. He had approached the Royal Geographical Society about the time of Speke's discovery of the Victoria Nyanza with a scheme for continuing David Livingstone's researches by investigating the valley of the Limpopo, but despite the Society's approval, the Government had rejected Baker's request for £1,000. Now the situation was reversed: Baker's new proposal, to explore the region of the Nile sources, filled the Society with confusion. It had already committed itself to Speke, Grant and Petherick, and, although Baker had now plenty of money with which to back his project, the inevitable opposition of two major expeditions was not considered wise.

Instead, the Society advised him to explore the Sobat from its confluence with the White Nile in the southern Sudan, but, dissatisfied, Baker turned away determined to ignore the Royal Geographical Society and its red herrings, just as it had so politely ignored his request for professional assistance.

Dr. R. C. Bridges has noted that the Society suggested to Baker that he might enlist Burton's help on the Sobat journey, and perhaps arrange a rendezvous with Speke and Grant at some preordained point on the route. In view of Speke's known estrangement from Burton it seems an extraordinarily tactless suggestion, but, as Dr. Bridges comments, 'Nothing ever came of an idea which would have made the famous Gondokoro meeting of 1863 even more enlivened'.[6] Of Petherick's frantic struggle against the shortage of funds, of Baker's quiet determined planning to discover the 'true' source of the Nile, Speke and Grant knew nothing until they finally arrived at Gondokoro. Apart from Petherick's promise to be there with boats in November 1861, it is tragic that no further word of his activities reached Speke in Africa. Had it done so, a bitter confrontation at the mission and its unfortunate train of consequences might well have been avoided.

It is significant that, from the beginning, Speke's *Journal of the Discovery of the Source of the Nile*, describing this second expedition, reads with a breadth and intensity of detail quite reminiscent of Burton. That Burton had influenced Speke's work is undeniable, but, perhaps more important, the satisfaction of command and good companionship, above all the motivation of his belief in the Nile source, had enlightened and inspired Speke's entire being. Under the guidance of Burton, Blackwood and Oliphant, he had become increasingly competent as a writer, and with this new skill came a noticeable expansion in the scope of his thought and observation.

Nevertheless, Speke dismissed the 116 days' trekking which spanned Kazeh and the coast, writing that it was in parts so similar to 'marching up the Grand Trunk Road in Bengal' it would have been 'an easy affair' had only desertions among the porters been eliminated. In fact, by the time the expedition reached Kazeh, 113 of its 115 porters had disappeared; the ranks of the Seedies had been reduced by 31; five Hottentots were too sick to work, another dead; and the hardy caravan-leader, Sheikh Said had collapsed with an old, unspecified complaint, which one suspects (allowing for Blackwood's natural caution), must have been venereal.

Although most of the deserters had not previously travelled with Speke, he believed that they had fled away forgetting his fair terms and guarantees of payment, and remembering only the harsher treatment meted out by Burton.

Abandoning for a moment his façade of the stoical hero, Speke wrote movingly of this and other hardships in a letter to Rigby from Khoko in the region of Western Ugogo. The opening sentence, quaintly expressed in a fashion common to many English-speaking Indians, lends weight to the rumour that on returning to London from Africa in 1863, its writer for a time affected a kind of broken English:[7] 'We are scarcely knowing what to do. Before us is the desert of M'Gunda M'Khali ... all famished, and without a grain of food to sell us; yet these are not a quarter of the difficulties we have had to contend against.'

On their inland journey Speke and Grant had suffered the effects of fever and the persistent discomfort of torrential rain. The mules acquired in Cape Town had all succumbed, save one;

the precious stores, including those sent ahead, had dwindled under the ravages of tribal taxes *(hongo)*, theft and the demands of insatiably avaricious chiefs. If, in these circumstances, Speke had occasionally chosen to alleviate hardship by disregarding it, the same cannot be said of Grant; he did not complain, but neither did he euphemise. Of one barren region he observed: 'Food was not abundant . . . we had to trust to chance and our rifles.' Despite the quantity of game, in certain areas it frequently proved difficult to find. The constant killing which preceded the enormous trading caravans, the movements of tribal groups and the disruption caused by inter-tribal wars and skirmishes with Arab ivory-traders, tended to scatter the animals far and wide about the axis of the expedition's route. Sometimes, in very desolate country, the travellers went hungry. 'One night [wrote Grant] our entire dinner consisted of two ears of Indian corn eaten with salt . . .'

Apart from the shortages due to famine, they fared better in the M'Gunda M'Khali wilderness. There, Speke ventured close enough to shoot a rhinoceros, using one of his lightest rifles, and further west, in the same locality, had several exciting adventures with buffalo. At one place, he was charged three times in the same day. Having located an unsuspecting herd, Speke had opened fire, wounding a cow and a bull; the cow he eventually killed, but before following up the bull he decided, after the style of his generation, to pursue the remainder of the herd.

'Their footprints being well defined in the moist sandy soil, we soon found the herd again; but, as they now knew they were pursued, they kept moving on in short runs at a time, when, occasionally gaining glimpses of their large dark bodies as they forced through the bush, I repeated my shots and struck a good-number, some more and some less severely. This was very provoking; for all of them, being stern shots, were not likely to kill, and the jungle was so thick I could not get a front view of them. Presently, however, one with her hind leg broken pulled up on a white-ant hill, and, tossing her horns, came down with a charge the instant I showed myself close to her. One crack of the rifle rolled her over, and gave me free scope to improve the bag, which was very soon done; for on following the spoors, the traces of blood led us up to another one as lame as the last. He then got a second bullet in the flank, and, after hobbling a little, evaded our sight and threw himself into a bush, where we no sooner arrived than he plunged headlong at us from his ambush, just, and only just, giving me time to present my small 40-gauge Lancaster. It was a most ridiculous scene. Suliman by my side, with the instinct of a monkey, made a violent spring and swung himself by a bough immediately over the beast, while Faraj bolted away and left me single-gunned to polish him off. There was only one course to pursue, for in one instant more he would have been into me; so, quick as thought, I fired the gun, and, as luck would have it, my bullet, after passing through the edge of one of his horns, stuck in the spine of his neck, and rolled him over at my feet as dead as a rabbit. . . .'

Now tracking back again to the first point of attack, we followed the blood of the first bull, till at length I found him standing like a stuck pig in some bushes, looking as if he would like to be put out of his miseries. Taking compassion, I levelled my Blissett; but, as bad luck would have it, a bough intercepted the flight of the bullet, and it went "pinging" into the air, while the big bull went off at a gallop. To follow on was no difficulty, the spoor was so good; and in ten minutes more, as I opened on a small clearance, Blissett in hand, the great beast, from the thicket on the opposite side, charged down like a mad bull, full of ferocity – as ugly an antagonist as I ever saw, for the front of his head was all shielded with horn. A small mound fortunately stood between us, and as he rounded it, I jumped to one side and let fly at his flank, but without the effect of stopping him; for, as quick as thought, the huge monster was at my feet, battling with the impalpable smoke of my gun, which fortunately hung so thick on the ground at the height of his head that he could not see me, though I was so close that I might, had I been possessed of a hatchet, have chopped off his head. This was a predicament which looked very ugly, for my boys had both bolted, taking with them my guns; but suddenly the beast, evidently regarding the smoke as a phantom which could not be mastered, turned round in a bustle, to my intense relief, and galloped off at full speed, as if scared by some terrible apparition.'[8]

In Ugogo, Speke and Grant 'foraged zealously for the camp, and, by killing saltiana antelope, zebra and warthogs, succeeded in giving to everyone a little meat'. Grant shot a giraffe at Makata which was completely gobbled up except for the bones; the ears were spitted and roasted over the fire, the hide turned into sandals and the stiff, black tail-hairs used for stringing necklaces. Then, near Magomba's village, on 30th November, a male and female of a new species of antelope fell to Speke's rifle, a further pair being added on 2nd and 3rd December. Describing the creature in his *Journal,* he wrote:

'These animals are much about the same size and shape as the common Indian antelope, and, like them, roam about in large herds. The only marked difference between the two is in the shape of their horns . . . and in their colour, in which, in both sexes, the Ugogo antelopes resemble the picticandata gazelle of Tibet, except that the former have dark markings on the face.'

It should not however be inferred from these remarks that the Nile expedition bore down upon the game country of East Africa like a great juggernaut, intent upon slaughtering animals in tremendous numbers. Quite the contrary: from September 1860 until December 1862, Speke recorded a total of only eighty-one head of big game killed by himself and Grant.* This figure, which is by no means excessive, excluded animals fired at which escaped with wounds, and did not include numerous smaller species such as foxes, ferrets, hyraxes, lizards and squirrels. Nor did it include the many birds shot, among them partridges, pigeons, plovers, and guinea-fowl. Grant noted:

'Of game-birds, the ordinary guinea-fowl . . . was the most common . . . Early in the morning they roost lazily in tall trees, and in the evening they may be found near cultivations, chasing insects or grubbing up sweet potato. We killed one rare species, red round the eyes and on the throat, having a standing-up purple collar of loose skin, a ridge of ostrich-like black feathers from the back of the head to the nostrils, weight about 3lbs., and in running it seemed to have a more compressed body than the ordinary species.'[9]

Whereas on his journey with Burton Speke had been often lonely and had received little respite or compensation for the

---

* In a letter to John Blackwood, dated 26–?–1863, Speke wrote: 'I think you had better put in the game bagged, for though it is small it shows the diversity of animals met with; moreover we were not a sporting expedition.'

cumulative depression caused by illness, meagre sustenance and bad weather, the relief of tension and the interest created by hunting revitalised both him and Grant. In this important daily activity the Hottentots had their share, Speke writing to Rigby that they 'love the gun and delight in hunting for specimens'.

But a still greater warmth distinguished a reference to Grant, of whom he remarked, ['he'] is a very dear friend, and being a good sportsman we get through our days wonderfully'.[10]

The example of such a united leadership was not always heeded by the expedition's senior staff. Bombay, whom Speke had described in 1858 as 'This wonderful man . . .' whose 'good conduct and honesty of purpose are without parallel', found himself rivalled by Baraka, the recruit of his own choosing, both for status and for his place in Speke's affections. In a letter to Rigby Speke extolled the newcomer's qualities and in so doing appeared to confirm the worst of Bombay's fears: 'We often think of you and the great service you have rendered to the expedition by giving us Baraka and the others . . . Bombay with all his honesty and kind feeling, has not half the power of command that Baraka has.'

Intelligent, swaggering, conceited, Baraka had imposed his personality upon the caravan from the beginning. He coveted Sheikh Said's authority as *cafila-bashi* and envied Bombay's intimacy with Speke. His hunger for promotion, although at first unmanifested, soon grew to be unquestionable, and likewise ambition swelled his belief in his own superiority. Fearful and uncomprehending, Bombay followed Baraka's every movement, Speke tells us, 'like a bird fascinated by the eye of a viper'; yet he need never have doubted his master's loyalty. Inevitably, Baraka's conceit made him difficult to work with, and he forfeited charge of Grant's division of the porters; thus, when declining health obliged Sheikh Said to withdraw permanently from his duties at Kazeh, it was Bombay whom Speke selected as his replacement.

After crossing a treeless plain whose starkness reminded Speke of the Crimean landscape, the expedition entered Kazeh on 25th January 1861, where it was delayed for fifty-one days.

The rains, which had flooded the river beyond and prevented their obtaining grain, checked their advance and made the task of procuring porters in sufficient numbers almost impossible. During this period, Speke and Grant were very hospitably entertained by Musa Mzuri, a merchant who had shown Burton's caravan much kindness on its earlier visits. In the *Lake Regions* Musa was depicted as 'a man of the uncertain "certain age" between forty-five and fifty, thin-bearded, tall, gaunt, with delicate extremities, and with the regular and handsome features of a high-caste Indian Moslem'. Like so many of his race, he was, according to Burton, 'fated by opium which so tyrannises over him that he carries pills in every pocket, and stores them, lest the hoard should run short, in each corner and cranny of his house'.[11] Musa's establishment resembled a small village; besides wives and slaves it contained more than three hundred men and women, and included his elderly father, an ex-patriot of over thirty years, who, unlike Musa, had retained a perfect fluency in Hindustani.

Speke arrived in the settlement just as another former acquaintance, Sheikh Snay, was preparing to leave with four hundred armed men, in pursuit of a young renegade chief, Manua Sera, whom the Arab had recently deposed. On becoming chief after his father's death, Sera had imposed a levy on every ivory-trader passing through his territory with the result that the Arabs had usurped his power by force and installed a weakling bastard brother in his place. Sera then took to the country, vowing vengeance on the Arabs, raiding, plundering and killing in an effort to regain his rightful position. Speke, who had encountered the rebel near Kazeh, had learned the details of his predicament and had managed to persuade him to follow the expedition to its destination, in hope of negotiating a peaceful agreement with his persecutors. Sheikh Snay, who paid no attention to Speke's intercessions, was eventually cut down and killed when his contingent closed with the approaching forces of Sera; but in spite of this, Speke continued to stand by the raider, and afterwards wrote that Manua Sera was 'as fine a young man as ever I looked upon'. Sera's heroic image was doubtless heightened by comparison with other non-idealistic, grasping chiefs of Uzaramo and Unyamuezi; with the drunkard, Magomba, of M'Gunda

M'Khali; and, in retrospect with the leechings of two neigh-bouring chiefs, Lumeresi of Uzinza and the mightier Suwarora of Usui. After leaving Kazeh, Lumeresi detained Speke for over two months, from 23rd July until 6th October 1861. At this point Speke had left Grant, who was ill with fever, camped at Ukuni, north of Kazeh, while he himself forged ahead in an anxious search for porters.* His approaches to the surrounding chieftains, such as Makaka, met with little success and generally resulted only in the payment of an expensive *hongo*, or transit fee. Speke was still further handicapped when, from a bad chest-cold contracted on the windswept plains, he developed a harsh racking cough, which rapidly worsened until he 'blew and grunted like a broken-winded horse'.

Night after night, heedless of his condition, he sat out in the darkness taking astronomical observations between breaks in the cloud, and persisted in this occupation even when his instruments were so soaked with dew as to be totally unreadable. At Lumeresi's, the combined effects of the cold and these nocturnal labours finally overcame him. His chest became choked with mucus and his heart felt so tightly inflated that at any moment it might explode; each rasping inhalation caused him agony and every fit of coughing ended with his vomiting 'streams of phlegm and bile'. His left nostril was quite blocked with mucus, his left arm hung limp and paralysed; pain rent his liver, lungs and spleen and delirious dreams filled the nights with every kind of lunatic fantasy and horror.

In the midst of his sickness, the chief remorselessly renewed his demands for *hongo*, and, when paid, affected an immediate dislike of the articles given him. Speke roared like a caged animal in his suffering and tried to counter this and Lumeresi's subse-quent threats by pleading and persuasion which he frantically alternated with outbursts of helpless anger. When his two Unyamuezi guides Bui and Nasib deserted, discouraged by Lumeresi's intimidations, the shock nearly killed him. Pros-trated by fever, depressed by the guides' disloyalty, frustrated by his captors' ceaseless demands, and without Grant to turn to for comfort and advice, Speke subsided at last into tears, like a lost child bereft of reassurance and direction.

* Speke eventually obtained seventy men.

At times desperation brought him close to madness when, being too ill to go shooting for relief, he instead resorted to the same insensate masochism that on Kivira island had encouraged him to stab himself deaf to kill the beetle. As an example of this, Speke attempted to cure his feverish cold by bleeding himself, thrusting a packing-needle hard against his side; but in the end the attempt failed, for the instrument was so blunt that neither he nor Baraka could make it penetrate the skin.

Speke, to his 'inexpressible delight', was reunited with Grant on 26th September, fourteen days after Grant had left Ukuni to join him. While overjoyed to see his companion again, Grant received a 'sickening shock' at his wasted figure, a fact which Speke acknowledged in the *Journal* (6th October 1861), writing: 'I believe I was a most miserable spectre in appearance, puffing and blowing at each step I took, with shoulder drooping, and left arm hanging like a dead log, which I was unable ever to swing.' Grant too, had had his share of illness. Between May and July he suffered from daily attacks of fever, each lasting six hours, after which, in July, colds followed, brought on by the same sharp winds that unknown to him had so badly injured Speke. When free of the attacks Grant usually wandered about shooting birds or hunting, thus occupying his mind and maintaining a reasonable diet.

In general he was treated kindly by the chief of the village and his elderly wife, who showed him the deference he expected and considered to be his due. The chief, like the rest of the men, passed the time in drinking, smoking and conversation, while the women, who were well-built, handsome and as a rule conscientious, worked hard in the fields by day and by night danced in huge laughing groups beneath the moon. Unlike Watutsi women, those of Ukuni did not disfigure themselves by excessive tattooing, an example of which Grant humorously described: 'Some of the Watutsi females [he wrote] were observed to have their shoulders and breasts very handsomely tattooed to imitate lady's point-lace in front, and crossed like a pair of braces behind.'[12] In these equatorial regions, as in other parts of the continent during the nineteenth century (indeed up to the present day), the idyll of native village life, when viewed in isolation, gave an incomplete and superficial picture of the true conditions. Although in no way less fascinating or beautiful, the more gracious aspects of primitive existence such as drumming, dancing, harvesting and hunting usually concealed a sinister background of murder, torture and terrible disease.

In Ukuni, Grant witnessed with dismay the swift judgements of tribal law, and recorded one particularly vicious sentence served upon the lover of a young adulteress. The youth was lashed to some railings and his genitals, having been smeared with grease and bound in rags, were set alight. The sentence was concluded with a couple of spear-thrusts, one administered by the chief's son, the other by his daughter-in-law, after which the punctured, smouldering body was dragged unceremoniously by one leg out of the village gates.

Yet throughout the months from May to September, Grant's life compared to Speke's was much less harrowing; that Grant felt deep concern for Speke's welfare and safety is true, most certainly, but during that time Speke, as we have seen, had desperate need of him. More than Speke, Grant had succeeded in accepting the enforced separation philosophically, and later reflected that they had seemed 'like two planets compelled by a fixed law to preserve their distances'. The traversing of Usui, a province south-east of the Nyanza adjoining Uzinza, was accomplished with considerable difficulty and lasted nearly a month. Pillage, petty theft and demands for *hongo* made by Suwarora's subchiefs, Vikora and Virembo, further depleted the stores and frustrated the leaders, while a tipsy squabble over the women divided Speke's servants, Bombay and Baraka.

Thus, the relief shared by Speke and Grant may be easily imagined when, on 15th November 1861, the course of their destiny altered, they finally threw off the shackles of Suwarora and his henchmen, and marched out through a country of 'wild rocks and crags' towards the welcoming green hillsides of Karagwe.

In England, the appearance of Burton's *Lake Regions* in the summer of 1860 had caused mixed reactions of excitement and disapproval among geographers and members of the public.

Not least of its consequences was the interest focused upon the character and achievements of Hanning Speke, for Burton had used the book to direct a merciless personal attack against the field-work of his former colleague. In bitter language he challenged the validity of Speke's claims regarding the Nile sources, highlighting the careless errors which littered the evidence. Of these, among the most damaging to Speke's case had been his statement that the north end of the Nyanza lay between latitudes 4° and 5° N., when it was already known and accepted that Egyptian expeditions had penetrated as far south as latitude 3° 22′ N., without ever having encountered the northern shore of the lake.[13]

Contemptuously Burton criticised Speke's arrogant manner and wrote mockingly of his superior disdain for native African and Arab merchant alike; with scorn he remarked upon the younger man's apparent inability to learn or converse in foreign tongues, his failure as a negotiator, and his incompetence in almost everything save for hunting and the knack for recording features of an unfamilar topography.

Referring to Burton's reprisals and part of the manuscript of *What led* . . . which he had recently sent to Edinburgh, Speke wrote to John Blackwood from Bagamoyo on 1st October 1860:

'I have heard today from Rigby . . . that Burton has published some bitter things concerning myself in allusion to the lake expedition, and I must now say that if he has been impinging my honor [*sic*] in any way, I shall be very sorry that I have glossed over many of his transactions in the late papers which I sent to you for publication.

Indeed I shall much regret their being published during my absence if you can possibly keep the public in suspense until my return without injury to yourself. It is a lamentable affair going into contest with one with whom I was associated for such a length of time, but it must be done if he has published *such* matter as he wrote to the Govt. unless he has also published my response which I am sure he would not do. . . .

If the spirits of Burton's victims could only raise their voices to England now and tell their tale without a fault what strange rebukes would appear against the would be injured man who injures without scruple yet feels more sensitively than most other men.

'I promise you not only a large book, but one that justifies my every action no matter from what side attacked. If for no other object I desire to return as speedily as possible to set men's opinions on a proper train for judging fairly between us.'[14]

Although, in anger, Speke had resigned himself to the prospect of a prolonged bitter feud, his mother in distant Somerset took a calmer and very different view. Georgina Hanning had always accepted her husband's belief that public wrangling was both vulgar and unnecessary, so that while she could appreciate her son's feelings she decided that there had been scandal enough in the family, considering her painful recollection of Benjamin's experiences in London and the more recent and widespread embarrassment of Burton's debt. In an effort to shield her son, and to spare her family further anxiety, she herself wrote to Blackwood the following September:

'Some months since we requested you to stop proceeding with my dear son Hanning's book, to which you kindly consented.
Hanning's reason was that he felt so indignant with Capt. Burton for what he did and said and wrote that Hanning felt it due to himself to expose his conduct, but since that we have been so strongly recommended to dissuade Hanning from ever bringing before the public that altercation, that we wish to put it out of his power to do so, and Mr. Speke and my other sons all think it would be advisable to have his book published as he left it.'[15]

Replying to the letter, Blackwood agreed, but on condition that the explorer be informed of this decision, a just and loyal proposal with which Mrs. Speke concurred. But as yet Blackwood had not received the furious letter written from Musa's house at Kazeh, which Speke had headed with grim humour, 'all right & ready to fight', and which continued: 'I could stand it no longer, so I have let fly at Burton's eye, and I think he has got it, as richly as he deserves. . . . Old Grant says the man ought to be hung, an opinion I must say I long ago arrived at.'[16]

In this state of impasse the issue rested, its settlement protracted by the slowness of communications linking Europe with the '*dark* regions' of Central Africa; in the interval, no alternative remained but the silence of interminable waiting. 'Would that there were means of communicating with our dear wanderer', sighed Speke's mother, 'but it is vain to wish – many months must elapse before we hear of his whereabouts.'[17] Try as she might, it would have been beyond her power to imagine the hardship or the strain her son had suffered; for, like a good son and a cheerful brother, Speke had purposely kept his letters to the family light and optimistic, so that in particular Georgina, with relief, could tell her friends, 'The last was good news'.

Upon entering the fertile valley which separated Usui from Karagwe, Speke and Grant experienced an immediate sense of pleasure and freedom from the 'harassing attentions of Negro tribes'.

The king of Karagwe, Rumanika, sent representatives to welcome the travellers and bade them make haste to the palace, saying 'wherever you stop a day, the village officers are instructed to supply you with food at the king's expense; for there are no taxes gathered from strangers in the Kingdom of Karagwe'. In the hills, they saw the little lake of Urigi, in bygone days part of an immense gulf of the Nyanza, after which, on 23rd November, they left the valley and climbed quickly up the slopes of the 5,000-foot N'yamwara ridge. It was an exhilarating journey: 'Oh,' Speke exclaimed, 'how we enjoyed it!' Two days later, descending from the summit of Weranhanjie hill, the caravan came in sight of Rumanika's palace which stood on the edge of another lake surrounded by large leafy trees.

'As to the lake', wrote Speke, '. . . I christened it the Little Windermere, because Grant thought it so like our own English lake of that name. . . .

To do royal honours to the king of this charming land, I ordered my men to put down their loads and fire a volley. This was no sooner done than, as we went to the palace gate, we received an invitation to come in at once, for the king wished to see us before attending to anything else.'[18]

The quiet, unaffected manner and striking appearance of Rumanika and his brother, Nyanaji, were a delight, and each quite as impressive as their hospitality. 'They had fine oval faces,' wrote Speke 'large eyes and high noses, denoting the best blood in Abyssinia.'

Stories of these aristocratic pale-skinned people had long ago reached the coast, and it was Richard Burton who at Kazeh reduced the evidence to fit the sleek Bahima from the pinnacled stronghold of Prester John. Apart from his dignity and kindness, the king's obvious love of his country touched Speke deeply. 'Rumanika begged us to be seated on the ground opposite to him, and at once wished to know what we thought of Karagwe, for it had struck him that his mountains were the finest in the world; and the lake, too, did we not admire it?' Graceful, too, by comparison with other chiefs, was Rumanika's acceptance of the presents which Speke and Grant had brought with them. How magnificent the scarlet broad-cloth looked; what beautiful beads he had been given and in such enormous quantities; only his neighbour Mutesa, the king of Buganda, had ever received gifts such as these!

Curious as Speke had been about Buganda, impatient as he was to reach the northern Nyanza to rendezvous with Petherick and head for home, Rumanika had little trouble in tempting him to break his journey at the palace. Here, in comfort and tranquillity he was able to relax and for the first time in many months examine his surroundings at leisure. He observed that while the children were as slender and attractive as the Bahima men, custom condemned the princesses of the royal house to stagger about like huge black whales, burdened by layers of undulating fat. The girls' almost obscene rotundity fascinated Speke, but poor Grant, who was suffering agonies from a swollen, horribly ulcerated knee, had fewer opportunities and perhaps less palate for contemplating the royal maidens.

Left to himself, Speke felt his fascination soon begin to exceed his natural sense of propriety. One of the king's sisters-in-law being especially vast, he made up his mind to measure her, promising in return to show the lady 'a bit of [his] naked arms and legs'.

'The bait took as I wished it,' he wrote, 'and after getting her to sidle and wriggle into the middle of the hut, I did as promised and then took her dimensions. . . . All of these are exact except the height, and I believe I could have obtained this more accurately if I could have laid her on the floor. Not knowing what difficulties I should have to contend with in such a piece of engineering, I tried to get her height by raising her up. This, after infinite exertions on the part of both, was accomplished, when she sank down again, fainting, for her blood had rushed into her head. Meanwhile, the daughter, a lass of sixteen, sat stark-naked before us, sucking at a milk-pot, on which her father kept her at work by holding a rod in his hand; for, as fattening is the first duty of female life, it must be duly enforced by the rod if necessary. I got up a bit of flirtation with missy, and induced her to rise and shake hands with me. Her features were lovely, but her body was as round as a ball.'[19]

The measurements of the princess fully justified his efforts: 'Round the arm, 1 foot 11 inches; chest, 4 feet 4 inches; thigh, 2 feet 7 inches; calf, 1 foot 8 inches; height, 5 feet 8 inches.' While the incident represented little more than a piece of admittedly gross, but innocent entertainment, in print it proved damaging to Speke's reputation. James McQueen, when writing the series of articles which in 1864 became his contribution to Burton's *Nile Basin*, corrupted the episode in order to blackguard Speke, for by then any weapon was anxiously sought and Victorian laws of libel were apparently more relaxed than the narrow code of prudish morality.

In a section of the book headed 'Manners and Customs', McQueen, quoting Speke's account, commented 'We believe none of our readers ever met with or ever heard of a piece of "engineering" as this, and we dare say will never wish to meet with such another'.

Burton fully approved of, and was indeed enthralled by, McQueen's outpouring of righteous abuse, declaring that while 'His literary labours in the cause of the Dark Peninsula have extended through half a century . . . hardly ever before has he shown greater acumen or higher spirit – to say nothing of his inimitable dryness of style. . . .' One should not forget, however, that McQueen's attack was published two months after Speke's death and, except from Grant, was in little danger of informed retaliation, for it is doubtful that Grant, the principal defender of Speke's honour and integrity, had been an eyewitness to any of the events described.

On 5th December, Speke received as a present from Ruman-ika a specimen of the now familiar sitatunga antelope or water-tragelaph, which proved similar to the species discovered on Lake Ngami by the missionary David Livingstone. The distinctive, spirited creature seemed to him well adapted to its semi-aquatic environment:

'so long were its toes, it could hardly walk on dry ground; while its coat . . . was long, and of such excellent quality that the natives prize it for wearing almost more than any other of the antelope tribe. The only food it would eat were the tops of the tall papyrus rushes; but, though it ate and drank frequently, and lay down very quietly, it always charged with ferocity any person who went near it.'[20]

After Speke's return to England, the creature's scientific designation, *tragelaphus spekeii*, was derived from his name, but while several skins and heads were brought back by the expedition, there is no evidence that any were actually shot either by himself or Grant.

At Rumanika's palace, Speke watched the 'New Moon Levee', a ceremony wherein district representatives paid the king monthly homage against the rhythmic throbbing of thirty-five drummers and the 'good rough Highland fling' danced by some of the girls. During frequent palavers Rumanika and he discussed religion, education and tribal lineage, the relative development of each other's countries and the means by which the Nile route into Central Africa and the Masai trade route might be opened up. On these occasions, Rumanika was especially impressed by Speke's novel reflections upon the Old Testament and certain of his remarks in regard to Bahima ancestry. Delighted, Speke wrote how the king

'dwelt on my theological disclosures . . . (tracing his descent from Abyssinia and King David) . . . with the greatest delight, and wished to know what difference existed between the Arabs and ourselves; to which Baraka replied . . . that while the Arabs had only one Book, we had two; to which I added, Yes, that is true in a sense; but the real merits lie in the fact that we have got the better *book*, as may be inferred from the obvious fact that we are more prosperous, and their superiors in all things, as I would prove to him if he would allow me to take one of his sons home to learn that *book;* for then he would find his tribe, after a while, better off than the Arabs are. Much delighted, he said he would be very glad to give me two boys for that purpose.'[21]

Owing to the freedom and facilities provided by Rumanika, Speke had become too involved with the court and was, besides, too concerned about the work that lay ahead, to explore seriously the country in the immediate vicinity of the Little Windermere.

One evening in November, strolling back to his camp at sunset, he glimpsed the distant peak of Mount Mfumbiro shining on the far horizon; but of the Mountains of the Moon, ancient rumours of which had originally attracted him to equatorial Africa, he saw no sign. Echoing the words of Rene Bere, Mr. Ian McMorrin has written in his most interesting book on mountains of the world that, while Speke observed the Virunga Volcanoes in 1858, 'the *Lunae Montes* eluded discovery'. 'Fittingly', Mr. McMorrin continues, 'the highest peaks [of the Ruwenzori] bear the names of the men who so eagerly sought them, although it is not without irony that the highest commemorates not the chief protagonists in the "Nile Duel" . . . but the explorer [H. M. Stanley] who first saw them'.[22] Speke believed that his Mfumbiro, 'said to be the highest of the "Mountains of the Moon" ', rose to a height of 10,000 feet; but the highest in fact, Mount Stanley, has twin peaks, Margherita (16,763) and Alexandra (16,749), and even Mount Speke (16,042) is six thousand feet higher than the explorer's published estimate.

Of greater interest to Speke in 1861 was a conversation in which Rumanika mentioned that Kamrasi, the king of Bunyoro, had been given beads of a pinkish colour not known to the Arab traders of the east coast. Eagerly he snatched at the scrap of evidence, convinced that the beads must have been brought to Kamrasi from Egypt by way of the Nile. It came as a sore disappointment when, having stirred Speke's imagination and revived his determination to reach Buganda as quickly as possible, Rumanika, speaking of the Kabaka, reminded him that on no account would Mutesa permit ailing travellers to enter his country. The Arabs and Swahilis had introduced venereal disease, which had yet to see its phase of popularity in Buganda, thus every foreign illness was diagnosed as such and potential carriers strenuously prohibited. Once again, as had happened three years before with Burton, Speke's plans were threatened with failure because of his responsibility to 'a sick companion'.[23] To make matters worse, Grant's poisoned leg, instead of improving with rest, defied applications of poultice, native medicines, even fresh gunpowder rubbed into cuts made in the swollen parts, and day by day grew steadily more malignant.

It is the measure of his strength of character as of the extent to which he accepted his position as a subordinate, that Grant neither complained excessively of his misfortune nor in any way made the next inevitable parting harder for Speke than was absolutely necessary. He instead acknowledged his leader's single-minded devotion to the main objectives and resigned himself to a further period of limited activity, during which he recorded his surroundings by sketching, painting in water-colours and taking notes. Even these quite moderate tasks could only have been performed with some restraint for, besides his infirmity, the index finger of Grant's right hand was missing (the result of an old wound), a disability which must have impaired, however slightly, his facility as a draughtsman.

Christmas in Karagwe came and went, celebrated by the king killing one of his finest long-horned oxen, which he then presented to Speke. At last, on 7th January 1862, a Moham-medan trader named Juma arrived at the palace bringing Rumanika lavish presents of slaves and ivory from the young Kabaka Mutesa, who also sent messages emphasising that he waited anxiously for the advent of the white travellers. Some days previous to Juma's arrival, there had come rumours of an unidentified expedition marching on the Victoria Nyanza from the north, exciting news which Speke and Grant instantly interpreted as meaning Petherick, for neither was then aware of any other possibility. Speke at once dispatched Baraka – he being missed least of all – with letters addressed to the Consul, and at the same time sent another slave off to the coast with a packet containing letters, reports for the Royal Geographical

Society and as many specimens as he could carry; but it was a matter of days later that the arrival of a large deputation of Baganda forced Speke's hand. On 10th January he bade farewell to Rumanika, to his stricken friend a reluctant *au revoir,* and marched away to the pirouette of flute and drum towards Buganda and one of the strangest adventures of his African career.

His expedition had already distinguished itself by making important botanical and zoological collections, gathering information on the Bahima and mapping large tracts of unknown country; but now Speke would add to it and to himself a permanent wreath of fame by becoming the first person ever to enter, and completely traverse, the extraordinary kingdom of Kabaka Mukabya Mutesa.[24]

NOTES

1. Speke to Dr. Norton Shaw, R.G.S. archives.
2. Speke to Dr. Norton Shaw, Madeira, 10th May 1860, R.G.S. archives.
3. Speke to Blackwood, H.M. Corvette *Brisk,* East London, 21st July 1860. N.L.S., MS. 4154: 'My sister will send you a paper which I had printed at Cape Town.'
4. Grant: *A Walk across Africa,* 1864, pp. 10, 11.
5. *Ibid.,* pp. 17, 18, 19. Speke and Burton met Roscher at Konduchi, whilst they were waiting for a ship. See also *Tanganyika Notes and Records,* No. 49, December 1957, p. 283 and fn.
6. Dr. R. C. Bridges: *The Uganda Journal,* p. 344 ref. Baker to Shaw, 20th November 1860: Council Minutes, 10th December 1860; Oliphant to Baker, January 1861.
7. Speke to Rigby, 12th December 1860, R.G.S. archives.
8. Speke: *Journal,* pp. 65, 66, 67 (Blackwood, 1863).
9. Grant: *A Walk across Africa,* pp. 36, 37.
10. Mrs. Charles E. B. (Miss Lillian M.) Russell: *General Rigby.*
11. Burton: *The Lake Regions,* vol. ii, p. 225.
12. Grant: *A Walk across Africa,* p. 99.
13. Burton: *The Lake Regions,* pp. 204–8. In *The Uganda Journal,* vol. 26, No. 1, March 1962, a very detailed discussion by Mr.

B. W. Langlands, pp. 1–22, examines 'Concepts of the Nile' pre-dating Speke's exploration and discoveries.

14. Speke to Blackwood, Bagamoyo, 1st October 1860, N.L.S., MS. 4154.
15. Georgina Speke to John Blackwood, Jordans, 25th September 1861, N.L.S., MS. 4164.
16. Speke to Blackwood, 1st February 1861, N.L.S., MS. 4731.
17. Georgina Speke to Blackwood, 25th September 1861, N.L.S., MS. 4164.
18. Speke: *Journal* (Blackwood, 1863, pp. 202, 203).
19. *Ibid.*, p. 229 (Blackwood, 1863, p. 231).
20. *Ibid.*, p. 221 (Blackwood, 1863, p. 224).
21. *Ibid.*, p. 236.
22. Mr. Ian McMorrin took on the difficult task of editing the *World Atlas of Mountaineering*, originally begun by his friend, the late Wilfrid Noyce. The volume was published by Messrs. Nelson, in October, 1969.
23. In the MS. draft of the *Journal*, N.L.S., MS. 4872, Speke has scribbled, then deleted: 'I only regretted I was burthened with a sick companion [Burton] . . . but I resigned myself to my fate feeling confident as soon as I returned to England and made all the circumstances of my discovery known, that I should soon return again – I was not wrong.'
24. Mr. B. W. Langlands: 'Early Travellers in Uganda: 1860–1914', *The Uganda Journal*, March 1962, pp. 55–71. See especially pp. 55, 56, 57: 'Speke was the first outsider to travel right through Uganda', p. 57.

CHAPTER 7

THE COURT OF MUTESA

It is important to understand something of the history of Buganda immediately prior to Speke's visit in order to appreciate its significance. In 1856 the king, Kabaka Suna, died suddenly leaving behind him the bewildering total of sixty-one eligible sons and a serious vacuum of doubt in the minds of the Prime Minister and his chief advisers as to which of them would be strong enough, yet for their purposes be sufficiently impressionable, to stand as his successor. At length they chose one of the least likely candidates, a quiet unassuming youth named Mukabya Mutesa, whose mother, the Dowager Queen, already exercised considerable control over the government of the country. The early years of the new reign were filled with uncertainty and threatened with continual opposition, but for much of the period the Kabaka's influence was slight, and responsibility for government was shared equally by his mother and the Prime Minister, or *Katikyro*, called by Speke Kamraviona, as chief officer of the Ganda state.

To prevent news of this internal unrest from reaching Buganda's neighbours, the kingdom was for several years completely closed to trade and every form of communication with the outside world.

In due course Mutesa, despite his somewhat feminine appearance and innocent demeanour, proved himself to be infinitely more capable and determined than anyone had ever imagined. By 1860 the power of the Prime Minister had diminished down to nothing and by February 1862, when Speke arrived, the influence of the Queen Mother had begun to show signs of a marked, if still strongly defended, decline.

Partly to satisfy his gruesome lust for blood which he expressed in ludicrous, fantastic forms, partly to endorse his supremacy by fear, Mutesa from time to time indulged in vast ritual massacres among his own people. One of these terrible affairs, called by the Baganda *kiwendos,* which occurred only a short while before Speke reached the palace, sacrificed 'fifty big men and four hundred small ones' and was probably no more than an outlet for the excitement Mutesa felt at the prospect of seeing the white man.[1]

The party of Baganda, headed by a royal officer or ambassador named Maula, led Speke down from the heights of Karagwe over a flat, swampy plain to the edge of the Kitangule river, which four years previously he had deduced as being a western feeder of the Victoria Nyanza. Because of a rainstorm and the superstitious natures of the ferrymen, Speke was unable either to take soundings, make drawings, or determine the width of the river with any accuracy, a disappointment which, although he did not realise it, came also as a foretaste of the future.

Greater than the restrictions imposed by language and the misunderstanding of his escort was Speke's over-riding anxiousness to reach Mutesa and thereby make his way to the source of the Nile. In consequence, he paid little heed to the western contours of the Nyanza beyond catching occasional glimpses of its shoreline from the Buddu hills on the journey into Buganda. In many respects he took both 'the shape and existence' of the lake very much for granted and made no serious effort to check his assumptions even though, in Karagwe, he could have done so by means of an easy two-day match to the east. As it was, on his maps he misplaced the west shoreline, showing it fully a third of the lake's total width too far to the east, and made no immediate effort to re-check his level of the lake surface, 3,740 ft., taken in 1858; in fact, despite the known inaccuracy of the instruments, this level had been only twenty feet above the true figure, but a subsequent estimate made at the north end of the Nyanza in 1862 went wildly wrong.

At Maula's village, where they halted, Speke learned to his dismay that, regardless of Grant's bad leg, Mutesa wished to see him also, and at once sent a message telling the patient Scot to wait for boats if he did not feel well enough to manage the journey by litter. Speke clearly realised that Grant's observations from a canoe would 'give us a much better knowledge of the lake', yet still one feels that he had acted with unusual caution by not ignoring Rumanika's warning and bringing his companion with him in the first place.

He did, however, attach great importance to the meeting with Mutesa. Having heard in Usui that the Kabaka wanted to open up a trading route across the Masai plains, and being hopeful that he might soon rendezvous with Petherick near the palace, Speke now contemplated only a rapid survey of the exact position of the Nile source and thereafter a straight march over the Masai to the coast.

Speke's plan was as confident and ambitious in its objectives as any ever conceived by his contemporaries. Having identified the source, he would have been prepared to postpone any further investigation of the Nile, although he should have, and indeed probably had, realised the importance of connecting the unknown source with the known section of the river. But after solving what to him seemed the major problem, he was eager to tackle others, and the difficulty and danger of the Masai route had attracted him ever since Burton had refused to attempt it in 1857.

Like Rumanika, the Kabaka had assured Speke that on his way to the palace provisions would be made available free to him and his men. Unfortunately, Speke's followers found the staple Buganda diet of plantains disagreeable and demanded grain, for which they were given currency in the form of beads. This gesture caused a dispute with the ambassador, Maula, the outcome of which was that Speke dispensed with him and took another of Mutesa's envoys, an amiable Usui chieftain called N'yamgundu.[2] Unfortunately, the change of escort was the indirect cause of a squabble between Speke and Bombay. Before N'yamgundu would lead the way to the palace, he insisted upon first rounding up some cattle which Mutesa had sent down for Speke and instructed Bombay not to break camp until his return. When he did not reappear the following morning, Speke began to fear that the delay might give Maula the opportunity of intimidating N'yamgundu, thereby needlessly prolonging the journey to Mutesa's capital. 'I waited', he wrote, 'restraining my impatience until noon, when as I could stand it no longer, I ordered Bombay to strike my tent and commence the march.'[3]

To Speke's astonishment, the normally faithful and obedient Seedy refused to co-operate. Describing the incident in the *Journal* Speke continued:

" 'How can we go?" said Bombay. "Strike the tent," said I. "Who will guide us?" said Bombay. "Strike the tent," I said again. "But Rumanika's men have all gone away, and there is no one to show us the way." "Never mind; obey my orders, and strike the tent." Then, as Bombay would not do it, I commenced myself, assisted by some of my other men, and pulled it down over his head, all the women who were assembled under it, and all the property. On this, Bombay flew into a passion, abusing the men who were helping me, as there were fires and powder-boxes under the tent. I of course had to fly into a passion and abuse Bombay. He, in a still greater rage, said he would pitch into the men, for the whole place would be blown up. "That is no reason why you should abuse my men," I said, "who are better than you by obeying my orders. If I choose to blow up my property, that is my look-out; and if you don't do your duty, I will blow you up also." Foaming and roaring with rage, Bombay said he would not stand being thus insulted. I then gave him a dig in the head with my fist. He squared up, and pouted like an enraged chameleon, looking savagely at me. I gave him another dig, which sent him staggering. He squared again: I gave him another; till at last, as the claret was flowing, he sulked off, and said he would not serve me any more. I then gave Nasib orders to take Bombay's post, and commence the march; but the good old man made Bombay give in, and off we went, amid crowds of Waganda, who had collected to witness this comedy, and were all digging at one another's heads, showing off in pantomime the strange ways of the white man. N'yamgundu then joined us, and begged us to halt only one more day, as some of his women were still at Kisuere; but Bombay, showing his nozzle rather flatter than usual, said, "No; I got this on account of your lies. I won't tell Bana any more of your excuses for stopping; you may tell him yourself if you like." N'yamgundu, however did not think this advisable, and so we went on as we were doing. It was the first and last time I had ever occasion to lose my dignity by striking a blow with my own hands; but I could not help it on this occasion without losing command and respect; for, although I often had occasion to award 100 and even 150 lashes to my men for stealing, I could not, for the sake of due subordination, allow any inferior officer to strike Bombay, and therefore had to do the work myself.'[4]

Through Speke's reaction to Bombay's quite understandable fear of imminent catastrophe, one sees in sharp relief that unreasonably overbearing attitude shared by so many Victorian explorers. It is to a degree excused by his appreciation of Bombay's status on the caravan, even if it did not prevent his administering the thrashing publicly; but perhaps there is a greater dignity in the Seedy's refusal to retaliate when, had he indeed been insensible with rage, such retaliation would have been inevitable. That Speke subconsciously regarded the apparent change in Bombay's behaviour as a kind of racial hazard rather than something spontaneous or accidental may be explained by his use of the word 'chameleon' when recalling the incident, but, whatever his feelings, it is certain that the second and particularly the third blow was superfluous, being delivered out of anger rather than necessity.

Further along the way, Speke's party encountered a scattering of cowherds led by Mutesa's officers, driving a hundred head of cattle to Karagwe as a present for Rumanika. It was a gift that plainly symbolised the Kabaka's joy at the coming of the white man, even more than it betokened his gratitude to Rumanika or sending him on so quickly. Speke wrote with some pride that already N'yamgundu had told him how Mutesa, on being given a silk handkerchief which Speke had sent ahead from Maula's village, had wrapped it around his head in ecstasy, crying out, 'Oh, the mzungu, the mzungu! He does indeed want to see me.'

Halting at a village close to the palace, Speke could scarcely believe his eyes at the surrounding devastation; acres of gardens and fields had quite literally been eaten bare by a succession of visitors to the Kabaka who had been forced to await his capricious pleasure. Determined that he, an important English traveller, would not be kept waiting like a common trader, Speke at once sent N'yamgundu off to arrange an interview with 'the father of the Nile' and was relieved to learn the following evening that Mutesa had become so wild with delight that he had decided to fast until Speke should see him, an indication of the haste with which Speke was expected to proceed. Three pages confirmed the message the next morning, urging Speke most excitedly to hurry and requesting, as a further titillation for their master, a few grains of the Mzungu's gunpowder.

After another night in the bush and another day of trekking, there arose at last in front of the party the low, closely-cropped hill on which stood the giant, thatched huts of the palace. Trembling with anticipation, Speke exclaimed, 'I had never seen . . . such a sight in Africa before.' The grandeur of the scene was hardly diminished by a light drizzle which had begun to fall, but the rain sufficed to detain Speke from going straight to the Kabaka himself, and the palace officers showed him instead a damp, dirty hut at the foot of the hill where he was told that he must stay. Fevered with excitement, but wholly conscious of his unique position as Mutesa's first white guest Speke rejected the hut he had been given and demanded another within the palace enclosure. 'I stuck out for my claims as a foreign prince,' he explained later, 'whose foreign blood could not stand such an indignity. The palace was my sphere, and unless I could get a hut there, I would return without seeing the king.'

Knowing the violence of the Kabaka's rages, poor terrified N'yamgundu begged Speke to be content, at least until he had met and spoken with Mutesa, but by contrast, the royal officers were not greatly impressed by their visitor's bravado. The court in their eyes represented the most refined, most sophisti-cated way of life in the whole world; their monarch, in whose hands lay the absolute power of life and death, was like a god. The fact that Mutesa had been enraptured by the news of Speke's approach merely defined him as yet another rival for the Kabaka's favour, and from the beginning it was as a rival, purely and simply, that the court determined to treat him.

In all, Speke spent four and a half months in Buganda at the court of the Kabaka, and devoted a section of 135 pages to the visit in his book, *Journal of the Discovery of the Source of the Nile*. This description is of the greatest importance to historians, for not only was Speke the first European to meet Mutesa and travel in his country, but the largely favourable report which he brought home helped to determine the European attitude to

Buganda from then on. It is equally significant that Speke entered the region in a peaceful manner; that his party came heavily armed is true, but only because of reports that warlike tribesmen, the Watuta, had been raiding at different places along the route.

From such impressions of the court as he had gleaned from the guide, N'yamgundu, who feared Mutesa, from Rumanika who considered the Kabaka to be a great and generous ruler, and from chief Irungu of Usui who lived in both Usui and Buganda alternately and whose loyalties were in consequence divided, Speke had a somewhat confused idea of what treatment to expect. His curiosity, however, was soon satisfied. On 20th February, the day after his arrival, Mutesa's pages announced that the Kabaka would receive him. Having arrayed twelve of the men in scarlet cloaks, each of whom carried a carbine, bayonet fixed, upon his shoulder, Speke walked to the palace, dressed in his best suit of clothes, as befitted his sense of panache as 'a prince' of Great Britain. The rest of the caravan brought up the rear, while Maula, N'yamgundu and Speke marched to either side of the procession. As a final touch, the leader of the porters paraded slightly ahead of everyone, holding aloft a fluttering Union Jack.

It is doubtful whether the crowds of Baganda pressing in on both flanks, covering their mouths with their hands in astonishment, and exclaiming 'Beautiful! beautiful!', had ever witnessed so peculiar a sight; yet sartorially, Speke felt himself somewhat drab compared to the brilliant display of the native audience.

'They wore neat bark cloaks resembling the best yellow corduroy cloth, crimp and well set, as if stiffened with starch, and over that, as upper cloaks, a patchwork of small antelope skins, which I observed were sewn together as well as any English glovers could have pierced them; while their head-dresses, generally, were abrus turbans, set off with highly-polished boar-tusks, stick-charms, seeds, beads or shells; and on their necks, arms and ankles they wore other charms of wood, or small horns stuffed with magic powder, and fastened on by strings generally covered with snakeskin.'

Speke was also surprised and not a little peeved to see his troop

Mutesa's palace, and one of Mutesa's cattle,
watercolours by Speke, 1862

Speke and Grant in 1863, with 'Bombay' in the background,
by Henry Wyndham Phillips

preceded into the palace enclosure by representatives of chief
Suwarora, led by Irungu, carrying a hundred coils of brass
wire as a gift for Mutesa. His grievance seems perfectly justi-
fiable when one realises that these very wires had been taken
from him in Usui during his unhappy bondage, and had formed
a considerable portion of his own intended present to the
Kabaka. Nevertheless, his offering was still relatively lavish.
It consisted of '1 block-tin box, 4 rich silk cloths, 1 rifle (Whitworth's), 1 gold chronometer, 1 revolver pistol, 3 rifled carbines,
3 sword-bayonets, 1 box ammunition, 1 box bullets, 1 box
gun-caps, 1 telescope, 1 iron chair, 10 bundles best beads,
1 set of table knives, spoons and forks'.

The huts comprising the palace were arranged in tiers
ascending the hill. Speke, unprepared for the strict ceremony of
the court, approached the second tier which formed the ante-
chambers to the throne-room, but instead of being shown into
one of the huts was asked to sit down, under the hot sun, on the
bare earth of the yard outside. As might be imagined, this
indignity, though unintended, struck the sensitive explorer as
cruelly insulting. '. . . I had made up my mind never to sit
upon the ground as the natives and Arabs are obliged to do,'
he complained, 'nor to make any obeisance in any other manner
than is customary in England. . . .'

This point of view and the other difficulties which confronted
Speke and his contemporaries have been resolved by John Allen
Rowe in an unpublished thesis on the Baganda, into three main
types: first, the essential difference in ideas and standards, for
instance of morality, honesty, honour; secondly the problem
of communication: in Speke's case this frequently led to complex
conversations relayed through three or more interpreters; and
thirdly the question of rank and deference.[5]

We have already seen all three of these factors in action and
have noted how Speke, unlike Burton, tended to preserve his
identity as an Englishman in Africa, only accepting the maxim
of 'when in Rome . . .' with the utmost reluctance. So it was
that, after a few minutes sitting on the hard ground exposed to
the hot sun, he rose to his feet in a fit of pique and, resisting all
attempts to make him stay, strode angrily down the hill
towards his camp. He had not gone far when one of the royal
officers came running after him imploring him to return.

Mutesa had heard of his withdrawal, was bitterly upset and refused to touch any food until Speke came back.

Fortunately for Speke, but perhaps more especially for the courtiers, Mutesa's fascination for the Mzungu had out-stripped his highly unpredictable temper, so that not only did he listen to his visitor's complaints, but allowed him to bring an iron stool to sit on, a concession until then unheard of in the kingdom. Agreement having been reached, the royal orchestra struck up a melody. In the background the nine-stringed Nubian harps twanged their jangling, metallic rhythms, as Speke advanced through the second tier of shelters, towards the Kabaka's private quarters. He was preceded as usual by a line of twirling flute-players and drummers, their instruments festooned with intricate bead-work and hung with skins of civet.

It was a spectacle worthy of Rider Haggard's romances; Speke sat on his stool, an umbrella fully spread above his head, directly facing Mutesa. In the *Journal* he wrote of the occasion:

'A more theatrical sight I never saw. The king, a good-looking young man of twenty-five, was sitting on a red blanket spread upon a square platform of royal grass, incased in tiger-grass reeds, scrupulously dressed in a new mbugu (toga). The hair of his head was cut short, excepting on the top, where it was combed up into a high ridge, running from stem to stern like a cock's comb.'

The young Kabaka's arms, legs and fingers were richly ornamented with amulets, charms and beads, and each alternate finger was encircled with a ring of brass or copper. He drank almost continuously from cups containing plantain wine, wiping his mouth with a piece of bark cloth and a square of gold-embroidered silk. Around him stood his chiefs of staff, his dark, Grecian-looking female sorcerers, his wives and sisters who administered his every need; close by was a separate symbolic grouping consisting of a white dog, a woman, a spear and a shield. Other officers, grouped in front of the throne, wore robes mostly made from cowskin, although a few, con-nected with the royal house, wore skins of spotted civet. Leopard skins lay on the ground among the squatting officers and ceremonial drums stood silently about like dim, truncated pillars.

Throughout the entire first meeting, not a word passed between Speke and the Kabaka. The two men sat, looking at each other across the tense space, the Kabaka admiring Speke's clothes, his umbrella (which he had to open and shut several times for his amusement), his wideawake hat, and the bright magenta cloaks of the armed escort. 'I longed to open conversation', he wrote, 'but knew not the language, and no one near me dared speak.' Presently, after enquiring if Speke had truly seen him, the Kabaka retired with ungainly loping strides to his private chamber. Intrigued by his curious walking motion, Speke asked Bombay 'if anything serious was the matter with the royal person', but it came as a mixture of relief and surprise to learn that Mutesa's ungainliness was deliberate, being an imitation of the regal posturings of the lion.

But the interview was not yet over. Having broken his long fast, Mutesa returned and immediately began a conversation, first with polite pleasantries, then with enquiries about Rumanika. After a while he again retired and the meeting place shifted, this time to another open hut, where, with Speke seated in front of him as before, the Kabaka once more asked whether he had seen him, 'evidently desirous of indulging his royal pride'. At that point as a sign of friendship Speke gave him a gold ring, wrought in the form of a dog-collar, taken from his own finger.

Mutesa thereupon made a tantalising response: if Speke desired friendship, how would he like to be shown a route which would take him to the East Coast in four weeks' marching? Speke anxiously pursued the question, but owing to the complex system of interpreting was too slow and the Kabaka meanwhile changed the subject. (Speke's messages were then being relayed first through Bombay, then Nasib of Kazeh, then N'yamgundu or Maula, and thence with considerable deference to Mutesa.) Thus the Kabaka's next question concerned not the Masai route but instead guns. The two-grooved Whitworth and all the other presents were ceremoniously handed over, after being touched by Nasib to prove that they were immune from witchcraft. Mutesa could scarcely contain his pleasure at the sight of so many gleaming mysteries and was still playing with them when torches flared up against the falling night, and the levee ended, the presents being thrown together into a blanket and borne away by slaves.

Three days passed before Mutesa would see Speke again. This time he was requested not to bring his stool, but, accepting the concession of the first day, to sit as other guests were obliged to do, on a pile of grass. Mutesa at once asked Speke to shoot four cows which slaves led into the courtyard, but as there was no ammunition available to demonstrate the Whitworth, he had to use the revolver, felling the unsuspecting creatures with five quick shots. The massacre brought loud applause but the *pièce de résistance* had yet to come. Mutesa, visibly impressed with Speke's performance, handed one of the carbines to a little page, commanding him to go to the outer court and kill a man! This the child speedily accomplished although, to Speke's horror, the cold-blooded and quite unnecessary murder excited no noticeable reaction in the onlookers; they had already grown so accustomed to atrocities of the kind that fear and indignation, if it existed, had long ago been dulled into acceptance, and, in any case, to dissent would have meant instantaneous execution.

A week or so after his arrival, throughout which he made endless efforts to communicate with Petherick and Grant, Speke was suddenly informed by the Kabaka that, according to the etiquette of the court, the dowager Queen Mother must receive a visit from him once in every three days. The gesture reveals how the Queen Mother, though fast losing her once tremendous influence, still merited some token of her power and position; apart from which, as Mutesa had hitherto demanded all Speke's attentions, the prospect of a change seemed welcome. Besides, Mutesa had no illusions about the extent of his authority, and Speke could see that if his plans were to succeed, even to the point of contacting Grant and Petherick, the sympathy and support of the royal lady might be very useful.

Carrying his status symbol, the umbrella, Speke visited the Queen Mother half a mile away in her private residence, a hutment surrounded by a fence of 'tiger-grass', which he observed so resembled that of her son that 'everything looked like the royal palace on a miniature scale'. As she had for some time been feeling ill, he brought with him the medicine chest in addition to an attractive present of wires, beads and cloth.

Speke wrote that 'Her Majesty – fat, fair and forty-five' received him in the customary silence, sombrely clad in a long, bark-cloth toga and seated on a carpet spread out upon the ground. . . . Eventually, the four female sorcerers who stood close to the Queen were dismissed and Speke was bidden approach, while beer was circulated among the assembly and pipes were lit. Speke sat as before on a modest 'throne of royal grass' entertained by a band of swaying drummers, flute-players and harpists who performed melodiously within the hut. After a while the court-hut was completely cleared save for Speke and a handful of the most important ministers, when the Queen Mother, who had meanwhile changed into another, coloured robe, proceeded to explain the nature of her illness to her visitor. She suffered, she said, from a combination of insomnia, stomach-upset, liver-pains and, worst of all, a lonely heart; her husband, the late Kabaka Suna, had been dead six years yet she still missed him dreadfully.

Speke at once reassured the Queen Mother that her sleeplessness was no more than 'a common widow's complaint' but stressed that in order to understand and cure her other maladies, he would have to examine her tongue, after which it would be necessary to take her pulse and possibly feel her sides. His original manuscript account of what ensued, which both Grant and Blackwood considered 'slightly indecent',[6] is much more pithy than the watered-down version published in the *Journal*. Quoting selected extracts from the first draft, we find Speke writing, 'The dreams and sleeplessness I told her was a common widow's complaint, caused by deprivation of her husband's company at night'. Continuing, he tells us that the Queen Mother, angered by her ministers' insistence that she should on no account submit to an examination, turned on them scornfully, crying, '. . . bosh! I will show my body to the Mzungu and bidding the Wakungu hide their faces lay prostrate ready for operation. I feel her and she likes it. . . .'[7]

There is no doubt that the Queen Mother was rapidly becoming much attracted to her handsome, bearded 'doctor' and the pathos of her middle-aged coquetry was only equalled by the daring of Speke's highly-effective intrigue. At the end of the interview she told him in Luganda idiom that she must see him again as the one brief visit could not satisfy her need. This request Speke translated for his first draft in a manner which, if acceptable to modern readers, would certainly have scandalised the public of Victorian England: '. . . but still she says her "belly" is not full of me', he wrote, 'I must return again two days hence, for she loves me much, excessively, she can't say how much'.[8] Subsequent visits to the Queen Mother's palace found Her Majesty at first no better, and then quite suddenly almost totally recovered. During the third audience, the native-brewed *pombe* flowed exceedingly freely, the wild music of the royal orchestra shrieked and throbbed at fever pitch, while the occupants of the court-hut leaped and danced about in unsuppressed orgiastic glee. The display of such flagrant debauchery depressed and sickened Speke who sat apart, observing the performance in silence and disgust. At last the sight of these intelligent, refined people so prostituting themselves, including the Queen Mother who lay 'drinking, pig-fashion' from a trough of beer, forced him to rise and take his leave. With an effort, as much as to the consternation of the assembled ministers, Speke managed to tell the Queen Mother that 'although I dragged my body away, my heart would still remain here, for I loved her very much'.[9] In making this bold declaration, Speke had sought to accelerate the slow-moving intrigue, the delicate playing-off of the Kabaka's affections against those of his mother, and the process by which he hoped to gain considerable local influence at the same time to achieve his objective of discovering the source of the Nile. Throughout the ensuing weeks he carefully divided his attentions between both parties, giving shooting lessons to Mutesa and with him making brief, crowded and only partially successful forays into the bush after game, enjoying meanwhile the hospitality and provocative conversation of his mother.*

Thus, by the end of March, two months after his arrival, Speke's life at the palace had begun to grow very pleasant. He had continued to correspond with Grant, whose leg was

---

* Cp. Speke's relationship with his own mother.

only slowly improving, but as yet had received no further word of the mysterious expedition to the north, nor made any significant advance towards a settlement of the Nile. He had likewise failed to communicate more profitably on the subject of the Masai route and in spite of being himself comfortably housed in a new royal hut, found difficulty often in keeping his forty-five followers content and properly fed. Contrary to his youthful habit of abstemiousness and the almost ascetic hunter's life which he had once led amongst the mountains and valleys of northern India, it would appear that in Buganda Speke had learned to appreciate more fleshly pleasures, pursuing relentlessly the comfort and ease from which he had formerly held such revulsion. More accurate it is to say that in achieving influence, the quest for which obliged him to be lenient in such unfamiliar directions as eating, drinking, coquetry and inactive leisure, he may have been seduced into temporary love of their intrinsic charms. Whereas on his first arrival at the palace, he had been lonely, friendless and possessed only of the most trivial amusements (such as watching the antics of a hen that used to lay her eggs on his camp-bed), he quickly invested himself with status, due in part to his dazzling prowess with his guns and rifles, in part to his mystique as a European, but also in a large measure to his personality and consequent success as the friend of both Mutesa and the Namasole, or Queen Mother. On 30th March, the Queen Mother presented Speke with two young Bahima girls, one named Kahala aged about twelve years, the other a little older. The older girl Speke named Meri, the native word for plantain. To begin with, the girls, to whom Speke referred as his specimens of Natural History, proved difficult, refusing even to eat, but after a time he could write that he felt a 'paternal love for these little blackamoors as if they had been my own offspring'.[10] The paternal attitude changed somewhat later, however, when, describing Meri's continual fretting, Speke burst out in the original manuscript draft of his *Journal*, 'Oh God, was I then a henpecked husband!'[11]

But fortunately his female interest was not confined to the two girls and their friends. At the first opportunity he commenced to flirt quite openly, though at a respectable distance, with the prettier members of the Kabaka's household, a reckless proceeding which suggests that, delighted with Mutesa's familiarity and exhilarated by his personal triumph Speke had foolishly thrown caution to the winds. Little wonder that the Prime Minister stared aghast at the explorer's unprecedented audacity, murmuring, 'Woh, woh! what wonders will happen next?'

On 7th April, the Kabaka again took Speke out shooting, followed as usual by his women, an orchestra and about one hundred of his advisers. To satisfy his own vanity, as much as to honour his companion, Mutesa was dressed in the European clothes which Speke had given him, even to a wideawake perched on top of his woolly head. The whole affair was of course a complete fiasco, for neither buffalo, the chosen game of the day, nor any other wild creature could have been successfully approached amidst such a clatter of music and shouting – though one gathers that the Kabaka, like Speke, was well aware of this fact. At one place the party came to a stream over which sagged the broken remains of a wooden bridge. To cross the stream there was no alternative but to wade through it. Taking instant advantage of the predicament, Speke gallantly invited each of Mutesa's women to ford the water straddled piggy-back fashion over his shoulders. The incredulous Kabaka at first gaped in awe, then, finding the humour of the situation to his liking, burst into fits of loud, crude laughter in which his relieved following heartily joined. Not one of the women refused Speke's outstretched hands, but the highlight of the escapade came when he carried over Lubuga, the most coveted member of the Kabaka's harem. She, more than any of the others, Speke imagined, had been particularly anxious 'to feel . . . what the white man is like'.[12]

A few days later, while walking on some grassland near the palace, Speke was 'accosted' by Kariana, the wife of one of Mutesa's ministers. After a brief introduction to the lady, Speke wrote 'I offered her my arm, showing her how to take it in European fashion, and we walked along, to the surprise of everybody, as if we had been in Hyde Park rather than in Central Africa, flirting and coqueting all the way'. Such surprising descriptions of intimacy with African women which are not to be found in the works of either Burton, Baker, Grant or Livingstone, annoyed the Royal Geographical Society and added fuel to the fires stirred up by Speke's academic opponents such as McQueen. Inevitably, the humour so manifest in his accounts completely evaded his narrow-minded critics, who either stated or inferred that implicit in these most superficial liaisons was an orgy of licentious living enacted at Speke's royal hut against the bloodthirsty backcloth of Mutesa's intemperate court.

There can be little doubt that, by writing in this vein, Speke secured for himself that questionable reputation which combined with his occasionally loose or inaccurate geography to damn him for a decade, a fate that was largely, if not entirely, undeserved. It is equally certain that, had he spent more time surveying the northern limits of the Victoria Nyanza and in pressing for an immediate exploration of the Nile sources themselves, the impact of subsequent adverse criticism would have been appreciably lessened.

On 14th April Speke wrote once more to Grant, about whose movements information was still confused and inexact. The very next morning, to his great joy, there came news that Mutesa's scouts had sighted the unidentified expedition far to the north, led by a bearded white man and accompanied by another, clean-shaven. Convinced that the bearded traveller must be Petherick, Speke wrote off a letter urging the Consul to hurry south as quickly as possible, but, rather presumptuously, cautioned him against wearing any kind of uniform on arrival lest he undermine Speke's bogus princely state. As if that were not enough, Speke begged his friend to expect and accept with good grace a position at the court inferior to that of his own! Yet, in spite of such strange advice, he felt thrilled at the proximity of the relief expedition and on 22nd April sent three servants, Mabruki (Bombay's brother), Budja and Bilal, to meet it, at the same moment dispatching another trio into the southern bush with a note addressed to Grant.

The explorer's spirits would have been considerably dampened had he but realised that a Maltese ivory trader, Amabile de Bono,[13] and not John Petherick, was leader of the northern party. Torrential rains, which had fallen also in Buganda, had meanwhile swelled the rivers, including the

Aswa which lay between Speke and Gondokoro on the Upper Nile. During this period, De Bono waited on at Faloro, but later returned to inform Petherick that he had neither seen nor heard anything of the Nile expedition, by now four months overdue. Petherick was quite naturally concerned at the news. His resources were already stretched to the utmost, a fact which more than ever obliged him to conserve his trading interests, else risk losing his livelihood altogether. Apart from ivory-trading, it was his supreme task as Consul for 'Inner Africa' to keep the Sudan as free as possible from slaving – the practise of which he justly abhorred.

Petherick had already battled up the Nile through fierce head-winds and troughs of calm, in an effort to compensate for time lost, having earlier missed the favourable flow of the river. His fair-skinned colleague the botanist Brownell had died of fever, a fate shared by Brownell's talented young assistant, Foxcroft. With the coming of the seasonal rains, the Nile waters rose in flood and the gallant Welshman, his wife and their companion, Dr. Murie, were brought once more to a standstill.[14]

Meanwhile at the palace, on 23rd April, Speke was summoned from his hut by breathless pages, and urged to make haste and join Mutesa for a three-day hippo-shooting cruise on the Nyanza. Being unprepared for the sudden start, Speke had no time to collect his notebooks, instruments, men or camping equipment, nor could he ascertain whether the Kabaka's message referred to the *Victoria* Nyanza or some other obscure lake or river, to which *nyanza*, as a general term, applied; thus a valuable opportunity for surveying the north-west portion of the lake was lost. The Cowes of Uganda, as Speke described it, began from the royal boathouse sited five hours distant from the palace on the west bank of a creek which he named in honour of Sir Roderick Murchison. As usual, the hunting element existed only as a motive and provided no more than an excuse, if such were needed, for further feasting, drinking and dancing, some of which towards the end of the cruise took place on a tiny islet in the Nyanza itself. On the first night, after a meal eaten at the boathouse, Speke noted with evident chagrin that Mutesa 'turned in with his women in great comfort, and sent me off to a dreary hut, where I had to sleep upon a grass-strewn floor'.

Again, it must be stressed that this slightly ambiguous comment should not lead one to imagine that its writer had turned soft as a result of the *good life* at Mutesa's court, for Speke could still work, sleep and travel in conditions as rough as those in which he had delighted ten years earlier. But in Buganda, he had felt obliged to concern himself with *status,* in part, perhaps, as a reaction to the treatment he had received from the Usui chiefs, and the bitter remark about his bed of grass was no more than a complaint that his assumed princely status had been ignored. It may have been partly restored however on the following day of the cruise, when the lake surface grew so rough that the Kabaka, who shared Speke's canoe, had more than once to grasp the explorer's tawny beard to keep his balance. The third day found the party debouched upon the islet, where one of the girls, thinking to please Mutesa, offered him a piece of freshly-picked fruit. Outraged by the simple gesture, the Kabaka threw a tantrum and ordered her immediate execution and, while his other women wailed and clamoured for mercy, the offender was brought bound and weeping to his side, whereupon the Kabaka seized a cudgel and began to strike the poor creature hard about the head. The last proved too much for Speke; at first dismayed and disbelieving, then filled with anger at Mutesa's senseless cruelty, he leapt forward and, holding back the Kabaka's arm, demanded that the girl be instantly released. In the horrified silence which followed, Speke realised that the action had placed his life in serious jeopardy, but the Kabaka eventually smiled, relaxed his uplifted arm, and, as a token of respect for his white companion's bravery, cast the sobbing girl aside.

Not only was Speke's relationship with Kabaka Mutesa fraught with continual if frequently petty misunderstandings, but the Queen Mother had begun to show her displeasure at the way he appeared to ignore her, having achieved reasonable terms of intimacy with her son and having already received her young girls into his quarters. When, almost as an afterthought, Speke visited her again on 7th May, the royal lady kept him waiting for fully five hours and in the end stalked out angrily to rebuke him: 'You won't call on me now I have given you such a charming damsel; you have quite forgotten us in your love of home'.[15] On the 11th, three letters arrived from Grant, saying that his native convoy had been too afraid to journey up to Buganda by water and were bringing him overland instead. Shortly after that, Mabruki, Budja and Bilal returned from Bunyoro with the news that Petherick had not reached that district, but was moored further north on the Nile, at Gani.

As if these disappointments were not enough, Mutesa's kitchen-boy continually misinterpreted Speke's request for fresh supplies, as a result of which there was now frequently little for him to eat; once in desperation he shot a few doves and breakfasted off these, a fact which greatly annoyed the Kabaka and caused the kitchen-boy to lose his ears! Yet his diet continued poor, in consequence of which, combined with his perpetual concern for Grant and Petherick, his domestic troubles and the effort of constantly intriguing with Mutesa and the Queen Mother, Speke contracted a severe, feverish cold. For several days he lay abandoned by the whimsical Kabaka with nothing to eat and only a dribble of beer to quench his thirst. He had only just begun to recover when on 27th May Grant was carried in to the tuneful rattle of musket-fire; despite his own weakness and Grant's still exceedingly painful leg, the reunion was everything that it might have been. In the *Journal*, Speke wrote of that happy occasion:

'How we enjoyed ourselves after so much anxiety and want of each other's company I need not describe. For my part I was only too rejoiced to see Grant limp about a bit, and was able to laugh over the picturesque and amusing account he gave me of his own rough travels.'[16]

Although his sojourn at the court of Buganda was shorter than Speke's had been, and his dealings with Kabaka Mutesa and the Dowager Queen more distant and more respectable, Grant derived considerable satisfaction from the experience. He made drawings of Mutesa in watercolour and pencil and remarked approvingly of the young man's personal cleanliness, 'clever-looking clear eyes', and 'good teeth'; the Queen Mother struck him as a pleasant, homely woman, in spite of the fact that, being only partially reconciled to her share in Speke's divided affections, she repeatedly kept the companions waiting for hours, seated 'amongst steaming natives', whilst deciding whether or not she would receive them. Perhaps the Queen Mother's rapidly waning authority within the kingdom, which was largely responsible for her fickleness, her undue concern to make her presence felt, also explains why, playing upon her vanity, Speke could have used her remaining influence with Mutesa to his advantage, when, by 1864, only eighteen months later, the Queen Mother had no power left to wield.

In most of its aspects Grant found the court impressive. He admired the industry and capability of the native craftsmen, the fine quality of their workmanship, and their knack of reproducing by sight even items so foreign to them as the white man's rifle-cases and articles of clothing. He and Speke gave drawing lessons to Mutesa who, being an apt pupil, afterwards amused himself between continual eruptions of entertainment by making little sketches on squares of bark-cloth *paper*. These flattering imitations of the European tradition were reciprocated by Speke's men, who sported the cowskin cloaks and bark-cloth robes of the Baganda. The atmosphere at the palace had never been more cordial, whilst good reasons for Speke to prolong his stay were many and valid: neither he nor Grant had made any kind of accurate survey of the Nyanza's shoreline, nor had they seriously attempted, with Mutesa's assistance, to circumnavigate so much as the northern extremity of the lake; furthermore, Grant was still unfit for marching, or indeed strenuous exertion of any kind. Yet still Speke seemed determined to lighten the burden of his responsibilities by leaving Buganda as quickly as possible. Before the expedition had left England, he had heard John Petherick swear that 'I would under no circumstances as long as I had life desert him [Speke] in the interior, and ... would keep boats for him at Gondokoro for an indefinite period.'[17] This extremely generous promise, which Speke had rightly accepted at face value, fully encompassed the otherwise imprecise provisions of the Royal Geographical Society's contract with Petherick. So convinced was Speke of the Consul's utter sincerity, so certain had he become that the reports of Mutesa's scouts had referred to Petherick and to no other, that June 1862 saw him at the pitch of desperation to be gone from the Kabaka's court. Even his once-cherished hope of traversing the Masai plains had long since been abandoned in favour of the promised rendezvous at Gondokoro; whilst above everything there remained the problem of the Nile itself.

It took much persuasion for Mutesa to agree to Speke and Grant's departure, but, having heard of the travellers' pressing desire to push up north through Bunyoro, he at length relented. (Rumanika had apparently insisted that Mutesa forbid Speke to enter Bunyoro and be instead sent back to Karagwe, but he, capricious as ever, conveniently demonstrated his superiority over Rumanika by ignoring the request and acceding to Speke's wishes.) Nor did Mutesa allow his visitors to leave empty-handed: sixty cows, fourteen goats and ten loads of butter accompanied them, in addition to a load of coffee, another of tobacco and at Bombay's suggestion, a hundred bark-cloth *mbugus* for the porters.* Speke's final meetings with the Kabaka were as usual polite, but tinged with sadness and a marked reluctance on Mutesa's part to accept the fact of the travellers' imminent departure; at each interview he would open conversation with the words, 'Well, Bana, so you really are going?' and painfully Speke in turn would have to assent.

It may be that something in the frank approaches, the bravery and open-hearted humour of John Hanning Speke had touched a chord of sympathy in the Kabaka's savage breast. If occasionally Speke had behaved with an unusual absence of decorum, or chosen devious rather than direct means to further his own immediate ends, such aberrations were more than compensated by his fairness, his patience and his customary kindness and friendliness towards Mutesa and the Baganda in general. With the result that the favourable impression made by Speke on the court of Buganda is probably greater than that of any other traveller in any other part of Africa, before or since. To which the example of Sir Samuel Baker in the Sudan might provide the only possible exception. John Allen Rowe has concluded nevertheless that Speke left Mutesa's country, his only legacy being 'a number of presents, the novelty of his white-skinned appearance, and little else of concern to the Baganda'.[18] But surely this cannot represent the

* As a memento of his visit, Speke himself received from Mutesa a beautiful little circular wooden stool or 'throne', now in the possession of Mr. Peter Speke.

whole truth. Dr. Bridges has noted that Mutesa took to wearing trousers and a hat and, like Speke, preferred henceforth to sit on a chair; that he promised Speke his men would now always fight with guns – and, to this end, actually formed a regiment of musketeers; that he began to comprehend that his kingdom was *not* the centre and focus of the world. The Kabaka told Speke, 'Bana, I love you, because you have come so far to see me, and have taught me so many things since you have been here.'

The explorer is spoken of still today, even in quite remote areas, and referred to as 'Sapiki' or remembered by the old-fashioned type of percussion gun he gave to Mutesa, known as the 'Makoowa Speke'. Most important of all, Speke opened the minds of the Baganda to the prospect of Western civilisation and to some extent prepared them for the influx of European travellers that was to follow: 'not many years will pass before you will see other Europeans coming to trade with this country', he had prophesied, 'coming from many different races of Europeans now unknown to you. From what I have seen of this country it contains much for Europeans to do.'

His final words upon the subject, 'When you see many Europeans here you must fear them no longer', whether or not they were actually heeded, nevertheless stood as the foundation for all Uganda's subsequent dealings with Europe in the future. At the same time, as we shall see, a whole new vision of trade and development within Central Africa had begun to spring up in Speke's fertile mind, to which the settlement of the Nile sources provided but one, albeit vitally important, key. May he likewise be forgiven if in his enthusiasm, sincere and benevolent as it was, he foresaw only the goodness and prosperity and not the evil and concomitant decay which would result from the breaking open of Africa's dark core.

Speke and Grant left Mutesa's palace on 7th July 1862. To mark the sad moment and to assuage his frustration and grief, the Kabaka killed one of his wives – an easy sacrifice. Then, at the foot of the tiered, royal hill, he reviewed the assembled Nile expedition for the last time. Profuse thanks and farewells were exchanged, the incomprehensible utterances of the Baganda mingling with the drawling voices of the expedition's two leaders. Thereafter, Mutesa turned and walked quickly up the hill to the palace, 'in gigantic strides', while the favourite among his women, the pretty little Lubuga, skittered merrily at his heels, waving and crying 'Bana! Bana!' until both she and Speke were out of sight and hearing.

NOTES

1. John Allen Rowe's unpublished MS. thesis and Speke's own on the Baganda.
   Speke: *Journal*, p. 263. From this account, the court assumed a quality in many respects similar to that of the Queen of Hearts in Lewis Carroll's *Alice in Wonderland*.
2. Speke: *Journal*, p. 275–6. 'N'yamgundu delighted me much: treating me as a king, he always fell down on his knees to address me, and made all his "children" look after my comfort in camp.'
3. *Ibid.*, p. 270.
4. *Ibid.*, pp. 270, 271, 272.
5. John Allen Rowe: *The Baganda*, unpublished MS.
6. See letter sent by J. A. Grant from Dingwall to John Blackwood, Monday (no date) 1863, N.L.S., MS. 4181.
7. Speke, original MS. draft of the *Journal*, pp. 319, 320, N.L.S., MS. 4872, Blackwood collection.
8. *Ibid.* In the published version Speke modified the Queen Mother's words, writing, 'Still she said I had not yet satisfied her . . .', p. 307.
9. Speke: *Journal*, p. 316.
10. *Ibid.*, p. 400.
11. Speke: MS. draft of the *Journal*. N.L.S., MS. 4872. See also the *Journal*, p. 402.
12. Speke: *Journal*, p. 353.
13. Amabile de Bono, a nephew of Andrea de Bono, a Maltese slave-trader who operated in the southern Sudan. B. W. Langlands, *The Uganda Journal*, 1962, p. 57, writes:
    'Amabile established a trading station at Faloro in the present East Madi count[r]y. Being a Maltese he was the first European to have entered the bounds of the present Uganda.' Ref: Thomas, H. B. and Scott, R., *Uganda* (1935).
14. See Brodie: *The Devil Drives*, pp. 220, 221; Petherick: *Travels in Central Africa*, 1869.

Speke photographed at St. Andrew's in 1864

The Speke Memorial, Kensington Gardens

15. Speke: *Journal*, p. 409.
16. *Ibid.*, p. 421.
17. J. Petherick: *Travels in Central Africa* (1869), Vol. II, p. 86: 'I personally promised Speke, not only to do my utmost to support him in his audacious undertaking, but, as long as life lasted, never to desert him.'
18. John Allan Rowe: *The Baganda,* unpublished MS.

CHAPTER 8

THE FOUNTAINS OF THE NILE

LED by Budja, and an escort provided by Mutesa, the expedition bore north-east through Namavundu, Nasire and Baja, beyond which one of Speke's men was killed while attempting to plunder wine-pots from a village. Knowing full well that progress would be soon slowed to the lingering pace of the cattle and goats, Speke decided that the caravan must be split into two sections; one half to shepherd the livestock and make its way to Kamrasi's palace, the other, led by himself, 'to trace up the Nile to its exit from the lake, and then to go on with the journey as quickly as possible'.[1] Writing in his *Journal* for 18th July, Speke explained the manœuvre, stressing that 'as it appeared all-important to communicate quickly with Petherick, and as Grant's leg was considered too weak for travelling fast ... I arranged that Grant should go to Kamrasi's direct with the property, cattle, and women, taking my letters and a map for immediate dispatch to Petherick at Gani, while I should go up the river to its source or exit from the lake, and come down again navigating as far as practicable'.[2] In spite of his plausible reasoning, it has ever since seemed hard and unfair that, in planning this hasty journey, in determining a gruelling and quite arbitrary pace of twenty miles a day, Speke denied Grant his rightful share in the discovery of the principal Nile source and thus poorly rewarded him for his many previous hardships, besides months of uncomplaining loyalty to his leader. While he admitted that he had 'yielded reluctantly to the necessity of our parting', Grant answered all those who later accused Speke of grasping selfishly for honours by writing unequivocally and with characteristic firmness, 'Nothing could be more contrary to the fact.'[3]

Be that as it may, a matter of days after Speke had turned

away towards the Nile, Grant had his favourite goat-boy tied to a tree and lashed twenty times for temporarily relinquishing care of his flock, a punishment of unusual severity delivered by one whose temperament was customarily so gentle.[4]

Crossing the three-mile-wide Luajerri drain Speke sighted the White Nile at Urondogani on 21st of July.

'Most beautiful was the scene,' he wrote, 'nothing could surpass it! It was the very perfection of the kind of effect aimed at in a highly-kept park; with a magnificent stream from 600 to 700 yards wide, dotted with islets and rocks, the former occupied by fishermen's huts, the latter by terns[?] and crocodiles basking in the sun, flowing between fine high grassy banks, with rich trees and plantains in the background, where herds of the n'sunnu and hartebeest could be seen grazing, while the hippopotami were snorting in the water, and florikan and Guinea-fowl rising at our feet.'[5]

In a wave of nostalgia for his beloved Himalayas, and as a token of respect for what he described as 'the holy river', he tried, though unsuccessfully, to induce Bombay and his men to shave their heads and bathe themselves in the Nile, as faithful Hindus embrace the waters of the Ganges.

Having celebrated the occasion by killing an antelope and several different birds, including a specimen of the hitherto unidentified long-tailed Goatsucker, but having failed to obtain any boats from the village of a neighbouring chief, Speke set off on foot along the left bank of the Nile toward some falls described to him by Mutesa. These falls, referred to by the natives of Usoga as 'the stones', he reached on 28th July, after four days' weary plodding through long grass, jungle and plantations devastated by elephant. A line of low rocks, which lay only forty miles due east of the Kabaka's palace, divided the flow of water out of the Victoria Nyanza and marked the birthplace of the Victoria Nile.

Strictly speaking, there was yet insufficient evidence to support this conclusion, for again it must be remembered that Speke's surveys had established and delineated no more than the southern, then latterly the extreme northern, limits of the lake; yet Speke felt certain that what lay before him, 'by far the most interesting sight I had seen in Africa', signified the end and the objective of his long journey.

'Though beautiful', he wrote, 'the scene was not exactly what I expected;* for the broad surface of the lake was shut out from view by a spur of hill, and the falls, about 12 feet deep, and 400 to 500 feet broad, were broken by rocks. Still it was a sight that attracted one to it for hours – the roar of the waters, the thousands of passenger-fish, leaping at the falls with all their might, the Wasoga and Waganda fishermen coming out in boats and taking post on all the rocks with rod and hook, hippopotami and crocodiles lying sleepily on the water, the ferry at work above the falls, and cattle driven down to drink at the margin of the lake, made, in all, with the pretty nature of the country – small hills, grassy-topped, with trees in the folds, and gardens on the lower slopes – as interesting a picture as one could wish to see.'[6]

More than this, Speke felt a solid comfort and satisfaction from the knowledge that his intuitive statement made in August 1858 had at last been proved to be correct. He could henceforward claim with renewed confidence that . . . 'The expedition had now performed its functions . . . that old Father Nile without any doubt rises in the Victoria Nyanza, and as I had foretold, that lake is the great source of the holy river which cradled the first expounder of our religious belief.'[7]

The falls he named after Lord Ripon who had been President of the Royal Geographical Society at the time of the expedition's departure, whilst the long neck of Nyanza from which the Nile ran out he called Napoleon Channel, thus reciprocating the honour bestowed upon him in 1860 by the French Geographical Society. Here, Speke's earlier revulsion against the heathen misery, the cruel oppression of mediaeval rulers like Suwarora and Mutesa and the bloody waste of inter-tribal wars, was transformed – to the surprise of Burton, for one – perhaps through the Biblical associations of the Nile, into an urgent desire to expose the natives of Central Africa to the Christian faith. 'What a place, I thought to myself, this would be for missionaries! They could never fear starvation, the land is so rich; and if farming were introduced by them, they might have hundreds of pupils.'[8] Inverting not only his religious beliefs, but the whole established order of his symbolism, the explorer

* In his unfinished novel, *Mount Analogue* (1959) the French author, the late M. René Daumal, has written: 'Long expectation of the unknown lessens the final effect of surprise.'

for a brief instant allowed his imagination to dwell on an idyll of peaceful domesticity, a theme unfamiliar to the period preceding his sojourn in Buganda: 'I . . . felt', wrote he, 'as if I only wanted a wife and family, garden and yacht, rifle and rod, to make me happy here for life, so charming was the place.'[9]

Having returned once more to Urondogani, Speke, through the influence of Mutesa, finally managed to procure five wooden boats in which he and his men set sail on 13th August, with the intention of exploring the Nile as far as Chaguzi in Bunyoro, the site of King Kamrasi's palace. Close to the inlet of Lake Kioga, the party was attacked by hostile tribesmen, subjects of chief N'yamyonjo, who menaced them with spears from either bank and grappled fiercely with one of Speke's boats from armed canoes. Two lucky gunshots felled two of the warriors, upon which the remainder fled, but since further exploration of the inlet would have been very dangerous Speke's tiny flotilla continued on its way downstream, thereby foregoing the possible discovery of Kioga.

Kamrasi, for his part, had kept Grant at a distance with no word of encouragement for twenty-two days. When Speke eventually rejoined Grant and, summoned at last, reached the palace on 9th September, it was only to be greeted by a sullen scoundrel 'inhospitable to strangers', a collection of damp, verminous huts and an infuriating and costly delay of two months, before, almost entirely drained of their resources, they were graciously permitted to proceed.[10]

Unlike his neighbour Mutesa, Kamrasi, who stood six feet tall, kept but little pomp or finery about his person. He was perhaps forty years old, shaven-headed and smooth-featured, and often carried a long spear with him when he walked, using it as a shepherd does his crook. The king's cold acceptance of Speke's presents contrasted dismally with the warmth displayed by Rumanika or even the childish pleasure exhibited by Mutesa, yet, as Grant has told us, Kamrasi was not totally unkind and presented the travellers with gifts of flour, coarse spirit and a bag of very pure, white salt.

Speke and Grant lived meanwhile off the milk and flesh of Mutesa's cattle, their diet supplemented by the sweet potatoes, flour and tobacco which Kamrasi's villagers willingly bartered in exchange for cattle-meat. When, in due course, he made enquiries as to the origin of the beautiful white salt, Speke was informed by Kamrasi that it came from an island on the Luta Nzigé,[11] a large stretch of water sixty miles to the west of Chaguzi. This exciting news confirmed another, similar story which Speke had already heard in Karagwe and later resulted in his communicating the existence of the lake to Samuel Baker at Gondokoro, together with remarkably accurate directions as to how best to approach it. Baker subsequently marched south and found the Luta Nzigé which he named, very appropriately, Lake Albert, considering it as equivalent of the consort to Speke's mightier Lake Victoria.[12]

On 1st November, Bombay rejoined the expedition dressed in trousers and cotton jersey, after a five-week trek which had taken him as far north as Petherick's outpost at Faloro. The Consul himself was then trading some eight days' march west of the river, but his agent, from whom Bombay had received the clothes, was there in charge of two hundred Sudanese porters, or 'Turks', each of whom carried an elephant rifle. The agent had told him that Speke would find Petherick's name cut into a tree to the north of Faloro, but, as neither he nor any of his men could read the letter which Bombay had brought for Petherick, they could not be certain that Bombay did indeed represent the expedition they had been detailed to assist.

Speke felt that he could delay at Kamrasi's no longer. Unburdening himself of everything he could possibly afford, he succeeded by this means in bribing Kamrasi into letting the expedition go, and on 9th November embarked on a voyage by canoe, through shoals of hippopotami, huge crocodiles and floating islands of papyrus, which terminated just above the Karuma Falls. After leaving the river on the opposite bank of the Karuma ferry, Speke and Grant marched north, touching the Nile only twice more, at Jaifa then at Apuddo, between Karuma and Gondokoro. Although it is now known that their route, having crossed the breast-shaped sweep of the stream above Karuma, followed its course thereafter fairly closely, the trek overland unfortunately provided geographers with no definite proof that the river down which the expedition sailed from Gondokoro was the same White Nile down which Speke had paddled from Urondogani, or from Kafu to the Karuma Falls.

On the third day of December, after a dry march through the naked tribes of Acholi, Speke and Grant came in sight of Faloro. Heralded by a sudden burst of fire, a pitch-black Sudanese, wearing Egyptian military uniform, came bounding out at the head of a procession playing on drum and fife, and eagerly embraced, even tried to kiss, Speke, who cautiously wrote that he just managed to avoid with a cheery hug, the somewhat 'unexpected manifestation of affection'.[13]

The officer, Mohamed Wad-el-Mek, after apologising breathlessly for Petherick's absence, served the travellers with a wholesome dinner of mutton, bread and honey, beer and coffee. Mohamed, who it transpired was employed not by Petherick but by De Bono, confirmed that Petherick was accompanied by his wife, who he confided had been accustomed to share her husband's camel in Khartoum, and told Speke that the name incised upon the tree was not his, but that of another traveller, who had retraced his steps afraid to penetrate the Bari country. Much to Speke's annoyance the Sudanese made excuses for not wishing to leave at once for Gondokoro, pleading that the Aswa river was too deep for them to ford and worse still, that no boats would appear at Gondokoro for a further two months. To risk the Bari natives with only forty men, as Speke immediately proposed, was, Mohamed assured him, suicidal. Meanwhile, he and over one hundred of his porters left Faloro, fully armed, to the strains of the same music that had welcomed the Nile expedition, returning eleven days later, dusty and triumphant, 'laden with ivory, and driving in five slave-girls and thirty head of cattle'.[14]

Speke, having heard during Mohamed's absence that this plunder had been seized from three burning villages, gathered together his men and remaining equipment and, leaving word for the ivory trader to follow, struck out with Grant for Gondokoro. The inhabitants of some villages they passed at first mistook them for the 'Turks' and scattered ahead of them into the bush. Their terror confirmed the rumours of Mohamed's excessive brutality, said little better for his master De Bono and, most disturbing by far, cast doubts upon the conduct of Consul Petherick about whose affairs Speke was already beginning to be suspicious.

At Apuddo they were shown the tree bearing the mysterious cypher, the name of a bearded European, which Speke dismissed as looking 'something like the letters M.I.' and which Grant reproduced as ΛΙΑΛ on page 346 of his book *A Walk across Africa*; Baker later identified the marks as belonging to the Venetian explorer, Giovanni Miani, who had journeyed to the southern Sudan in 1860.[15] By the time Speke's party had been caught up by that of Mohamed, the latter had amassed such a quantity of ivory that more than six hundred porters were required to transport it.[16] The huge caravan, a thousand strong, had in consequence little difficulty crossing the Bari country and a half-hearted attack by the tribesmen was easily repelled. On 15th February, two weeks beyond Apuddo, Speke and Grant, accompanied by Mohamed, entered Godonkoro, more than thirteen months after the original appointed time. Mohamed at once introduced them to an acquaintance, a Circassian merchant named Kurshid Aga, but Speke, refusing to be sidetracked as he had been at Faloro, wrote grimly:

'Our first enquiry was, of course, for Petherick. A mysterious silence ensued; we were informed that Mr. De Bono was the man we had to thank for the assistance we had received in coming from Madi; and then, in hot haste, after warm exchanges of greeting with Mohamed's friend, who was De Bono's agent here, we took leave, to hunt up Petherick.'[17]

As they walked down past the mission to where some boats lay moored, a figure was seen hurrying excitedly towards them; for a moment Speke thought it must be the Consul; but it was not: in another instant who should be shaking them by the hand and pouring out a flood of welcome but Samuel White Baker, the sportsman whose broad, friendly face Speke had not seen since they parted from the P. & O. steamer at Aden in 1854.[18] 'What joy this was I can hardly tell,' wrote Speke. 'We could not talk fast enough, so overwhelmed were we both to meet again.'

For a few moments Petherick was forgotten. Over food and drink Baker gave them news of home, of the American Civil War, whose basis, slavery, was now a cross borne by Speke himself, and, to Speke's great sorrow, of the passing of H.R.H. Prince Albert, to whom he had been introduced by Sir Roderick Murchison and who had taken so personal an interest in the expedition. In his turn, Baker heard the thrilling account of Speke's successes, but, as Speke has inferred, with hopes to add to them achievements of his own. Baker had, therefore, another entirely private motive for remaining at Gondokoro: having learned of the approaching ivory caravan, he had waited to off-load the massive contents of his three Nile *dyabirs** on to the shoulders of some of Mohamed's porters. Similarly, Petherick's absence he must have found disturbing for, expensively provisioned and anxious for adventure, he could hardly have welcomed – whether or not out of moral obligation – the prospect of a prolonged stay at Gondokoro even if, as he said, it was 'a charming country'. Baker's near-predicament was in no way lessened by the failure of another expedition led by three courageous Dutch ladies, Mrs. Tinné, her daughter Alexandrine and the Baroness van Capellan, who, inspired and concerned by Speke's heroic endeavours, had arranged a costly undertaking aimed at relieving him,† but fever drove them back to Khartoum.[19]

The fate of these good ladies, the solicitude of Baker, set against the fact that Petherick had seemingly neglected his sworn duty and, financed by public money[20] (which included £100 donated by Speke's father), was even then trading at N'yambara, seventy miles to the west of the Nile, turned Speke's mood of disquiet at the Consul's absence into one of anger.

When Petherick finally arrived on 18th February, it was to find

---

* Dyabirs [*sic*] or 'dhahabia' – a type of sailing-boat commonly used on the Nile.

† In England, Petherick had been misreported dead, and nothing had been heard of Speke since 30th September 1861. An account of the Tinnés and Baroness van Capellan is given in Speke's Nile diary – the '3rd Voyage down the Nile from Gondokoro to Khartum' and more recently in *Travels with Alexine* by Penelope Gladstone (John Murray, 1970).

his work done for him, his money and effort wasted and his reputation all but destroyed by the insinuations of Mohamed and the Circassian both of whom, be it noted, he had previously jailed for slaving and both of whom were his bitter rivals in the business of the ivory trade. Gossip spread by Kurshid Aga implied that Petherick, apart from attending to his commercial rather than public interests, had been likewise involved with slavery for gain. Influenced by this talk, Speke afterwards drew a slighting comparison between Petherick, De Bono and Mohamed, writing that the former, by neglecting to pursue the river route south from Gondokoro, 'had missed a good thing', for 'he would not only have had the best ivory-grounds to work upon, but, by building a vessel in Madi above the cataracts, he would have had . . . some hundred miles of navigable water to transport his *merchandise*'.[21]

Pathetically, the Consul offered Speke the use of his boats, besides cloth and as much of his food as he could carry, but to no avail; Speke drew most of his provender from Baker and accepted only ninety-five yards of cloth from Petherick's agent, after which, on Petherick's arrival, several yards more, for which he bitterly offered to pay. Disregarding the sufferings endured by the Welshman and his brave wife,* their immense outlay of expenditure of which the public subscription formed only one quarter, to say nothing of the fact that his own expedition was, if to an extent unavoidably, more than a year overdue, Speke had grown unrelentingly hardened towards his erstwhile colleague and friend. He became distant and withdrawn, yet maintained a veneer of brittle politeness, 'Though naturally I felt much annoyed at Petherick', he wrote, 'for I had hurried away from Uganda, and separated from Grant . . . solely to keep faith with him – I did not wish to break friendship, but dined and conversed with him. . . .'[22] Mrs. Petherick's account of their first meal together at Gondokoro made no secret of the explorer's want of sympathy. She recalled how

'During dinner I endeavoured to prevail on Speke to accept our aid, but he drawlingly replied, "I do not wish to recognise the succour-dodge." Mrs Petherick commented angrily, "Never mind, his heartlessness will recoil upon him yet." '

* Cf. Burton's comment given on page 65.

And indeed it did.[23]

Grant, throughout, behaved like a gentleman, outraged nevertheless that Speke had been apparently deceived, but perhaps more than usually subdued by the news of a death in his family which had come by letter with the Pethericks.

From Gondokoro in Baker's boats, he and Speke, accompanied by their nineteen 'Faithfuls', as Speke described the porters who had stood by them throughout the entire journey from the coast, sailed down the Nile to Khartoum.[24] There, Speke found a letter from Murchison informing him that the Royal Geographical Society had awarded him its Gold Medal for 1861, in belated recognition of the discovery of the Victoria Nyanza three years before; from Khartoum it was that Speke sent the Society his historic telegram, telling them 'The Nile is settled'. Recalling this cryptic message in his book *The Nile*, Laurens Van Der Post has stated that Speke 'reported his discovery to London in such terms of explorer's authenticity that they are . . . poetic', and suggests that they ring with the same 'scorched temper' that distinguished Sir Edmund Hillary's cry upon conquering Mt. Everest in 1953, 'We've done her, the bitch'.[25]

From Khartoum, Speke also wrote a letter to Petherick, sinister in its striking similarity to that written to Burton in 1859 from Cairo. In it he promised that the Consul should not suffer by his late misfortunes, and concluded by sending 'Grant's best wishes, conjointly with my own, to Mrs. Petherick and yourself, for your health and safety in the far interior.'[26] Once again a colleague of Speke's, misguided by a written reassurance, would return from Africa to find in England a climate cold and unfriendly and a reception quite the reverse of the expected.

In Cairo, where they stayed at Shepheard's Hotel, Speke and Grant fêted, photographed and showed off the 'Faithfuls', including Bombay, at *tableaux vivants*, public concerts and parties not least of these a reception at the Viceroy's palace on the island of Rhodes.

Hard as he had been on the defaulters, several of whom had, since their desertion, been taken into custody and imprisoned, Speke showered an equal generosity upon this staunch remnant of the original caravan. Bombay he appointed their captain, giving him three group photographs, with three others of the four women, to serve as passports for their return journey from Suez, through Aden, to Zanzibar. Each man received the equivalent of three years' pay and Speke further arranged with his old acquaintance, Lambert Playfair, who had succeeded Rigby in 1861 as H.B.M. Consul, that each should have a portion of 'a grand "freeman's garden" to be purchased for them' there. Last of all, should any wish to marry, a dowry of ten dollars should immediately be paid over to him.

Thus, Bombay and his eighteen comrades regained their homes, after a memorable voyage via Mauritius and the Seychelles, where they were taken to a circus and given gifts of money. In later years they and their descendants played roles of recurring importance in the journeys and discoveries made by other famous travellers – Bombay, for instance, accompanied Henry Morton Stanley – but for them all, and in particular Bombay who knew him best and longest, Speke's position of supreme regard remained unchallenged to the end. It is, furthermore, to Speke's everlasting credit that the nineteen, to a man, 'volunteered to go with [him] again, should [he] ever attempt to cross Africa from east to west through the fertile zone'.[27]

In the summer of 1863, Speke and Grant returned to England, to greater acclaim, but an acclaim embittered by the tongues of renewed controversy. As before, Speke displayed unwavering confidence in the validity of his discoveries, and in the closing chapter of the great *Journal*, wrote

'I had now seen quite enough to satisfy myself that the White River which issues from the N'yanza at the Ripon Falls is the true or parent Nile; for in every instance of its branching, it carried the palm with it, in the distinctest manner, viewed, as all the streams were by me, in the dry season, which is the best time for estimating their relative perennial values.'[28]

Forty years later, Sir Harry Johnston summed up the conclusions reached by Speke at the end of his splendid, though latterly somewhat scarified, expedition:

'As it was, Speke's theories have been shown subsequently to have been very near the whole truth. The Victoria Nyanza is the main source of the Nile, though that river finds another reservoir in the great swampy lakes of Kioga and Kwania (which again receive much of the drainage of Mount Elgon), and a most important contribution from the Albert Nyanza; for this last lake is the receptacle of the Ruwenzori range.'[29]

Yet in fairness Johnston felt bound to temper his praise of Speke's remarkable achievement with what is, at this point in the explorer's life, a prophetic sentence, and one which then, as now, contained the enduring sadness that is aftersight: 'At that time, however, Speke's theory was not sufficiently supported by evidence, and was certainly open to attack, the more so because he had blundered by giving the Victoria Nyanza so many outlets.'[30]

The arrival of Speke's telegram in London dispelled the widespread fears that he and Grant had come to grief, and caused great rejoicing when Murchison read it to a meeting of the Royal Geographical Society. The subsequent arrival of the explorers themselves intensified popular speculation upon the hazards through which they had come, and set up a wave of patriotic feeling founded upon the belief that Great Britain had solved one of geography's most persistent enigmas. At a special meeting of the Royal Geographical Society convened on 23rd June at Burlington House, Piccadilly, the crowds of well-wishers so exceeded the capacity of the auditorium that in the resulting commotion the glass of several windows was shattered.[31]

It may have disappointed some that, in his hour of triumph, the quality of Speke's oration scarcely matched the spirit of the occasion and even then could not exclude a passing defamation of Burton;[32] but the platform was always his least favourable ground, besides which, soon after returning, he had received news that for many months past his father had been seriously ill.[33]

The following evening Speke recounted his adventures to H.R.H. The Prince of Wales 'and a most select audience'; Queen Victoria sent him a message of congratulation and the

King of Sardinia gave orders for the striking of a special commemorative medal. To Speke's delight, the India Office paid off all the debts incurred by the expedition, which overran the original grant by more than £1,000. The East India Company's Army voluntarily extended his paid leave for a further year, until July 1864, but the Royal Geographical Society, having already bestowed upon him its highest award, the Gold Medal, could give no more except in words of praise from Murchison.[34]

In Somerset the ceremonies arranged several months later were no less impressive. Indeed Taunton's ovation outdid even the first tumultuous reception at Southampton in June; church bells rang out above the music of brass bands and waves of cheering, and a contemporary engraving shows Speke standing in an open carriage, acknowledging with graceful motions of his top-hat the enthusiastic acclamation of the crowds which thronged the streets.[35] Addresses delivered by civic leaders followed the procession and, after a speech of welcome read by the senior bailiff, Mr. Ballance, Speke was presented with two magnificent gold vases, now in Taunton Museum, each embossed with the flowers of the Nile.

According to a local newspaper report the explorer replied, saying 'He wished he had words with which he could express the feelings of his heart; but really this great demonstration had quite overpowered him.'

After further cheers, Speke went on to describe his discoveries, explaining how the names for the lake, the hill, the archipelago and the creek had been derived, and defying anyone to circumvent the Victoria Nyanza in an effort to disprove the truth of his statements. He spoke briefly of his ambitions for the development of Africa's 'fertile zone' and concluded by declaring his intention 'to explore the whole of Africa himself' so that missionaries and settlers might not be led astray by false reports of different regions.[36] One suspects that, in failing to circumnavigate the Nyanza, Speke felt inwardly guilty of an omission serious enough to warrant remedy; making allowances for the emotion of the occasion, his challenge might have been designed as a palliative to his own conscience, whilst, by its confidence, dousing the criticisms of his geographical opponents.

After a civic luncheon Speke, together with his brothers, Benjamin and William, returned to Jordans along roads strewn about with flowers and here and there arched over with banners of welcome. At Ashill, two hundred horsemen, a party of county dignitaries, and a procession numbering at least two thousand people, waited to greet him.

Turning at last up the tree-lined drive to Jordans, Speke's carriage swept him home to the strains of yet another band playing 'See the Conquering Hero Comes', a piece composed originally in honour of the Duke of Cumberland. To his waiting family, he may have seemed at first little changed, only older looking and somewhat worn, his hair, beard and eyebrows bleached by the tropical sun, the skin of his face and hands burned several shades darker, and perhaps, when not engaged in conversation, having a strange, haunted look about the eyes.

That same evening, a supper party was held in marquees erected on the lawns, with a bonfire and a huge display of fireworks; while, beyond the gates of Jordans, Somerset blossomed for days with flags and bunting determined not to stint its hero, as much as to shake itself free of the cobwebs and chaff now highlighted by his fame.

Despite the strength of Speke's heroic image in the country, three sources of antagonism threatened him, each different yet interlinked and each quite as menacing as the javelins from which he had once fled across the Somali shore.

First, a strong geographical opposition, led by Burton, attacked the core and substance of Speke's claims. The faction might easily have been quashed by the Royal Geographical Society, save that Speke had erred by suppressing his expedition's results instead of immediately publishing them in the Society's Journal; as Dr. R. C. Bridges has explained, Speke's tendency in this and other respects to sheer away from its once paternal influence caused Murchison and other powerful members of the Royal Geographical Society to withhold their support. In 1862, Speke had written to Murchison from Mutesa's palace at Bandowarogo: 'My dear Sir Roderick, As you have proved yourself a good father to me by getting up this Expedition, so I hope you will consider me a worthy son . . .'[37] This relationship had continued, indeed flourished, between 1859 and 1863, but when, after a lengthy interval, it became evident that Speke was determined to ignore its repeated requests for a scientific paper, the favour and support of the patron body rapidly declined.

James McQueen, destined to emerge as one of the explorer's most savage detractors, maintained that a state of impasse had been reached because Speke 'forbade anyone to . . . seek out the particular point [viz. the Nile source, A.M.] until Blackwood had told the world where that point was to be found'.[38] To the council members of the Royal Geographical Society, Speke's behaviour appeared mysterious and inexplicably curt, as much as it was unprecedented and dismaying; yet from Speke's own point of view he had behaved with perfect consistency. In a letter dated 12th October 1859, which John Petherick reproduced in volume two of his *Travels in Central Africa*, Speke had urged him to write for Blackwood and not the Society: 'The Royal Geographical Society have not the means of spreading anything about, whereas Blackwood has a larger circulation than anybody else. Again the Royal Geographical Society is slothful to the last degree, but Blackwood does not want a week to produce a map, a paper, or anything else.'[39]

This rather unfair comparison has been used by several commentators to imply that Speke only desired quick fame, that his motives were entirely selfish, that his intentions were concentrated upon gain. While the first of these criticisms is reasonable, it is arguable that the second and third overlook the significance of Speke's altruistic meditations by the banks of the Nile. From them it is clear that, in his eyes, the discovery of the source of the Nile would facilitate the introduction of Christianity, the Western system of trade and education, and with these a 'civilised' code of morals into a society baulked by superstition and heathen principles. Like the quest for the sources of the Nile, the idea of an Afro-European trade along that river may have originated in discussions with Burton, who, it will be remembered, contemplated a trade route linking the east and west coasts of Africa as early as 1853. Speke seems to have imagined, however mistakenly, that to delay publication of his journal by the popular press even for the brief period required to compose a report for the Royal Geographical Society, might fatally impair the progress of the movement towards Africa, a movement demanding his guidance and participation.

As at the conclusion of his expedition with Burton, the combined effect of hardship, illness, mental strain and physical deterioration, with, on this occasion, the compensation of instant success over riding other distant but clear memories of past failure, caused Speke to clutch desperately at the discovery, make its identity ultra-personal and see its outcome as too immediate, too subjective a responsibility. Thus, angered and goaded by opposition, determined that neither his discovery nor his mighty vision of Nile trade should want for lack of publicity, increasingly inspired by the image of himself as promoter of Central Africa's future development, Speke again spurned the most important of his benefactors and again rushed headlong into general publication.

The third source of opposition, Petherick, was to a greater extent than the others one of Speke's own making. In May 1863, Petherick reported Speke's offhand treatment of him at Gondokoro, at the same time absolving Grant from any blame. The Consul's letter, followed by another plea for justice written by his wife, elicited a sympathetic reply from Murchison, but one insisting that, before the unfortunate circumstances of Gondokoro could be settled, a complete report would have to be studied by a committee of the Royal Geographical Society.[40] Meanwhile, Speke, contrary to the assurances of his letter from Khartoum, had provided Murchison with sufficient evidence to connect Petherick, circumstantially at least, with participation in the slave-trade. In a speech delivered at Taunton on Christmas Eve, the same year, Speke foolishly made public his worst suspicions, still unproven, thereby inviting still more violent criticism and alienating himself even more completely from the Royal Geographical Society, whose committee had not yet had an opportunity of assessing Petherick's official evidence.[41]

On 19th February 1864, Speke wrote to Norton Shaw a prim letter implying that, yet again, the use of money was a root-cause of his antipathy toward the Consul: 'I have the honour to request you will solicit the President and Council of the

Royal Geographical Society to institute an enquiry into what Mr. Consul Petherick has done with money entrusted to him for the purpose of aiding my late Expedition; and also to ascertain what steps he took to render me assistance. . . .'[42] Judging from letters to Playfair and others, it would appear, as Dr. Bridges has suggested, that Speke was also determined to retrieve the one hundred pounds which in his absence his family had contributed to the Petherick fund.[43]

In April, Petherick's report was read to a meeting of the Royal Geographical Society. Sir Roderick Murchison commented favourably upon it and described as most unjust the allegations that the Consul had been guilty of abetting, much less participating in, slavery.

'The implication of all this,' comments Dr. Bridges, after a thorough investigation of the case, 'was that the Royal Geographical Society had obtained value for their money: Speke's charges were largely rejected'.[44] There the affair rested. The Foreign Office, however, had been influenced enough by rumour to withdraw Petherick's consulship, and its subsequent official absolvency did little to remove the clinging smear so rashly daubed upon his character by Speke. When, in May 1865, the Royal Geographical Society presented its Gold Medal to Samuel Baker, Petherick, who had by then returned to London, assumed this to confirm the Society's suspicions, possibly actual belief, in his guilt and opened the case a second time. In so doing, he achieved little. Baker, meanwhile, and unknown to the Royal Geographical Society, had proceeded south on Speke's instructions and had discovered the Albert Nyanza, hence fully justifying the award. Had Baker been less successful, then Petherick's position might have been a stronger one. But it reflects small credit on the Royal Geographical Society and Home Government that not one penny of compensation was ever paid to the professionally-ruined claimant, whose eventual reimbursement came at last from the coffers of indignant Egypt.[45]

NOTES

1. Speke: *Journal*, p. 455.
2. *Ibid.* p. 458.
3. Grant: *A Walk across Africa*, p. 247.
4. *Ibid.*, p. 248. Mrs. Brodie, *The Devil Drives*, p. 219, uses the beating of his cattleman by a powerful Seedi as a 'striking personal parable' describing Grant's true feelings at being abandoned by Speke. I have used the (more literal) example, which immediately follows the incident in Grant's own text, for a similar purpose.
5. Speke: *Journal*, p. 459.
6. *Ibid.*, pp. 466, 467.
7. *Ibid.*, p. 467.
8. *Ibid.*, p. 470.
9. *Ibid.*, p. 470.
10. Although Sir Harry Johnston's *Nile Quest* portrayed Kamrasi as a scoundrel, Grant, while offering no excuses for the king's rough and habitually sullen manners, wrote 'Kamrasi was not unfriendly'.
11. The meaning of the name Luta Nzigé is 'dead locust'. See Brodie: *The Devil Drives*, p. 220.
12. Baker reached Lake Albert (Luta Nzigé) in March 1864.
13. Speke: *Journal*, p. 579.
14. *Ibid.*, p. 588.
15. Grant: *A Walk across Africa*, p. 356; B. W. Langlands (*Uganda Journal*, March 1962), p. 57, note on Miani.
16. Speke: *Journal*, p. 597. In fact, of some 600 porters, 300 carried ivory alone.
17. *Ibid.*, p. 601.
18. *Ibid.*, p. 601, 2.
19. *Ibid.*, p. 603.
20. Royal Geographical Society archives.
21. Speke: *Journal*, p. 608.
22. *Ibid.*, p. 607.
23. Petherick: *Travels in Central Africa*, 1869.
24. Speke wrote modestly on p. 548 of the *Journal* that 'in other circumstances, it might have been worth while to describe' the river journey. The MS. version of the Nile diary is in fact included with the *Journal* MS., N.L.S., MS. 4872, and will be reproduced in full in the forthcoming edited volume of Speke's letters.
25. Eliot Elisofon and Laurens Van Der Post: *The Nile*, 1964.

26. Petherick: *Travels in Central Africa,* Vol. II, pp. 132–3.
27. Speke: *Journal,* p. 612.
28. *Ibid.,* p. 610.
29. Sir Harry Johnston: *The Nile Quest,* 1903, p. 171.
30. *Ibid.,* p. 171.
31. See Dr. R. C. Bridges: *Speke and the R.G.S., Uganda Journal,* March 1962, p. 37.
32. *Proceedings of the R.G.S.,* Vol. 7, pp. 109, 182–96, 212–23.
33. Bridges: *Uganda Journal,* March 1962, p. 37; *The Weekly Chronicle and General Advertiser for Somerset, Dorset and Devon,* Saturday 10th October 1863.
34. Speke to Blackwood, N.L.S., MS. 4185.
35. R.G.S. archives. Newspaper cuttings book.
36. Contemporary newspaper report, R.G.S. archives.
37. Speke to Murchison, R.G.S. archives.
38. A newspaper article of 1863 commented: 'Some persons had expressed doubts as to the reality of the importance of that discovery [the source of the Nile] . . . Captain Speke had, with the utmost modesty, said "Wait for my book".' The newspaper considered Speke's reply to be 'most just and reasonable'. R.G.S. archives.
39. See also Bridges: *Uganda Journal,* March 1962, p. 40.
40. See Bridges: *Uganda Journal,* March 1962, pp. 37, 38.
41. *Ibid.,* pp. 37, 38.
42. R.G.S. archives.
43. Bridges: *Uganda Journal,* March 1962, p. 38.
44. *Ibid.,* p. 38.
45. *Proceedings of the R.G.S.* (new series), vol. 4, p. 200.

CHAPTER 9

ENGLAND AND THE AFTERMATH

DURING the expedition of 1860–3, Speke had corrected and partially re-written the two copies of article proofs which were finally included in *What led to the Discovery of the Source of the Nile*, published in 1864. On his return to England he also brought with him preliminary notes from which he prepared the first draft of the longer *Journal*, the book describing the events of his most recent journey. In the succeeding race for publishing rights, John Murray of Albemarle Street led the field with a tempting offer of £2,000 cash and a share of profits, but Speke had not forgotten his friends in Scotland, the Blackwood family. In a letter to John Blackwood, he carefully detailed the terms of Murray's offer, and affirmed his desire that Blackwood, and no one else, should have his book. Replying on 23rd June 1863, Blackwood wrote 'I was very much pleased with your determination and the feeling that I should be the publisher of your book and I shall take care that you are not the loser thereby . . . I will guarantee you the £2,000 Murray offered and similar arrangements as he proposed for the contingent profits. . . .'[1]

The manuscript of the *Journal* was completed in 'a thoroughly good room' at Strathtynum, Blackwood's house near St. Andrews, where Speke was permitted to work quickly and free from interruption; later, recalling the visit, Blackwood has mentioned that, at intervals, when he had grown tired – or perhaps when his eyes had begun to hurt him – Speke used to sit back from the table, light a cigar and wait for its aroma to beckon in his host. Then they would smoke and talk until Speke felt like resuming his narrative.[2]

After some weeks, the precise dates are as yet unknown, Speke travelled south for the homecoming celebrations in

Somerset; then, on 21st November, as work on the proofs entered the final stages, John Blackwood sent a letter to Jordans criticising some levels shown on Speke's maps and map-sections and in particular advising caution in his treatment of Petherick and the slave trade. He wrote:

'I will again send you the strips* about Petherick for reconsideration. Both old B. and I think that it is not worth while to publish what you call the "succouring dodge". It comes like a drop of bitterness at the End, but that does not matter so much as your use of the word "Turk" as applied to Petherick. Substantially your statement comes to this that you met and dined with him, not quarrelling or showing that you were offended, and then when you come home you publish a statement or rather expression which is infinitely more damaging than if you had cut him on the spot. Consult your brothers or anyone about this and I am sure they will agree with me.'[3]

Even Grant, Speke's staunch and unfailing supporter, while hoping that 'care will be taken that Speke's peculiar style of expression be not altered', could not disguise his concern at the freedom of several passages and remarked, 'I hope he will consent to have certain alterations made as, in its present form, many parts are . . . too slangy for the general public . . . it strikes me he sadly wants the advice of a friend'.[4] Acting upon Blackwood's recommendations, Speke grudgingly modified his reference to the Consul to 'two chilly lines', although the published account of Petherick's activities was still misleading and left Speke open to charges of ungenerosity. 'I have . . . corrected my proofs as best I can', he wrote, 'I wish to God I had never seen the beast for both he and his wife are writing against me in the most blackguardly style.'[5] Apart from the problem of Petherick, Blackwood greatly feared that Speke's levels for the Nile (which at one point appeared to make a ninety-mile stretch of the river flow uphill!) 'might discredit the whole book', and strongly advocated that he leave out both 'the table and the sections of heights on the Map'. Speke, on the other hand, considered his figures to be 'all right', save for one or two, and showing a lack of

* i.e. the proof-sheets.

concern similar to that of the lion for the circling jackal, reassured Blackwood with enviable breeziness,* 'Don't fear critics, we will put them to shame if they wag their tongues.'[6] Unfortunately, as many a lion has discovered, the jackal, too, possesses strong and efficient teeth.

The subsequent criticism of Speke's calculations quite vindicated Blackwood's more sober judgement. Apart from other geographical detail, the inclusion in the *Journal* of a notorious forgery, an old Hindu map previously described by Rigby in the 1844 *Transactions of the Bombay Geographical Society*, drew scornful cries from eminent theoretical geographers, including W. D. Cooley and Dr. Charles Beke, and caused Blackwood to 'drop it' from the second edition of the *Journal*; but damage had been done that its omission could ill repair.

From November until Christmas Speke's life consisted of long spells of solitary writing relieved only by a succession of exhausting official engagements. 'Do you see the flag flying?' he complained, half-serious, in a note to his publisher. 'These awful dinners are killing me.'[7] By December, he was fast growing impatient for the publication of his book and, fearing lest it be delayed by the steady pace of his companion, who in his Highland retreat near Dingwall laboured hard to finish off the illustrations, wrote again to Blackwood, suggesting briskly, 'If you like I will ginger up Grant'; but such action proved unnecessary. Soon enough the *Journal* was ready. As a final gesture, partly motivated from belated caution, partly in favour of an old, tried friend, partly out of native cunning, Speke requested that a copy be sent immediately to Laurence Oliphant. Oliphant 'knows', he wrote confidingly, 'what will *take* with the geographers who support, sit in carpet slippers and criticise those who labour in the field'.[8]

The *Journal of the Discovery of the Source of the Nile* appeared before the public on 16th December 1863. The title, considered in certain quarters as presumptuous, was, at best, an improvement on the unwieldy, if more comprehensive, original, *Speke's discovery of the source of the Nile and life in Africa with Captain Grant*. To cater for the Christmas market, the first impression of 4,000 copies was increased to 7,500 from which

* Cf. pp. 19, 41 (note 22).

Speke received his own copies a week in advance, including extras ordered for 'all the maids in the kitchen' at Jordans, who, he assured Blackwood, 'were dying to read it'.[9]

The reaction to the much-awaited *Journal* was, unsurprisingly, varied. Theoretical geographers and hydrographers sneered at Speke's map and chuckled at the notion of the Nyanza spewing out its waters from four distinct and separate outlets, like the gargoyles of a cathedral. They dismissed with scorn the latitudes estimated for the northern shore of the lake, fastened angrily upon the Hindu map and badgered the author for his blind assertion that the Nile, which he claimed to have seen pouring out over the shallow Ripon Falls, was the same river as he had met again at Apuddo, Jaifa and Gondokoro. He had neither traced the river's course entirely, nor had he produced any evidence to prove that the Nyanza, whose extreme ends only he had mapped, was in fact a homogeneous sheet of water.

The Scotsman, while applauding what it described as Speke's 'frankness, simplicity, and directness', quite failed to appreciate his 'carelessness and roughness of expression'. The paper's reviewer considered that 'Captain Speke is little given to moralising and not much more to describing – he merely narrates, and narrates with an even excessive plainness . . .'; but admitted nevertheless that 'his narrative is of adventures of unsurpassed interest'.[10]

The Athenaeum – a journal of literature and the arts – of 19th December, in a lengthy review, agreed, its correspondent noting that 'The tale is left in its naked form: naked as one of Captain Speke's equatorial kings.' A penetrating commentary attacked what its writer regarded as Speke's obliviousness to historical precedent, his lack of recognition for the groundwork provided by his contemporaries, men like Burton, Beke and Desborough Cooley. It revolted against his caricature of Petherick as the enterprising villain and maintained that the Consul's efforts had merited gratitude and praise instead of condemnation. 'Of all these labours', sighed *The Athenaeum*'s reviewer, 'Captain Speke is the prodigal, and, as some will think, the ungrateful heir.'[11] There followed criticism of Speke's measuring experiment upon the fat princess at Rumanika's palace and several cynical allusions to the explorer's relationship with Mutesa's mother, to say nothing of his two Baganda virgins. *The Athenaeum* felt that, in particular, the latter experience must have placed 'a young, unmarried man like Captain Speke' in an extremely 'awkward position'. On the very day on which *The Athenaeum* review was published, Speke, considerably upset, wrote a firm rejoinder to its editor.

> 'I . . . do not think I deserve the imputations for want of generosity which you have cast at me. Burton although I asked him to go . . . with me twice, once at Kaze and once at Ujiji not only refused . . . but absolutely did his best to dissuade me from going alone.
>
> Petherick's book I never read and moreover do not wish to read it as it is well known that he never used an instrument by which he could tell where he went to – what I have written regarding him I am sorry I was obliged to.'[12]

The reference to Petherick, made at the height of Speke's campaign against him, still reflected some of the caution insisted upon by Blackwood. It was only after the Christmas Eve speech at Taunton and the resulting letters of reprisal which the Consul's father-in-law, D. B. McQuie, addressed to the editor of *The Times*, that Speke in an impetuous reply destroyed the last remnants of the discreet veil behind which, with Blackwood's help, the facts of the Gondokoro episode had been hidden. Writing into the very quick of the truth, Speke stated how 'On meeting Mr. Petherick . . . I did not conceal my feelings . . . speaking out plainly before Mr. Baker, Capt. Grant and Dr. Murie'.[13]

The letter, although it concurred with Mrs. Petherick's account, startled Blackwood by its bluntness and caused him to express the hope, in a note dated 1st February, that Speke had not 'been firing off any more letters to the newspapers'. After suggesting that Speke might publish 'a general reply to reviews impinging his statements or theories', Blackwood concluded, with the desperate plea: 'If you draw anything up send it here.' It seems ironic that at this moment, when his advice and consolation might have been most appreciated, Grant was travelling on the continent and thus avoided the initial wave of interrogation, academic turmoil and dispute. Incensed by what he still genuinely believed to have been Petherick's deception, dispirited by recurrent attacks upon his own geography, inwardly peeved and disappointed that Grant's trip abroad had coincided with publication of the *Journal*, Speke, who was himself busy 'hunting' Petherick and the critics, wrote disapprovingly to Blackwood, 'Much better I think had he stopped at home and done a little hunting first.'[14] In actual fact, had it not been for a mistake on the part of Blackwood, Grant's excursion would have served one useful purpose. He and his friend, the eminent Gaelic scholar J. P. St. Clair, both of whom supported Speke's scheme for developing Central Africa, felt that Speke '*ought* certainly to see the Emperor' Napoleon of France, whom Speke hoped 'to excite . . . to open up Western Africa tracking into the interior from the Gaboon'.[15] To this end, Grant proposed that he deliver a special copy of the *Journal* to the Emperor, on his way through France to Italy, as a prelude to Speke's own intended visit to Paris later in February 1864. Unfortunately, a petty disagreement with Speke over the colour of the book's binding and the delay caused by Blackwood sending an ordinary edition to Paris instead of the special one, prevented Grant, whose time in France was limited, from carrying the proposal through. Grant, the botanist, had suggested that the *Journal* should have a green binding, while Speke, the hunter, had specified 'English scarlet'.

Sales of Speke's book, like its reception by the public, in due course proved to be inconsistent. John Blackwood had thought to dispose of 10,000 copies, but by February 1864 was finding difficulty in clearing the remainder of the first impression. By the end of that month, however, the once more rising distribution persuaded Blackwoods to print a further 2,500, even although, unknown to them, the zenith of the book's popularity was rapidly approaching and many copies were left on their hands.

Meanwhile, Blackwood had agreed to publish Speke's Somali diary, sections of which had already appeared in the 'Maga', 'as a small volume', although it would 'not have a sale anything like the book' and, at the same time, had encouraged

Grant to prepare his own account of 'Camp Life' on the expedition, a personal narrative intended to supplement the wider-ranging *Journal*. Both projects immediately caught Speke's interest, snapped him momentarily out of his depression and forced him again into solitary retreat, re-writing and recomposing the old material. Much of it must have made painful reading, kindling once more the embers of resentment which, for nearly a decade, had smouldered deep within him. In the phases of their flame, revived by every familiar sentence, heightened by every phrase, Speke might have perceived the sallow, mocking features of Richard Burton and still have heard, through the void of recollection, the echo and re-echo of Burton's sarcastic laughter.

Four and a half years of bitter estrangement unrelieved by argument or correspondence had distorted out of all proportion the magnitude of wrong for which each of the former companions held the other responsible. Had Burton and Speke been spared the aggravating sympathy of friends, had they been able to come face to face in private to argue, or even, as Speke implied at the crudest level, to fight each other bare-fisted, this honest action could have purged their stagnant hatreds and removed a considerable weight of enmity from their hearts.

But Burton, like Speke, had been abroad. In December 1863, he landed in England from Consular postings in Fernando Po and the Cameroons, episodes which he described very fully in two two-volumed works, *Wanderings in West Africa* and *Abeokuta and the Cameroons*. After spending Christmas with his wife Isabel, Burton returned in January 1864 to Dahomey in West Africa and a further eight months of separation.

At Jordans, Speke continued with the work of revising the Somali and Lake Tanganyika diaries, whilst advancing his plans for the development of Central Africa. Because of this, and because Grant had been unable to present Napoleon with the special *Journal*, Speke postponed his visit to Paris until March and instead wrote, then had printed off and circulated, two broadsheets, one outlining his *Scheme for opening Africa*, the other *Considerations for opening Africa*. Writing in the *Uganda Journal*, the former Chief Justice for Zanzibar, Sir John Milner Gray, has described in detail both the advertisements and the meeting, which followed their publication at No. 6 Grosvenor Place, London W., the home of the Marquess Townshend.

'In the Considerations', writes Sir John Gray, 'Speke agreed that the experiences of Livingstone, himself, and the Arab traders had shown that there was a belt of fertile land in equatorial Africa, which "is the only part of Africa worthy of serious consideration" and that European countries should concentrate on opening this particular zone.'[16]

Having explained the routes by which the zone might be approached, Speke went on to direct the attention of the Missionary Societies to the three kingdoms ruled by Mutesa, Rumanika and Kamrasi. He spoke passionately of the horrors of the slave-trade, particularly vile when Central African chiefs became induced into inter-tribal bloodshed in the slavers' cause, and suggested that some use should be made of the free Africans in the prevention of slavery, rather than leaving them to bargain with the Arab and Swahili caravans, which too often led to compromise. The 'Scheme' contained eight major points for African development, which are as follows:

1. That our Government be petitioned to use its influence, conjointly with the Egyptian Government, to suppress the illegitimate tendencies of the White Nile trade; and, for that purpose, to establish an alliance with the Bari Negroes at the foot of the cataracts above Gondokoro,

2. That our Government be petitioned with the European Governments to support a United Church Mission, to be sent via Suwakin on the Red Sea to Berber on the Nile, and thence up the Nile to the foot of the cataracts above Gondokoro; whence, by land, they would march up the Nile to the kingdom of Unyoro,

3. That the Missionaries composing the Mission be selected not for the purpose only of preaching to the Wahuma (Bahima), but for general instruction; and that they shall be bound to be self-supporting after the first two or three years, or until a trade can be instituted with Egypt,

4. That after a certain time, and [sic] the King of Unyoro can see and understand that legitimate trade is the best thing for the

maintenance of his Government, and the prosperity of his people,

4. detachments of Missionaries should be sent further on to the kingdom of Uganda and Karagwe,

5. That our Government be petitioned to make arrangements with the Sultan of Zanzibar, to put a full stop to the slave-trade in his dominions,

6. That our Government be petitioned to recognise all persons convicted of taking part in slavery as conniving at murder, and to treat them accordingly; for without bloodshed slaves cannot be caught,

7. That our Government be petitioned to form a chain of Negro Depots round the East and West sides of Africa, in sufficient numbers to half man our men-of-war, and yet to have a strong reserve at each depot; who shall all be educated and brought up for the holy purpose of liberating their fellow country men from the thraldom of slavery; as it is obvious that the great sums of money now spent, with a view to suppressing slavery, are doing more harm than good,

8. That as much as possible, Negroes should be educated and employed in all British services, and taught to abhor the slave-trade, which they have hitherto been taught to consider legitimate from the fact that they are purchased with European articles of merchandise.[17]

Sir John Gray concluded: 'I have not been able to find any reference to this meeting in the contemporary press. Speke was a very poor and unready speaker at public meetings and perhaps he failed to make a good impression. Possibly his audience showed a polite interest in what he had to say and then departed, fully convinced that something ought to be done in regard to the opening of Africa by somebody other than themselves.'

Speke's plea for the slave and invitation to missionary and trader alike preceded by over a decade Stanley's famous summons to the missionaries which the *Daily Telegraph* published in 1875. That Stanley's delivery was more polished is not disputed, yet Speke's failure at Grosvenor Place must be explained by other reasons. He was passionately dedicated to his theme, he held the floor, his audience, among whom the broadsheets had been distributed, came to Speke's lecture already partly informed.

If only Speke had not thrust Africa, its unfamiliar geography and the need for Government intervention in the slave-trade upon his listeners in so confused a manner, the speech might have scored heavily; as it was, the gathering dispersed having received an incoherent description of many schemes, each a complex and costly operation in itself. Yet to Speke, in whose mind each proposition rang with that clarity and certainty born of actual experience, the negative reaction of his audience must have been as mystifying as it was desperately disheartening.

At the end of March 1864, Speke travelled over to Paris. This, his first visit to the French capital, secured no significant promotion of his plans, so that having been entertained at the British Embassy, done some sightseeing and spent the few days very luxuriously at the expensive Grand Hotel, the explorer, bored and frustrated, returned to London. Throughout April, May and June, Speke's correspondence with John Blackwood was concerned mainly with the progress of the Somali book and with Grant's smaller effort, upon which the latter was said to be 'working famously'. By 9th July, Speke could report that 'Grant, I am happy to say, has got out 5 chaps', and among other details, was by then sufficiently far ahead to consider even the frontispiece of his own volume, which he conceived as a compound illustration showing '3 scenes Somali . . . like the buffalo fight' in the *Journal*.

It was at this point only, having concentrated exclusively on personal affairs since the previous June, that Speke interrupted other work to fulfil his obligation to the Royal Geographical Society by submitting a report for its journal. While he could scarcely have bettered Burton's scholarly thesis describing the expedition of 1856–9, Speke would have been well advised to take pains with his paper, for in so doing he might have mustered reinforcements sufficient to choke the loudest opposition to his theories regarding the Nile and, later in that same year, expose the slanderous *Nile Basin*, written by Burton and James McQueen, who, as a friend of Petherick's father-in-law, McQuie, had a vested interested in securing Speke's ruin.

Speke, instead, merely dashed off a hurried summary on the hydrography of the Upper Nile, which quite failed to meet the criticisms of this aspect of his discovery, a subject to which *The Athenaeum* of 1863 had devoted considerable attention. One of its correspondents, Colonel Greenwood, strongly backed by another, Professor Jukes of Dublin, wrote several letters denouncing Speke's claim to the Nyanza's many outlets. In a significant reply, the then Assistant-Secretary of the Royal Geographical Society, Hume Greenfield, revealed the increasingly equivocal position adopted by the Society, by writing to *The Athenaeum*, 14th June 1863:

'It is perhaps rather early either to impugn or defend the discoveries of Capts. Speke and Grant at the sources of the White Nile . . . I would caution all and sundry who refuse their belief to anything that transcends our limited experiences of the abnormal manifestations of natural forces, that nothing can be more dangous in science than to say, "This cannot be." '[18]

Upon receiving Speke's notes, Sir Roderick Murchison instantly rebelled at their 'brief and imperfect character', and a committee of the Royal Geographical Society decided that, while the paper had better appear in the journal, a preface should explain its inadequacy and footnotes draw attention to its feeble content. In the preface the Council regretted

'that so very important a subject should be illustrated in their Journal, only by a short memoir . . . As the author has not transmitted . . . any other material or diary of his travels, the reader must look for further information to the published work of Captain Speke, respecting the important expedition with which he was entrusted, and in which he has been supported throughout by the President and Council of the Society . . .'[19]

This admonition and a host of alien footnotes, some of which compared the paper unfavourably with that of Burton's, was proof enough that his careless draft had insulted Murchison and, at a critical moment in Speke's career, alienated the Society. Indeed, the break with the Royal Geographical Society was but the consummation of a year scarred and worn by dispute and controversy, added to which, by midsummer, the task of writing and correcting the Somali proofs had become so unpleasant an imposition, it was with evident relief that Speke announced to Blackwood his intention to revisit India during the coming autumn. In an emphatic letter dated 11th July 1864, he wrote, 'As I shall have to leave England for the East next October, I am now buying a battery of guns and rifles.'

Another note sent from Jordans on 18th July was more explicit: 'I shall only go out to India for 6 months shooting and then will return on Furlough for 3 years.'

He added, with disgust, 'I am sick of proofs. . . .'[20]

In August, the month in which Burton returned to England from Dahomey, Speke again crossed over to Paris where he once more put up at the Grand Hotel, this time accompanied by his friends, Lord Cowley and Laurence Oliphant. The visit elicited the warm praise and interest of the Emperor who seemed 'delighted with the prospects' of an expedition which he and Speke discussed, whereby Speke 'worked up' the upper reaches of the Nile while a French party headed inland towards the Victoria Nyanza from the Gaboon. No doubt due to Oliphant's presence, the otherwise successful sojourn was clouded by a stream of fresh criticism against Burton, in which, referring to his Somali book, whose second half comprised the events leading to the discovery of the Victoria Nyanza, Speke urged Blackwood not to be 'afraid on my account of what I have written for it only exists between B the B and myself whether we fight it out with the quill or the fist. He was cut by his Regiment for not accepting a challenge and now my Regiment expects me to tackle him in some way or other to say nothing of my own feelings of honour.'[21] Remembering Burton's treatment of him in *The Lake Regions,* it comforted him to picture his former commander as a coward. In 1861, from the house of Musa Mzuri at Kazeh, Speke had sent a furious letter to Blackwood, exclaiming, 'What a vile dastardly wretch it is not to have had it out with me at home . . . but as he has taken up the pen instead of a pistol, we will have it out so. . . . He has brought it on himself.' In the same letter, he had gloated over a snippet of gossip furnished by Rigby. 'Rigby tells me an amusing story about Burton's first entre in Yankee land, when, at Salem, he met with an Editor whose feelings Burton had abused in his book and no sooner did he land there than the said Editor called him out and B vanished the same night – how like him!!! – '22 These extracts, better than any other, explain Speke's willingness to revive in print the scenes of past miseries and hardship. They show his by then almost masochistic urge to work over the old Somali and Tanganyika ground, whipping himself into a rage with each reflection upon former disagreements, scraping the scabs off old and partially covered wounds. It was the need to consummate the literary duel that drove Speke on.

In consequence, his second book, *What led to the Discovery of the Source of the Nile*, is a far more personal narrative. Its scale being much reduced, the nuances of mood and the force of its emotional impact are more concentrated. Across the bared image of the abban, Sumunter, Speke lashes his dislike of Petherick and Burton, while, for argument's sake, the plundering Somali may be said to represent Speke's moral and scientific antagonists. Cornered and beaten, Speke crouches, all but lost until, in the last stages of his agony, he manages to rise from the blood-stained beach to strike free and flee for safety. The Somali book struck that blow for the freedom of his spirit and India waited at the end of the long dark spring and summer to welcome him home.

Apart from its range of feeling, personality, simplicity and lack of inhibition together form the essence of the book's greatness, assuring its place, along with that of the *Journal*, among the outstanding works of nineteenth-century travel and exploration. Yet, ultimately, it was against all these qualities that its author spoke out in an extraordinary letter written from North Wales on 25th July, a letter which ignored even the debt incurred by Grant's unswerving loyalty and unfailing spirit of acquiescence. 'I shall never travel with a male companion again in wild country', Speke wrote, 'and certainly shall never again think of writing a personal narrative since it only leads to getting abused.'23

With the return of Burton to England in August, the Nile controversy began to approach its climax, thereby providing fuel and entertainment for the summer or vacational meeting of the Royal Geographical Society, which took place annually as Section E, 'Geography and Ethnology', of the British

Association convention. In 1864, an important meeting was arranged for 16th September, to be held in the hall of the East Wing of the Mineral Water Hospital, Bath. According to custom famous travellers and explorers were invited as guests to address a selected audience. Sir Roderick Murchison, and Greenfield's successor as Assistant-Secretary of the Royal Geographical Society, H. W. Bates, therefore arranged that Speke and Burton should be pitted against each other for a public debate on the Association's platform, as much, one suspects, to teach Speke a lesson for cold-shouldering the Society as to attempt to resolve the interminable controversy over the Victoria Nyanza and the Nile.

The advantage in this confrontation lay with Burton. He possessed all his faculties, was a practised, often brilliant, speaker, logical and unhurried in his delivery, a man not easily flustered. Immediately upon receiving Bates's invitation, Burton set about putting the finishing touches to his latest theory that Lake Tanganyika was the true source of the Nile and, with this carefully-prepared ammunition, waited out the interval, secure and confident, until the contest.

Speke, for his part, was in a weaker position. He detested public speaking and knew instinctively that Burton's presence on the platform would put him off. He was deaf in one ear and his delicate eyesight presented a further deficiency invariably exaggerated by any kind of mental strain. Six months of uncongenial literary work, spliced with a surfeit of geographical and personal antagonism, found Speke, by September, in an impaired physical condition, nervous, and considerably depressed. The forthcoming voyage to India and the possibility of a further African expedition during 1865, financed by Napoleon, alone sustained his spirits.

Had Speke's case for associating the Nile and the Victoria Nyanza been free of doubt, he would still have found the debate an awkward experience; but to argue a theory based essentially on instinct and inspiration, against an eloquent rationalist such as Burton, whose wit and innuendo could be so devastating, was no pleasant prospect. True, he would soon enough be out of it, safe in the forests, soothed by the gentle air of the Indian hills, but in the meantime Speke felt obliged to accept the Royal Geographical Society's challenge for the sake of honour and justice, miserable as the experience was certain to be.

He must have realised too, that should Burton utterly destroy him, the future of his development plan for Central Africa would be precarious, and the French perhaps influenced into withdrawing their vital support.

Contrary to Burton's calmness, Speke continued to pursue his philosophy of violence, a reaction linked with his already long-established practice of shooting as an antidote to crisis or frustration. Laurence Oliphant, the sinister mediator, the disrupter of friendships, conveyed to Burton the fact that Speke had threatened in a flash of temper that, should Burton dare to appear on the stage at Bath, 'he would kick him'. Burton's response must have delighted the sadistic Oliphant: 'Well, *that* settles it!' he cried angrily. 'By God, he *shall* kick me.'[24] The battle was on.

On the morning of Thursday 15th September, the day preceding the Burton–Speke debate, a preliminary meeting was held at the Mineral Water Hospital with all the participants present. Speke travelled to Bath from Neston Park, the estate owned by his cousins, the Fullers, near Corsham in Wiltshire. The sight of Burton after so many years and so many harsh and unrepentant exchanges seems to have opened yet another well of conflict in Speke, exposing a sudden anguish and momentary remorse. For an instant the chasm separating the two men was bridged by a mutual, instinctive response to each other's presence. Writing on page 389, volume one, of her *Life of Sir Richard Burton*, Isabel Burton has brought us very near to the tension of that highly charged atmosphere. The climax came when she and her husband were asked to take seats quite close to Speke.

'He looked at Richard, and at me, and we at him. I shall never forget his face. It was full of sorrow, of yearning, and perplexity. Then he seemed turned to stone. After a while he began to fidget a great deal, and exclaimed half aloud, "Oh, I cannot stand this any longer." He got up to go out. The man nearest him said, "Shall you want your chair again, Sir? May I have it? Shall you come back?" and he answered, "I hope not" and left the Hall.'[25]

That was Speke's last appearance in public. Discounting an

unfinished letter,* and an almost inaudible exhalation made as he lay in one of his cousin's fields, the curt rejoinder, 'I hope not' was the explorer's last recorded utterance. By four-thirty on that same day, Thursday 15th September 1864, Speke was dead.

The following morning, 16th September, the conference hall was packed in anticipation of some lively dialogue between the principal contestants. Burton and his wife stood alone on the platform, he grasping a sheaf of notes. After a delay of almost half an hour, Sir Roderick Murchison, the members of the Royal Geographical Society Council and a troop of distinguished guests, among them David Livingstone, walked slowly into the hall from a private meeting from which Burton only had been excluded. When all was quiet, Murchison announced that Speke had been killed accidentally the previous afternoon, while out shooting partridges on the Fuller estate.

The effect upon the audience was electric, especially Burton, for whom the news came as a tremendous blow. He 'sank into a chair', wrote his wife, 'and I saw by the workings of his face the terrible emotion he was controlling, and the shock he had received'.

Fortunately, Burton had also come prepared to read a lecture on the ethnology of Dahomey, which he now did, at Murchison's request, to fill the gap; but when he spoke it was 'in a voice that trembled' and with a view to disposing of the paper 'as briefly as he could'.

Isabel Burton later recollected that 'When we got home he wept long and bitterly, and I was for many a day trying to comfort him'.[26]

* A letter written by Speke to Mr. Tinné, 14th September 1864, from Neston Park, Corsham, Wiltshire and now part of the manuscript collection of the R.G.S., London. The letter concludes, 'There is no richer land in the world than the Equatorial regions and nothing more of importance to the interests of Egypt than that of opening up these lands to *legitimate* commerce.' This letter, so strongly reflecting Speke's hopes for the development of Equatoria, is hardly the sort to have been written by one contemplating an early death. Moreover, the last phrase thrusts hard again at Petherick and takes up a previous remark: 'No doubt a consul is much wanted in the Soudan but then he should not be a trader, for no one can trade honestly in those regions.'

Speke was buried in the little church of Dowlish Wake, near Jordans, some forty-five miles from Bath, at a small family funeral attended also by Murchison, David Livingstone and Grant. *The Times* of Saturday 17th September included a report of the British Association's proceedings as well as the inquest held on Speke's death. On Monday 19th the same newspaper paid a warm tribute to Speke and his achievements, but quite rightly avoided any reference to the dispute with Burton.

The *Evening Star* of 17th September was more outspoken: praising Speke's discoveries and applauding his fearless example, the paper commented: 'The late Captain Speke was not a man of genius; he was not even a clever book-writer. . . . He was a simple Indian officer who had a taste – a too fatal taste – for field sports. . . .' Having compared Speke to James Bruce, Sebastian Cabot, Mungo Park and David Livingstone, the *Evening Star* completed its emotional obituary with some acid criticism of the Government.

'If, however, Downing-street was indifferent to his claims, there was at least one high personage who appreciated his services. The King of ITALY sent him a gold medal – a noble and graceful act, which forms a striking contrast to the ungracious conduct of the dispensers of patronage and honour at home. But living or dead, he could have no better title than which he had gained for himself – the title of discoverer of the sources of the Nile.'

The Sherborne Journal for 22nd September spoke emphatically of the surprise element in Speke's death, while *The Bath Chronicle* published the following week expressed condolence for the Speke family, observing that 'the sources of consolation are very great . . . Sympathy with the mourners is universal'. The *Chronicle* was correct. Even many of Speke's most entrenched opponents, the object of their opposition gone, had suffered a sudden change of heart. Mysteriously, malevolence and enmity were translated into messages of sympathy for the family, even into speeches of admiration for the gallantry and manly tenacity of Speke himself.

Four days after his death, a review of *What led* . . . was printed in *The Daily Review*. The article began, 'This work would have been precious as a gift, it becomes almost sacred as a legacy . . .' and continued: 'He has just – or he has little more than – lived to complete his own portraiture, – that of a singularly high-spirited fearless, single-hearted gentleman, ever true to his purpose, and . . . a born adventurer'.[27]

On 29th September, William Speke, the explorer's elder brother, wrote to John Blackwood in Edinburgh:

'. . . We are all recovering as well as we can from our awful affliction. I never experienced such a blow in my life, as we were out together shooting partridges shortly before the accident, in the best of health and spirits. I cannot tell you much in the short space of a letter, in looking over his papers I found a letter unfinished to Mr. Tinné expressing regrets for his loss and anxiety about his friend Baker. It was also a marvellous dispensation of Providence that a letter was written on that day, perhaps that hour from the Chairman of the Geographers at Bath stating that the Committee of Section E had recommended that Govt: be moved to grant honorary distinctions to Capt. Speke and Capt. Grant, a knighthood and civil CB to my brother, the latter distinction to Grant with a pecuniary reward to them. It would have been a great pleasure to him to have been allowed to receive it. Nevertheless it is a consolation to us and perhaps a satisfaction to them'.[28]

Speke had in fact written to Murchison on 7th March requesting that the Royal Geographical Society should recommend some formal recognition of his services by the Government, but he was not sufficiently popular with the Society at that time for much to be done. Dr. Bridges, who has stated that 'Murchison had approached the government on Speke's behalf in 1863', and had made only 'lukewarm' overtures to Palmerston in 1864, did not have sight of William Speke's letter. It is possible that the Royal Geographical Society Council believed that any distinction conferred on Speke might alleviate some of the tension surrounding the Nile question, or, a less likely explanation, they perhaps felt that he had been over-harshly treated. Whatever their motive, as William Speke's letter concluded, '*The Times* article, as well as Sir Roderick Murchison publicly and Livingstone told Grant privately that undoubtedly he [Speke] was the discoverer of the Source of the Nile. What then need we care for malevolent detractors.'

Livingstone's latest judgement was the complete antithesis of a former opinion that Speke had 'turned his back' upon the true fountain of the Nile, which, Livingstone, like Burton, had imagined to be Lake Tanganyika. It must therefore have surprised and gratified the famous missionary that, some time after Speke's death, he received from Speke's family the welcome though entirely unsolicited donation of two thousand pounds, the proceeds of the *Journal*, for the furtherance of his travels and researches.

John Blackwood, Speke's publisher, was deeply grieved at the tragedy, for, as William Speke had observed, he and Hanning were 'no ordinary friends'. In volume XCIV of the 'Maga', October 1864, Blackwood painted an idealistic picture of the dead wanderer very different from others drawn by Petherick, Burton, and later McQueen.

'In the best sense of the word he was very amiable. The charm of his sweet temper and kindly ways fell on all those who came into intercourse with him; and it was a sincere and fundamental amiability. . . .

By the friendly hearth, in fact, he had so much good-humour, docility and pliability about trifles, that people who saw no more of him might have formed the utterly mistaken notion that he was infirm of purpose and wanting the hardness of character necessary for great achievements. And so he realised that fine old idea of chivalry, in which the hero in the field became a lamb at home.'

As Blackwood had long since discovered, one of Speke's most potent charms was his disarming, childish innocence. With children themselves 'he took and communicated enjoyment; and their sports were actually sport to the hunter of the tiger and the hippopotamus'.

There was one unforgettable occasion when Speke kept 'an illustrious table' waiting while he played out of doors with their sons and daughters, yet it was not one of these, but a more private, more picturesque recollection of Speke that Blackwood held most precious. One quiet summer evening in 1859, the two men were strolling and smoking under the trees in Blackwood's garden at St. Andrews, deep in discussion of the second expedition in search of the Nile.

'It was remarked to [Speke] that he had already risked his life to an extent far beyond the average dangers which the human being is likely to escape, and he should consider the feelings of those to whom he was dear – of his parents especially – before setting forth again. With a light in his eye never to be forgotten, he expressed the inner force that was driving him on to his discovery. He knew, he said, that he had hit the Source of the Nile, he must complete his work. How would he feel if any foreigner should take from Britain the honour of the discovery? – rather die a hundred times!

It is fortunate for the world [Blackwood ended], that the triumph preceded the catastrophe.'[29]

J. A. Grant was hard at work on his account of the expedition when the news of Speke's death reached him in Scotland. Sadly he wrote that with its coming, 'the first dark cloud connected with our African expedition had suddenly appeared'.[30] Grant's book, entitled *A Walk across Africa*,* was published by Blackwood towards the close of 1864. In memory of his companion, Grant insisted that those parts of the text with which he had been concerned at the time of Speke's death should be fenced with a black border, and pages 347, 348, and part of page 349 are so treated.

If Speke had become a controversial figure during the last five years of his life, the controversy which sprang up over his death was undoubtedly the greater, and one which has never been satisfactorily resolved. A cynical remark of Burton's contained in a letter to Frank Wilson in Fernando Po summarised the wilder strains of contemporary speculation: 'Nothing will be known of Speke's death; I saw him at 1.30 p.m. and at 4 p.m. he was dead. The charitable say that he shot himself, the uncharitable that I shot him.'[31] Thereafter, despite the unanimous verdict of the inquest, that 'the deceased died from an accidental discharge of his own gun after living a quarter of an hour', two schools of opinion rapidly formed, each sharply divided: the one favouring death by misadventure, the other proposing suicide. What were the circumstances of Speke's

* Lord Palmerston is quoted as having remarked, 'You have had a long walk, Captain Grant'; hence the title of Grant's book.

'bad end', as Burton called it, for reports vary? How did the tragedy come about? Is there any reasonable conclusion to be drawn from the available evidence; in short, how was John Hanning Speke killed and why?

NOTES

1. John Blackwood to Speke, from 4 Burlington Gardens, London, W., Wm. Blackwood & Sons Ltd., Edinburgh, letter-book.
2. This note is included with MS. in the Speke *Journal*, N.L.S., MS. 4872.
3. Blackwood to Speke, 21st November 1863, Blackwood letter-book, Edinburgh.
4. Grant to Blackwood, from Dingwall, 1863, N.L.S., MS. 4181.
5. Speke to Blackwood, Jordans 7 — (?) 1863, N.L.S., MS. 4185.
6. Speke to Blackwood, Jordans, 30th March 1863, N.L.S., MS. 4185.
7. Speke to Blackwood, Jordans, 12 — (?) 1863, N.L.S., MS. 4185
8. Speke to Blackwood, 4 Burlington Gardens, W., no date, N.L.S., MS. 4185.
9. Speke to Blackwood, Jordans, 12 — (?) 1863, N.L.S., MS. 4185.
10. R.G.S. archives. Newspaper cuttings album.
11. *The Athenaeum*, No. 1886, 19th December 1863, pp. 829–32.
12. Speke to the Editor of *The Athenaeum* Jordans, 19th December 1863, N.L.S., MS. 4185.
13. *The Times* newspaper.
14. Speke to Blackwood, 14 — (?) 1863, N.L.S., MS. 4185.
15. Speke to Blackwood, 6th August (?) 1864, Grand Hotel, Paris, N.L.S., MS. 4185. In a letter, undated, sent from 106 Jermyn Street, London, S.W., Grant wrote: 'My dear Speke, As your book may now be said to be "out" what would you say to deputing me while at Paris to present a copy of it in your name to the Emperor! It would prepare him for your visit in February and probably obtain for us some French honours which you know I have often said I'd much prize. . . .'
16. *Uganda Journal*, September 1953, vol. 17, no. 2, p. 150, article entitled 'Speke and Grant'.
17. *Ibid.*, pp. 150, 151.
18. *The Athenaeum*, 14th June 1863.

19. Bridges, *Uganda Journal,* March 1962, p. 40.
20. Speke to Blackwood. Letters written from 79 Eccleston Square, London, S.W. (the home of Mr. C. Murdoch, Speke's brother-in-law), N.L.S., MS. 4185.
21. Speke to Blackwood, 6th August (?) 1864, Grand Hotel, Paris, N.L.S., MS. 4185.
22. N.L.S., MS. 4731. Letter written on blue, squared paper, 1st February 1861.
23. N.L.S., MS. 4185, 25th July 1864 (?).
24. Isabel, Lady Burton, *The Life of Sir Richard Burton,* vol. 2, p. 426.
25. *Ibid.*
26. *Ibid.*
27. R.G.S. archives. Newspaper cuttings book.
28. William Speke to John Blackwood, Jordans, 29th September 1864, N.L.S., MS. 4185. See also Bridges: *Uganda Journal,* March 1962, p. 41 and accompanying references.
29. *Blackwood's Magazine,* 'The Death of Speke', Vol. XCVI, pp. 514–16, October 1864.
30. J. A. Grant: *A Walk across Africa,* p. 347.
31. Brodie: *The Devil Drives,* p. 226; Byron Farwell: *Burton,* p. 241.

CHAPTER 10

ๆ๛๛๛๛๛

THE FINAL OFFERING

๛๛๛๛๛๛

A SHORT article written for the *Uganda Journal* (March 1949) by the well-known East African historian, Mr. H. B. Thomas, has compared conflicting reports of Speke's death, showing how some, such as that by Sir Harry Johnston and the *Dictionary of National Biography* 1921–2 reprint, got almost every detail wrong. Prior to publication of Mr. Thomas's article, *The Times* archives together with the *Encyclopaedia Britannica* (11th edition 1910–11) contained the most accurate accounts of the general circumstances; but, apart from one or two small details, Mr. Thomas's report supersedes both these authorities and for the last twenty years has remained by far the best in existence. He writes as follows:

'At about 2.30 p.m. . . . . Speke set out from his uncle's house in company with his cousin, George Fuller, and a gamekeeper, Daniel Davis, for an afternoon's shooting in Neston Park. He fired both barrels in the course of the afternoon, and about 4 p.m. Davis was marking birds for the two guns who were about 60 yards apart. Speke was seen to climb onto a stone wall about 2 feet high: for the moment he was without his gun. A few seconds later there was a report and when George Fuller rushed up Speke's gun was found behind the wall in the field into which Speke had jumped. The right barrel was at half-cock: only the left barrel was discharged. Speke who was bleeding seriously was sensible for a few minutes and said feebly, "Don't move me". George Fuller went for assistance leaving Davis to attend him; but Speke survived only for about 15 minutes, and when Mr. Snow, surgeon of Box, arrived he was already dead. There was a single wound in his left side such as would be made by a cartridge if the muzzle of the gun – a Lancaster breech-loader without a safety-guard – were close to the body; the charge had passed upwards through the lungs dividing all the large blood-vessels over the heart, though missing the heart itself. . . .

'Speke's body had been removed to the residence of his brother, Mr. W. Speke, J.P., at Monk's Park, Corsham, within a mile or so of Neston Park, and here an inquest was held that afternoon (16th) by the coroner of the Liberty of Corsham (in which parish Neston Park was then situated) and a jury "composed of respectable inhabitants of the place". A unanimous verdict . . . was recorded.'[1]

Two further points, both included in the report of the inquest which appeared in *The Bath Chronicle* for Saturday 17th September, are, firstly, that according to evidence given by George Pargiter Fuller, the wall upon which Speke had stood was 'a low part of a loose stone wall, at that place, about two feet high', and that Davis, who 'was making birds for my master and the deceased, who were shooting . . . was about 200 yards to their right, standing in a field'.

It is also worth noting that Fuller, who was 'about 60 yards from the place', was walking in front of Speke and that, after the fatal shot was fired, Speke did not jump from the wall, but, according to Fuller who actually saw him, 'fell into the field'. The element of mystery was further intensified when on 20th March 1921 George Fuller, by then a very old man, sent a letter to *The Times* in response to an article which the paper had printed about Burton, quoting Burton's famous comment to Frank Wilson. Fuller's letter concluded, 'The verdict was "Accidental death by explosion of a gun". Being the only living eye-witness of that sad accident, and having been in company with Speke on the day of his death, I can testify that Burton could not have seen Speke on that day, and that the death occurred before 1.30 p.m.'

Although a brave attempt to remove the slur of suicide from his cousin's name, Fuller's letter made matters more complicated than ever by introducing a new time for the shooting and one which so obviously conflicted with the published report on the inquest. From 1921 until the present day no new evidence has emerged to either clarify or further confuse the known facts, that is until quite recently when, by the generous permission of Mr. Peter Speke, it has been possible to examine a memorandum, accompanying a letter written by George Fuller to his nephew Walter Speke, and dated 23rd January 1914. In it, Fuller contradicted still more completely details given as of part his original evidence in 1864: for example, the 'Lancaster breech-loader' became a muzzle-loader; Speke instead of being 'without his gun' was seen on top of the wall holding on to the weapon by its muzzle end; whilst the date of the accident was given as 1st September, instead of 15th September. More important by far is the fact that Speke's gun, picked up it was said in 1864 with the right hammer at *half-cock,* was reported by Fuller fifty years later as having been found with that hammer at *full-cock,* i.e. ready for firing.

Mrs. Brodie, in her admirable biography of Burton *The Devil Drives,* has dismissed as 'decent camouflage' the reconstruction offered by *The Times* of 19th September 1864, that the left hammer of Speke's gun 'must have struck against a stone or hitched a bough, and the blow just lifted the hammer, and then allowed it to fall back upon the pin of the cartridge'. Mrs. Brodie, having built up a strong case for suicide, while cautiously reminding the reader that 'We cannot on the evidence assert that it was deliberate suicide', has defined the latter as 'a supreme act of hate', in Speke's case whereby 'his own act of self-destruction . . . would seal Burton's mouth forever, thus destroying *him*'.[2]

The theory is an interesting one constructed and expressed with great lucidity, but unfortunately depends in part upon an error of fact, in that Mrs. Brodie has described how Speke's gun 'was held against his chest', when the shot charge really entered Speke's body under his left armpit,[3] traversing the chest at an angle and shredding the blood-vessels over the heart. In order to have delivered its charge at such an angle, the barrels of Speke's Lancaster must have been so aligned as to have made it practically, if not entirely, impossible for him to reach the left trigger, even when standing in balance on flat ground. But consider how much more difficult it would have been to effect so unlikely a means of discharging the weapon when upright upon a broken country dyke, the stones of which, Fuller's evidence assures us, were 'loose', and foothold therefore unsteady.

The barrels of Speke's gun were probably twenty-eight to thirty inches long, in common with similar shotguns of the period, which in itself would make the triggers difficult to reach;[4] but even supposing Speke had envisaged, indeed carried out, such a precarious method of self-execution, it seems inconceivable that he should have stretched his arm still further in order to reach the left or rear trigger, when, especially in an awkward stance, so much more pressure could have been applied, and so much more expeditiously, to the right. Speke could not have shot himself by this or any other method unless he had first cocked fully the hammer firing the left barrel, for he could not readily have eased the hammer off unless by engaging it, or, if fully cocked, the trigger, on a twig or a projection of stone. In either event this mode of suicide appears an unlikely one, in particular for a man so accustomed to killing and having behind him possibly twenty-five years' experience of firearms.

A remark made by George Fuller (whose memorandum will be given presently in full) seems to bear out this argument, in that it utterly contradicts the supposition made by the editor of *The Times* in 1864 and shared by many another since, that Speke's 'great familiarity' with shotguns had 'produced the momentary incaution'.

Burton himself reinforced this when writing eight years later in *Zanzibar* that

'The calamity had been the more unexpected as he was ever remarkable for the caution with which he handled his weapon. I ever make a point of ascertaining a fellow-traveller's habit in that matter, and I observed that even when our canoe was shaken and upthrown by the hippopotamus he never allowed his gun to look at him or at others.'[5]

Discounting for a moment practical considerations, the usual arguments favouring suicide are: that Speke feared a disastrous outcome of his verbal duel with Burton at Bath; that this and Speke's extreme state of nervousness is proved by his sudden departure from the hall on the morning of the 15th; that antagonism and controversy had induced unendurable depression, the climax of a depression cycle extending back as far as Speke's early youth. Although each of these arguments is reasonable in itself, it is uncertain that together or singly they provide a good enough reason for Speke to have taken his life.

From the outset, Blackwood has written, Speke 'knew . . . that he had hit on the Source of the Nile', while nothing in Speke's published or reported accounts makes any doubt of this fact. Having failed to establish beyond question the connection between the Nile and the Victoria Nyanza in 1863, Speke, after returning from India could, and would have done so, backed by France, in 1865, as his reply to the bailiff of Taunton had indicated. Undeniable though it may be that Speke detested the prospect of an intellectual brawl with Burton in public, when, as Isabel Burton's story showed, the very proximity of Burton made Speke nervous and uncomfortable, he would have almost certainly endured the debate if only for the sake of Central Africa and his own avowed responsibility to his discovery. It might be added that, although the past four years have seen assembled more new Speke material than has ever collected together previously, there still remain too many been blanks up to 1854 to permit of depression theories being profitably constructed. Thereafter the comparatively few facts known about Speke render theories of the kind both dangerous and misleading and can only emphasise to future commentators the inadvisability of applying psychoanalysis, complicated enough with living persons, to someone a hundred and five years dead, whose case history is, to say the least of it, incomplete.[6]

One might also argue that Speke's notorious vanity, referred to frequently by Burton, and his truly Old Testament-like sense of justice and morality, would have made it exceedingly hard for him to contemplate suicide seriously. At the time of the conference, his attitude was positive and bravely extrovert, even as we have noted, violently so. As was customary in moments of stress, he had gone out shooting, once with his brother William, then with his cousin George Fuller and only an immutable transgression which occurred during the second of these excursions in any way altered the successful, established pattern of a lifetime.

George Fuller's *Memorandum*, a unique, and in some respects eccentric, eye-witness account of Speke's death, was compiled, 'for family use only', in response to a request made by Walter Speke's aunt, Matilda Pine-Coffin. In the accompanying letter dated 10th February 1914, Fuller wrote, 'She thinks that such a memo: coming from me . . . would be satisfactory to the members of your family in order to show not only how this accident really happened, but also to contradict the vile and wicked slander set up by Burton at the time with the view to advertising himself as an authority on the discovery of the Source of the Nile.'[7]

The document itself, which covers three and a half sheets of paper a trifle larger than standard quarto size, is written in handwriting resembling Speke's own, clearly and legibly and with only minimal alterations. The memorandum begins:

'It was on the 1st of September 1864 that Hanning Speke – my first cousin – met his tragic end when shooting partridges with me in ––––––– Farm near here.

A memorial stone still records the spot where he fell. . . . The Geographical Society was holding its annual meeting at Bath on the day of his death. In consequence of his deafness Hanning Speke did not attend that meeting, although much pressed to do so. I well recollect his doubts on the subject of absenting himself from that meeting, and the reasons he gave for not accepting the invitation urged upon him.

His natural modesty led him to avoid appearing as a sort of hero at such a gathering. He also knew that Burton was to be present at it, which circumstance made him doubt whether his presence would be acceptable at the same time with Burton.

It was no secret at this time that Burton had no scruples in putting Hanning in the shade as far as he could by exaggerating his own exploits to an extent which Hanning knew to be as untrue as they were undeserving of praise in many respects. Hanning therefore preferred a peaceful day's partridge shooting with me to a possible wrangle with Burton whose character he knew too well. There are many persons who have only heard of Hanning's death through the reports circulated by Burton. These reports, being so untrue, your family must necessarily be pained at hearing any repetition of them. In order to contradict these wicked reports I am induced again to put on record the scene which so vividly rests in my memory.

Hanning's gun was made by one of the best makers of the day, a double-barrelled muzzle-loading one, with an extremely light pull to the trigger.

While shooting with him on that day, the only day I ever shot with him, I was apprehensive of an accident because he used the gun in the same way as he was accustomed to use a rifle, which, as you know, has a heavy pull on the trigger and is [not] usually kept broken for safety.

I do not think that Hanning for many years before that day had shot with anything but a rifle. He did not seem to have acquired the usual precautions exercised by sportsmen accustomed to the use of muzzle-loading double-barrelled guns.

My gamekeeper, who was with us, and I, both noticed this carelessness in the use of the gun by Hanning. We therefore avoided being very close to him when walking the fields, and in crossing the wall where the accident happened both the gamekeeper and I were at some distance from Hanning.

The gamekeeper saw Hanning on the top of the wall holding the gun in his left hand at the muzzle and supporting himself on the wall with the stock of the gun on the wall. At the moment I was not looking toward Hanning but on hearing the report of a gun I immediately looked round, thinking that Hanning had fired at the partridges we were expecting to find near that spot.

On seeing Hanning on the wall with his hand clasping the muzzle end of the gun, and observing him in a falling attitude I knew that something serious had happened, and went immediately to his assistance.

When I reached him blood was flowing in a stream from near the heart where the shot had entered his body.

In a few minutes he expired from loss of blood.

The cause of the accident must always remain a mystery, but, [from?] what both the gamekeeper & I saw, there cannot be a shadow of a doubt on one fact, viz: that Hanning could not have possibly pulled the trigger of the gun himself. The trigger must have been touched by the butt of a stone, or in some way the exposed part of the trigger must have come in contact with some other force. The wound itself indicated that the charge of shot entered his left side below the armpit in an upward direction, thereby showing the position of the gun to have been such as to have made it impossible for Hanning to have touched the trigger.

The hammer of the lock on the other barrel was at full cock when the gun was picked up.

These facts correspond with the evidence taken at the inquest, and should be an answer to the report, or rather inuendoes, made

by Burton at the meeting of the Geographical Society, viz: that
Hanning committed suicide rather than meet Burton who came
prepared to contradict Hanning's history of the discovery of the
source of the Nile. . . .

Hanning was a traveller as a sportsman in search of wild game,
Burton was a traveller as an author in search of a reputation.'[8]

It has been deemed essential to give Fuller's description of
the actual shooting *in extenso*, especially as has been noted, this
account sent to Walter Speke differs so widely from several of
his original statements. In view of his age, one need not perhaps
be too critical of Mr. Fuller's inability to recollect exactly
abstract phenomena such as the date, or indeed, as happened
seven years later, the time at which the incident occurred.
Nor is it so unlikely that he should have forgotten that Speke's
gun was a breech-loader and not a muzzle-loader, particularly
as they had never shot in each other's company on previous
occasions. On this point, the original testimony of the gamekeeper, Davis, is more likely to be reliable in the absence of
the actual weapon itself for which many fruitless searches have
been made. More probable it is that concerning Speke's
progress up to and over the stone wall Fuller's memory served
him faithfully, for his graphic account of what both he and
Davis saw has in it the ring of truth and is, of the whole
narration, the part most logically and most precisely described.
It also tallies with the evidence given by Fuller and Davis at the
inquest, if one assumes, and it appears reasonable to do so,
that in Fuller's case his observations are logically pursued,
whilst in the case of Davis, a minute time-lapse had occurred
which was not considered vital enough to be elaborated upon at
the inquest.

If we combine the statements made by Fuller and Davis in
1864 with the contents of the memorandum, the following
pattern of events will be seen to emerge:

Speke, observed by the keeper from an eighth of a mile away,
went up to the wall, 'his gun in his hand'. According to Fuller
(1914), Davis then saw Hanning 'on top of the wall holding the
gun in his left hand at the muzzle and supporting himself on
the wall with the stock of the gun on the wall'. Such observations
in such detail would be quite normal for a keeper to have

made, and are perfectly feasible, even at two hundred yards. Davis (1864) testified that, having watched Speke approach the wall, 'Almost immediately afterwards I heard the report of a gun'. It was at that moment Fuller (1914) turned and saw Speke falling forward, 'his hand clasping the muzzle end of the gun'. Accepting this use of the reported facts, it can only be that the gun was fired while in a near to vertical position, a conclusion not borne out by the expert testimony of the surgeon, Mr. Thomas Fitzherbert Snow.[9] On the other hand, allowing a difference in time, however slight, for the firing of the shot, the sound of which would have reached Davis only a fraction earlier than his eyes could have registered the sight of Speke apparently supporting himself on the wall with the gun-stock, it is quite possible that as Speke turned his body while drawing the fully-cocked Lancaster up at his side as he stood on the wall, a point of stone or a piece of stick engaged the left trigger and fired that barrel into his side. If indeed both hammers were at half- instead of full-cock, the same piece of stone or branch could as easily have lifted and dropped the left hammer, producing an identical result. It is more likely, and despite Fuller's remarks on Speke's use of the gun, more in character with him, that he laid down the loaded shotgun *before* getting up on the wall, muzzles foremost lest they pick up mud or dirt. Whether or not Fuller saw him holding the weapon *after* the shot was fired is less important in this sequence of events, as the fact of whether Speke dropped the gun, or brought it down with him as he fell cannot influence the actual cause of his death. The fact that neither Davis nor his master *saw* the gun discharge makes it impossible for any definitive statement to be made and, for the sake of reason, an element of doubt must always be allowed. But from the evidence as much as from the events of Speke's life leading up to the shooting itself, it is the opinion of this writer after some four years' acquaintance with the facts, that Speke neither contemplated suicide, nor did he kill himself, and that his death was entirely accidental.

The memorial stone which still marks the site of the shooting is very simply and unequivocally worded:

HERE
THE DISTINGUISHED AND ENTERPRISING
AFRICAN TRAVELLER
CAPTAIN JOHN HANNING SPEKE
LOST HIS LIFE
BY THE ACCIDENTAL EXPLOSION
OF HIS GUN
SEPTEMBER 15TH 1864.[10]

Grant, though he afterwards reproached himself for not joining Speke at Bath and thereby perhaps preventing 'this calamity', contributed a final word of sentiment to Speke's passing: he wrote

'Had the toll of the funeral bell reached the shores of the Nyanza, as it touched the people in the valley of Ilminster, there is one at least – the King of Uganda – who would have shed a tear for the untimely death of the far distant traveller who had sought and found his protection.'[11]

NOTES

1. H. B. Thomas: 'The Death of Speke in 1864', *Uganda Journal*, vol. 13, No. 1, March 1949, pp. 105–7.
2. Mrs. Fawn M. Brodie: *The Devil Drives*, p. 226.
3. This fact I discussed with Mrs. Brodie during the visit referred to by her on page 10 of *The Devil Drives*. I also demonstrated to her the various theories which commentators had devised to explain Speke's death, but at the time was, myself, still open-minded as to the possible cause and motive.
4. I have been assured of this in conversation with Mr. Peter McKenzie, the expert on muzzle-loading guns, Mr. D. W. Perkins and Mr. J. W. Barrett a former director of John Rigby and Co. Ltd., Gunmakers, London, W.
5. Burton: *Zanzibar*, vol. 2, p. 398.
6. There is almost no surviving documentation of Speke's life from the time of his birth until 1844. From then until 1854 we are largely dependent on scant references in *What led . . .*, his letters to John Blackwood and the brief notes in Vol. 2 of Burton's

Zanzibar. Thus the first 27 of Speke's 37 years remain, virtually, still unrecorded.

7. Letter made available by courtesy of Mr. Peter Speke.

8. Memorandum written by George Pargiter Fuller, 23rd January 1914, and made available to the author by Mr. Peter Speke. Although a vast over-simplification, Fuller's last-quoted sentence draws a neat distinction between his cousin and Richard Burton which contains important elements of truth.

9. Surgeon Snow's testimony appears in the *Bath Chronicle*.

10. *Memorandum*, 23rd January 1914, page 1.

11. Grant: *A Walk across Africa*, p. 349.

EPILOGUE

WHATEVER the depth of his private grief, Burton, unlike Grant or even some of Speke's former opponents, did not indulge in sentimentality or allow controversy to die. Assisted by James McQueen, he renewed his attack upon Speke's claims and exploits in *The Nile Basin*, a slender scurrilous little volume published only a short while after the accident. Although in his preface Burton stated that he did not 'stand forth as an enemy of the departed' and was careful to notice Speke's 'noble qualities of energy, courage, and perseverance', both press and public considered the haste with which the book appeared was indecent, whilst by association with McQueen's brutal journalism, the reputations of both Burton and Petherick in whose defence McQueen had so vigorously written suffered a decline instead of gaining strength.

In a lengthy dissertation which identified Lake Tanganyika as 'Ptolemy's Western Lake Reservoir', Burton proceeded to discredit Speke's discoveries on five main issues:

'There is', Burton wrote, 'a difference of levels in the upper and lower part of the so-called Lake. This point is important only when taken in connection with the following.

The native report that the Mwerango River rises from the hills in the centre of the so-called Lake.

The general belief that there is a road through the so-called Lake.

The fact that the southern part of the so-called Lake floods the country for thirteen miles, whereas the low and marshy northern shore is not inundated.

The phenomenon that the so-called Lake swells during the dry period of the Nile and *vice versa*.'[1]

Here again Burton questioned not merely Speke's assertion
that the Victoria Nyanza flowed into the White Nile, but the
very existence of the lake itself. In *The Westminster Review*,
April 1864, he had written:

'on his first journey, in 1858, Captain Speke merely visited the
southern extremity of the lake in about 1° 30' S. lat. On his second
journey, he and Captain Grant, though they skirted the north-
western side of the lake, did not reach it except at Murchison
Creek, in 0° 21' 19" N lat., and 32° 44' 30" E long . . . so that, in
point of fact, the Nyanza was actually visited at only two points,
the one at the north, the [other] at the south end.'[2]

At every opportunity throughout the remainder of *The Nile
Basin*, Burton's co-author, McQueen, in a series of articles
reprinted from the *Morning Advertiser*, dwelled upon Speke's
reputedly licentious life in Africa, but one suspects only reveal-
ing in himself a repressed preoccupation by continual references
to the scanty bark-cloth *mbugus* worn by the native women,
Speke's preference for attractive young maidservants and his
alleged sexual adventures with a variety of others ranging from
the Queen Mother of Buganda to Consul Petherick's cook.

After smashing the framework of Speke's geography to
pieces, in one instance by highlighting that ninety-mile stretch
of the Nile which the explorer, against Blackwood's advice, had
shown apparently running uphill, McQueen continued his
tirade by denouncing all connection between the Nile and Lake
Victoria, reiterating meanwhile that Speke – as distinct from
Petherick – had wasted not only time but public money by
'drinking pombe, flirting or coquetting, and collecting harems'.

Sneeringly McQueen suggested that, at the so-called source
of the Nile, an hotel might be established, advertised as 'THE
RIPON FALLS HOTEL. Speke and Mtesa. Pombe and
Mbugus always Ready'.

Though the text of Speke's *Journal* had provided McQueen
with much material for his venomous critique, he maintained
that Speke 'should never have allowed such narratives to have
issued from his mouth, or stained his pages with such rubbish...'
Sound advice indeed, but perhaps advice from which the
critic himself might also have profited. Likewise it should be

borne in mind that it was McQueen's posthumous attack, rather than the explorer's own account of his travels, that for years left enduring blemishes on Speke's largely undeserving character.

Nine years later, in 1873, following extensive explorations on the Upper Nile, the German botanist, Dr. Georg Schweinfurth, a man skilled in languages, zoology and anthropology, besides other disciplines, published his classic work entitled *The Heart of Africa*.[3] Unfortunately for Speke's geographical reputation, which by then had sunk very low, the map by which Schweinfurth illustrated his adventures agreed entirely with Burton's assessment of the Lake Victoria region, in that it was shown covered by no less than five separate 'lakes and lakelets'.[4]

It was not for a further two years that Henry Stanley, having completed the exploration of Lake Tanganyika with Livingstone in 1871, revisited Africa to establish the identity of the great and mysterious river known as the Lualaba, which, until his dying day, Livingstone had believed to be the Upper Nile. Stanley's huge and well-equipped expedition, paid for by *The New York Herald* and the London *Daily Telegraph*, included among its provisions an iron boat which his porters carried in sections from Zanzibar. At the southernmost tip of the Victoria Nyanza, Stanley's boat was assembled, and in it he managed to circumnavigate the entire lake. By this means, wrote Sir Harry Johnston, 'Stanley not only ascertained the approximate area and shape of the Victoria Nyanza, but he was able to define with some approach to accuracy its principal islands and archipelagoes. After his journey there was no longer any doubt as to Speke's great discovery. The question was settled once and forever.'[5]

Stanley's expedition not only vindicated Speke, but, by tracing the Lualaba's course west, eventually proved that Lake Tanganyika was 'the head reservoir not of the Nile, but of the mighty Congo'.[6] Defeated at last, the tenacious Burton reserved until 1881 his acknowledgement of Speke's ultimate victory and in 1890 wrote a letter from his death-bed in which he told Grant that every harsh word he had ever uttered against Speke was withdrawn.[7]

To these aging travellers, the urgency and mad rage of the Nile dispute must have appeared by then a little absurd, sad, almost intangibly remote. They probably retained quite accurate memories of Speke's appearance, assisted no doubt by photographs, but just as likely had forgotten* such sensations as the touch of his hand and had perhaps begun to lose all clear recollection of his voice. In far-off Zanzibar, Bombay, despite the fact that fame is said to have made him excessively conceited, unlike Grant or Burton experienced no distractions capable of blurring his master's image. In the end, Bombay's reverence for Speke's memory was perhaps equalled only by that of Grant, for on hearing of Speke's death the faithful Seedy is reported to have said: 'Now my father is dead and my right arm is cut off.'⁸

During the winter of 1864, a bust of Speke was made from the death-mask by the sculptor, Edgar George Papworth, while another was executed by Adolfo Pieroni of Lucca, the famous medallist. In an article which appeared in *Fraser's Magazine*, February 1869, Isabel Burton described a visit which she and Burton made to Papworth's studio at 36 Milton Street, Dorset Square, London. In it she recalled how Papworth indicated the 'drawn-down mouth and the deepen'd eye' of the death-mask lying on the floor and, turning to Burton, said: 'I only took the cast after death, and never knew him alive; but you who lived with him so long can surely give me some hints.'⁹ Thereupon, it is said, Burton took up the sculptor's pencil and completed Speke's likeness with a few deft strokes.

After this story came a poem of twenty-three stanzas, each of six lines, which, inspired by the sight of the death-mask, explores Burton's ties with Speke, their mutual sufferings in Africa and the precarious friendship destined to be short-lived. After comparing the poem to *The Kasîdah*, and another, earlier lament, Mrs. Brodie considers that only Burton himself could have written it, such is the richness of its 'oblique allusions', and such the intimate understanding of its subject. In the final

---

* Cf. J. L. Borgès: 'The Aleph', from *A Personal Anthology* (1968), p. 154. 'Our minds are porous with forgetfulness.'

stanzas, the poem distinguishes 'a true friendship with men' and Burton's relationship with Speke:

'But 'twixt man and man it may not so hap;
Each man is his own and proper sphere:
At some point, perchance, may the lines o'erlap;
The far rest is far as the near is near –
Save when the orbs are of friend and friend
And the circle's limits perforce must blend.

But the one sole point at which he and I
Could touch, was the contact of vulgar minds;
'Twas interest's forcible, feeble tie,
Which binds, but with lasting bonds ne'er binds;
And our objects fated to disagree,
What way went I, and what way went he?

Yet were we comrades for years and years,
And endured in its troth our companionship
Through a life of chances, of hopes, and fears;
Nor a word of harshness e'er passed the lip,
Nor a thought unkind dwelt in either heart,
Till we chanced – by what chance did it hap? – to part.'[10]

Set against the attentions of the country and his friends, the recognition accorded to Speke's achievements by Government was, in the words of Sir Harry Johnston, no more than

'the paltry satisfaction of granting to him through the Herald's College supporters and an additional motto to his coat of arms. By this grant the family is now entitled to add a hippopotamus and a crocodile as supporters to their shield, a crocodile to the crest, the flowing Nile to their coat of arms, and the additional motto, 'Honor est a Nilo''.'[11]

But if politicians had in the end shown themselves inadequate and feeble, then the gesture made by the President and Council of the Royal Geographical Society was infinitely nobler. Sir Roderick Murchison moved that a 'Monumental Pillar should be erected in some happily chosen spot'. In which connection the *Exeter Gazette*, describing a dinner given for Burton, chaired by Lord Stanley, observed approvingly that in his speech Burton not only withdrew his sharper criticisms of Speke but 'promised to do all in his power' to aid work on the memorial.[12]

In response to Murchison's appeal, a simple obelisk of red polished granite was erected in Kensington Gardens, London, close to one of the main avenues leading north to the Bayswater Road.[13] Totally starved of embellishment, the inscription* incised on its west face implied the perpetuation of Speke's fame, whilst, in its simplicity, it reflected only the straightforwardness and none of the complexity inherent in his character. The inscription reads

'IN MEMORY OF
SPEKE
VICTORIA NYANZA
AND THE NILE 1864.'

As a consequence of recent researches made by Mrs. Hughes, archivist to the Royal Geographical Society, six letters concerning the Speke Memorial have come to light. In the earliest of these, written soon after Grant's death, his friend, General J. Shaw Stewart, addressed himself as follows to the then President of the Society, Sir Mountstuart E. Grant Duff:

15 April 1892.

'My dear Sir Mountstuart

I know the thought has occurred to other friends of the late Colonel Grant besides myself that it would be a graceful act to add his name to Speke's on the monument in Kensington Gardens.

The R.G.S. is preeminently [sic] the Body from whom any such proposal should emanate, and if the suggestion has not already been made I will be glad if you will kindly give it consideration.

The inscription on the west side of the monument is somewhat to this effect –

* More informative is the inscription cut on the three exposed sides of Speke's tomb, in the family vault at Dowlish Wake:
Sacred to the Memory of
JOHN HANNING, second son of WILLIAM & GEORGINA SPEKE
who died Sept. 15, 1864. Aged 37 years.
The top of the dark marble sarcophagus, embellished with hippopotamus, crocodile, birds and what is presumed to be 'lake sedge', bears the inscription: *E Nilo praeclarus.*

In Memory of
Speke –
Victoria Nyanza
and the
Nile.
1864.

I think some words such as these might be placed on the east side –

Also in Memory of
Grant
Speke's Companion
and Friend.'[14]

When asked for his opinion, Mr. K. R. Murchison, who felt that the 'placing of Grant's name on the Speke monument' was not either 'enough or most suitable', wrote 'I suppose before anything is decided some communication will be made to the *Speke* family to ascertain their opinion and wishes upon the subject'.[15]

The eminent geographer, Francis Galton, upheld this viewpoint and advised J. Scott Keltie of the Royal Geographical Society 'that Speke's representatives shd be asked for their approval to the suggested addition of Grant's name, in a subordinate fashion, to the monument. Also whether they have any other views on to [*sic*] making the monument representative of Nile or African Exploration generally always of course retaining its distinctive character as having been originally erected in memory of Speke.' Galton concluded his letter: 'this latter question is asked because an idea has been expressed, that if any such addition could be effected it wd. add much to the importance of the monument, but no serious consideration has yet been given to that idea.'[16]

On 3rd August 1892, Galton wrote again to Scott Keltie, this time enclosing a letter dated 30th July, which he had received from Grant's widow, Margaret. With a restraint so characteristic of her late husband, Mrs. Grant cautioned Galton, 'I hardly think the name of another could be added *now* – after a quarter of a century and I doubt the Speke family liking it although they are all *very great friends* of ours and were deeply attached to their Brother's friend – still – they might not like to divide the honor. They are very jealous of his fame.'[17]

Then followed an interval of almost five months until, on Christmas Day 1892, Speke's brother-in-law, Sir John Dorington, replying to Francis Galton from Lypiatt Park, informed him that he would 'communicate with Mr Speke & the other members of the Speke family & will let you know shortly what their views are on the matter you bring before me. It is clearly one in which their wishes are of paramount importance. . . .'[18]

Although the precise terms of the Speke family's reaction are not known, they can scarcely have differed much from the very deferential views advanced by Margaret Grant. No additions were made either to the obelisk or to its inscription; thus in death, as in life, Grant's status relative to Speke remained unaltered.

Yet, so unfaltering was Grant in his praise, and so tenaciously loyal to Speke's memory,[19] that it is impossible to conceive that much, if any, true dissatisfaction derived from his self-perpetuated role.

It remains only to be said that, of all known descriptions of the Speke Memorial, by far the most perceptive has been devised by Mr. H. B. Thomas who wrote in the concluding paragraph of his article, 'The Death of Speke in 1864':

'There is something particularly fitting in its situation, with G. F. Watt's "Physical Energy" on the one hand, and Sir George Frampton's "Peter Pan" on the other; for Speke's nature displayed a truly remarkable blend of indomitable courage with the spirit of perennial youth.'[20]

NOTES

1. R. F. Burton and J. McQueen; *The Nile Basin*, 1864, pp. iii, iv.
2. *The Westminster Review*, April 1864.
3. Dr. Georg Schweinfurth: *The Heart of Africa*, 1873.
4. *Ibid.* and Sir Harry Johnston: *The Nile Quest*, p. 223.
5. Sir Harry Johnston: *The Nile Quest*, 1903, p. 226.
6. Brodie: *The Devil Drives*, p. 231.
7. Sir Harry Johnston: *The Nile Quest*. No mention of this is made in *The Devil Drives* (1967).
8. R.G.S. archives. Bombay died on 12th October 1886, aged, according to Sir Henry Stanley, sixty-two or sixty-three.

9. William Speke to John Blackwood, 15th November 1864, N.L.S., MS. 4185; Mrs. Fawn M. Brodie: *The Devil Drives*, p. 228. Another bust of Speke was executed by Adolfo Pieroni (1832–75), the famous medallist, a native of Lucca. Pieroni formerly studied under Onestini and Casale.

10. See Brodie: *The Devil Drives*, pp. 228, 229; Lady Burton: *The Life of Sir Richard Burton*, vol. I, p. 391.

11. Sir Harry Johnston: *The Nile Quest*, p. 170.

12. N.L.S., MS.

13. The obelisk is approximately twenty feet high, with its main shaft divided into three sections. The shaft is square in section and relatively slender, with a long, tapered point. It stands upon a stepped base of three levels and is surrounded by a low iron railing. The inscription is cut on the west side facing the avenue.

14. Letter from General J. Shaw Stewart to Sir Mountstuart E. Grant Duff, P.R.G.S., 15th April 1892, R.G.S. archives.

15. K. R. Murchison Esq., writing from 'Brockhurst', East Grinstead, Sussex, 23rd July 1892, R.G.S. archives.

16. Letter from Francis Galton to J. Scott Keltie, from 42 Rutland Gate, S.W., 25th July 1892. R.G.S. archives.

17. Letter from Mrs. Margaret Grant to Francis Galton, black-bordered paper, Househill, Nairn, N.B., 30th July 1892, R.G.S. archives.

18. Letter from Sir John Dorington Bart., M.P., Lypiatt Park, Stroud, Buckinghamshire, 25th December (1892), R.G.S. archives.

19. Mr. John Guille Millais: *Far Away up the Nile*, London 1924. In a footnote to page 82, Mr. Millais wrote of Grant, 'I knew him well for three years when he lived near Nairn, N.B., and had many delightful talks with him of old days in Africa. His loyalty and affection for Speke were unbounded.'

20. H. B. Thomas, O.B.E.: 'The Death of Speke in 1864', p. 107, *Uganda Journal*, vol. 13, no. 1, March 1949.

BIBLIOGRAPHY

Baker, J. N. L., *A History of Geographical Discovery and Exploration.* London, 1931.

Baker, Sir Samuel White, *Ismailia.* 2 vols. London, 1874.

Baker, Sir Samuel White, *The Albert N'Yanza.* 2 vols. London, 1866.

Borgès, J. L., *A Personal Anthology* (translation). London, 1968.

Brodie, Fawn M., *The Devil Drives.* New York, 1967.

Bruce, James, *The Travels to Discover the Source of the Nile in the Years 1768–1773.* 7 vols. London, 1790.

Burke's *Landed Gentry*, pp. 2370–2. London, 1952.

Burton, Sir Richard Francis, *First Footsteps in East Africa.* London, 1856.

Burton, Sir Richard Francis, *The Lake Regions of Central Africa.* 2. vols. London, 1860.

Burton, Sir Richard Francis, *Abeokuta and the Cameroons Mountains: An Exploration.* 2 vols. London, 1863.

Burton, Sir Richard Francis, *Zanzibar: City, Island, and Coast.* 2 vols. London, 1872.

Burton, Sir Richard Francis, *Two Trips to Gorilla Land and the Cataracts of the Congo.* 2 vols. London, 1876.

Burton, Sir Richard Francis, *Wanderings in Three Continents.* London, 1901.

Burton, Sir Richard Francis, and McQueen, James, *The Nile Basin.* London, 1864.

Burton, Lady (Isabel), *The Life of Capain Sir Richard F. Burton, K.C.M.G., F.R.G.S.* 2 vols. London, 1893.

Cameron, V. L., *Across Africa.* 2 vols. Leipzig, 1873. Another edition, enlarged and corrected, London, 1885.

Cooley, W. Desborough, *Inner Africa laid Open.* London, 1852.

Cumming, Roualeyn Gordon, of Altyre, *Five Years of a Hunter's Life in the Far Interior of South Africa.* 2 vols. London, 1850.

Daumal, René, *Mount Analogue* (translation). 1959.

Drayson, Capt. Alfred W., *Sporting Scenes Among the Kaffirs of South Africa.* London, 1858.

Edwardes, Allen, *Death Rides a Camel.* New York, 1963.

Farwell, Byron, *The Man who Presumed, A Biography of Henry M. Stanley.* New York, 1957.

Farwell, Byron, *Burton.* London, 1963.

Gladstone, Penelope, *Travels with Alexine.* London, 1970.

Grant, J. A., *A Walk across Africa.* London, 1864.

Gudsow, Agube, *The Princess Biaslantt.* London, 1926.

Gudsow, Agube, *The Unknown Land* (unpublished MS.). N.D., *c.* 1940.

Harris, Sir William Cornwallis, *The Wild Sports of Southern Africa.* London, 1839.

Hassall, Christopher, *Rupert Brooke: A Biography.* London, 1964.

Henderson, Philip, *The Life of Laurence Oliphant.* London, 1956.

Hodson, Major V. C. P., *Officers of the Bengal Army, 1758–1834.* 4 vols. London, 1946.

Hurst, H. E., *The Nile.* London, 1952.

Johnston, Sir H. H., *The Uganda Protectorate.* 2 vols. London, 1902.

Johnston, Sir H. H., *The Nile Quest.* London, 1903.

Johnson, The Rev. T. B., *Tramps round the Mountains of the Moon.* London, 1908.

Loftus, E. A., *Speke and the Nile Sources.* London, 1954.

McMorrin, Ian, and Noyce, Wilfred, *World Atlas of Mountaineering.* London, 1969.

Millais, J. G., *Far Away Up The Nile.* London, 1924.

Moorehead, Alan, *The White Nile.* London, 1960.

Moorehead, Alan, *The Blue Nile.* London, 1962.

Murdoch, Mrs. Sophia (née Speke), *Records of the Speke Family.* Private edition, 1922.

Petherick, John, *Egypt, the Soudan and Central Africa.* London, 1861.

Petherick, J. & K., *Travels in Central Africa.* 2 vols. London, 1869.

Playfair, Sir R. L., *A History of Arabia Felix.* Bombay, 1859.

Rainsford, Prof. O., *Livingstone's Lake.* London, 1966.

Richards, Charles, *Some Historic Journeys.* London, 1961.

Richards, Charles, and Place, James, *East African Explorers.* London, 1960.

Rüppell, W. P. E. S., *Atlas zu der Reise in nordlichen Afrika, Zoologie.* 5 vols in 1. Frankfurt, 1826–8.

Russell, Mrs. Charles E. B., *General Rigby, Zanzibar and the Slave Trade.* London, 1935.

St. John, Charles, *Wild Sports and Natural History of the Highlands.* London, 1846.

Schweinfurth, Dr. Georg, *The Heart of Africa.* 2 vols. London, 1873.

Skelton, R. A., *Explorer's Maps 1856–91.* London, 1958.

Speke, Capt. John Hanning, *Journal of the Discovery of the Source of the Nile.* London, 1863. 2nd Edition, London, 1864. 1st American edition, New York, 1864. 1st French edition, Paris, 1869. Subsequent editions in English: London, 1906. London, 1912. London, 1937.

Speke, Capt. John Hanning, *What Led to the Discovery of the Source of the Nile.* London, 1864.

Stanley, Sir H. M., *How I Found Livingstone in Central Africa.* London, 1872.

Stanley, Sir H. M., *Through the Dark Continent.* 2 vols. London, 1878.

Stanley, Sir H. M., *In Darkest Africa.* 2 vols. London, 1890.

Stanley, Sir H. M., *Autobiography.* London, 1912.

Stanley and Africa, etc. (Baker, Burton, Speke, Grant . . .). 662 pp. London, N.D.

Thomas, H. B., and Scott, R., *Uganda.* London, 1935.

Thomson, Joseph, *Through Masailand.* London, 1885.

Tinné, J., *Geographical Notes.* London, 1864.

Trotandot, John, *Rambles, Roamings and Recollections.* London, 1870.

Van Der Post, Laurens, and Elisofon, Eliot, *The Nile.* London, 1964.

Ward Rowland, *Horn Measurements of Great Game.* London, 1892.

Waterfield, Gordon (editor), *First Footsteps in East Africa.* (new edition with additional material). London, 1966.

Wemyss Reid, T., *The Life of Richard Monckton Milnes.* London, 1890.

JOURNALS AND PAMPHLETS

Baker, Prof. J. N. L., 'Sir Richard Burton and the Nile Sources'. *English Historical Review* (1944), vol. 59, pp. 48–61.

Baker, Prof. J. N. L., 'John Hanning Speke'. *Journal of the Royal Geographical Society,* vol. CXXVIII, part 4, 1962, pp. 385–8.

Bridges, Dr. R. C., 'Speke and the Royal Geographical Society'. *Uganda Journal,* vol. 26, No. 1, March 1962, pp. 23–43.

Cooley, W. D., 'The Geography of the White Nile'. *The Athenaeum,* No. 1866, August 1863.

Gray, Sir John, 'Speke and Grant'. *Uganda Journal,* vol. 17, No. 22, September 1953, pp. 146–60.

Harlow, Prof. Vincent, 'Burton and Speke Expedition Centenary'. *Tanganyika Notes and Records,* No. 49, 1957, pp. 312–18.

Ingham, Prof. Kenneth, 'John Hanning Speke: a Victorian and His Inspiration'. *Tanganyika Notes and Records,* No. 49, 1957, pp. 301–11.

Langlands, B. W., 'Concepts of the Nile'. *Uganda Journal,* vol. 26, No. 1, March 1962, pp. 1–22.

Mukasa, H., 'Speke at the Court of Mutesa I'. *Uganda Journal,* vol. 26, No. 1, March 1962, pp. 97–9.

Pike, A. H., 'Notes on the Exploration of the Sources of the Nile'. *Tanganyika Notes and Records,* No. 49, 1957, pp. 223–5.

Risley, R. C. H., 'Burton: an Appreciation'. *Tanganyika Notes and Records,* No. 49, 1957, pp. 257–300.

Speke, John Hanning, 'Journal of a Cruise on the Tanganyika Lake and Discovery of the Victoria Nyanza Lake'. *Blackwood's Magazine,* vol. 86, pp. 339–57 *et seq.,* 1859.

Speke, John Hanning, 'Discovery of the Victoria Nyanza'. *Travel, Adventure and Sport,* vol. 1, 1859.

Speke, John Hanning, 'My Second Expedition to Eastern Intertropical Africa', 19 pp. pamphlet. *Private edition.* Cape Town, 1860.

Speke, John Hanning, 'Captain Speke's adventures in Somali Land'. *Blackwood's Magazine,* vol. 87, pp. 339–57 *et seq.,* 1860.

Speke, John Hanning, 'Captain Speke's discoveries in Central Africa'. *Cape Monthly,* vol. 7, pp. 159–67, Cape Town, 1860.

Speke, John Hanning, 3rd Voyage down the Nile from Gondokoro to Khartum. (Unpublished MS.) Contained as pp. 483–520 in the manuscript of the *Journal.* National Library of Scotland, MS. 4872, Blackwood Collection. (This section is 15,984 words in length.) 1863.

Speke, John Hanning, 'The Upper Basin of the Nile'. *Journal of the Royal Geographical Society,* vol. 33, pp. 322–46, 1863.

Speke, John Hanning, 'Captain Speke's Welcome'. *Blackwood's Magazine,* vol. XCIV, pp. 264–6, August 1863.

Speke, John Hanning, 'Captain Speke's Journal' (review). *Blackwood's Magazine,* vol. 95, pp. 1–24, 1864.

Speke, John Hanning, 'Scheme for opening Africa', 1864, and 'Considerations for opening Africa', 1864. *Handbills, privately printed.*

Speke, John Hanning, 'The Death of Speke'. *Blackwood's Magazine,* pp. 514–16, October 1864.

Thomas, H. B., 'Giovanni Miani and the White Nile'. *Uganda Journal,* vol. 6, pp. 174–94, 1942.

Thomas, H. B., 'The Death of Speke in 1864'. *Uganda Journal,* vol. 13, No. 1, pp. 105–7, March 1949.

Wenban-Smith, W., 'Diary of the 1857–1858 Expedition to the Great Lakes'. *Tanganyika Notes and Records,* No. 49, pp. 247–55, 1957.

'The Mystery of the Nile.' *The Athenaeum,* No. 1861, p. 843, 27 June 1863.

'Nile Basins and Nile Explorers.' *Blackwood's Magazine,* vol. XCVII, pp. 100–17, January 1865.

The Nile Centenary Festival. Brochure printed by the Uganda Argus, Ltd., Kampala 1962.

NOTE

I have referred to *Tanganyika Notes and Records,* Nos. 51, 52, 55, 57, 58 and 59, and to the *Uganda Journal,* vol. 17, 1953, pp. 150–51.

The various biographies of Sir Richard Burton have also been consulted, including those by F. Hitchman, 1887; Georgiana Stisted, 1896; Thomas Wright, 1906; W. P. Dodge, 1907; H. J. Schonfield, 1936; and Seton Dearden, 1936.

Where it is referred to in the Chapter Notes, the National Library of Scotland is given as N.L.S.

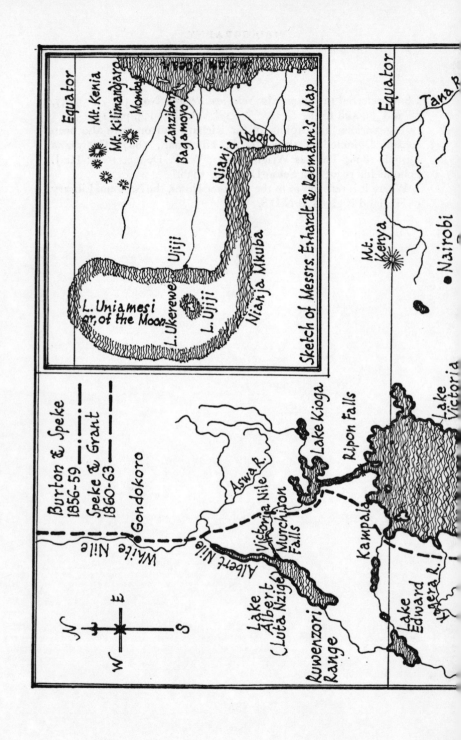

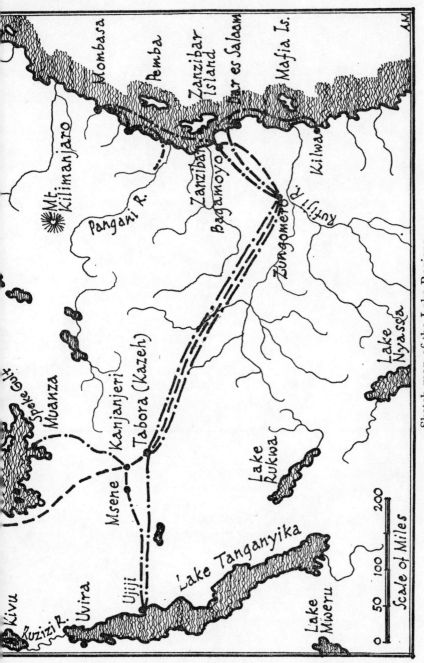

Sketch map of the Lake Regions
showing the routes taken by Burton, Speke and Grant,
drawn by the author

INDEX

Abdullah (son of Sultan Gerad), 23, 37
Aden, 5; Speke's arrival at, 8, 9, and
    return to, 12; Speke's convalescence
    in, 43–4; Speke leaves for England, 94
Albert, H.R.H. Prince, 116, 175
Anderson, 53
Anthropological Institute, the Royal,
    78 n
Apuddo, 172, 174
Artemise, the, 63
Ashill, 13, 181
Athenaeum, The, 190–1, 197
Aynterad, 33
Ayyal Nuh, the, 48

Back, Admiral Sir George, 52
Bagamoyo, 63, 122
Bahr-el-Ghazal, the, 107
Baja, 168
Baker, Sir Samuel, 123–4, 164, 172,
    174–5
Balyuz, the (el Balyuz), 33–4, 36, 42 n,
    47
Bamford Speke, 13
Bandawarogo (*see* Mutesa, Speke at
    the Court of)
Baraka, 121, 129, 133, 141
Barnstaple Grammar School, 14
Barrett, J. W., 218 n
Bates, H. W., 200
Bath Chronicle, The, 203, 210
Beke, Dr. Charles, 189, 190
Berbera: Burton plans expedition
    from, 6–8, 32–5; Burton's camp
    ravaged at, 31, 36–40; and Sheikh
    Shamarkay, 33, 36
Bilal, 159, 162
Bir Ahmed, 5
Blackheath College, 14
Blackwood, John: seeks to publish

Speke's Indian diaries, 19, 20, and
Speke's Nyanza diaries, 102–5,
    107–8; questions Speke's discretion
    over Burton, 114; takes over John
    Murray's commitments, 187; his
    assistance to Speke, 187–8; his
    remonstrates with Speke, 191;
    encourages publication of Somali
    diary, 192–3, 196; his grief at
    Speke's death, 205
Blackwood's Magazine: articles on
    Speke's expedition, 19; effect on
    Royal Geographical Society, 107;
    Burton's criticism of Speke's
    articles, 110
Blissett rifle, 82, 127
Blyth, Edward, 54
Bombay (city), 53
Bombay (Speke's companion): first
    impression on Speke, 61; at Msene,
    69; attitude towards pay, 79;
    nurses Speke, 90; joins Speke's
    expedition, 121; Speke's affection
    for, 129; squabbles with Speke,
    146–8; at Cairo, 177; leaves Speke's
    service, 178; learns of Speke's
    death, 224; other references, 63, 68,
    71, 84, 93–4, 133
Bridges, Dr. R. C., 106, 124, 165, 181,
    184, 204
Brisk, H.M.S., 120
British Association, the, 106
Brodie, Mrs. Fawn M.: on Speke's
    death, 41 n; states Speke was con-
    temptuous of Africans, 65; on naming
    of Lake Victoria Nyanza, 66; on
    Speke's inhibitions, 78 n; describes
    Speke's discovery, 85–6; on
    Oliphant's influence on Speke, 97 n;
    concerning Speke's effect on Burton,

239

Elphinstone, the, 53, 57
Encyclopaedia Brittanica, 13, 209
Erhardt, 52, 53, 68
Espec, William, 13
Evening Star, the, 203
Exeter Gazette, the, 225

Faloro, 160, 170, 173-4
Faraj, 127
Farhan, 11, 26
Forte, H.M.S., 113, 115-16,
Foxcroft, 160
French Geographical Society, Speke's
    Gold Medal from, 116
Frij, 121
Fuga, 60-1, 105
Fuller, George, 209, 210; his account
    of Speke's death, 211, 214-16, 219 n
Furious, H.M.S., 94, 98

Gaetano, 63, 71
Galton, Francis, 227-8
Geographical Society, the Royal:
    instructions to Burton about Lake
    Nyassa, 62; considers Speke's
    approach to source of the Nile, 100;
    Speke's neglect of, 106; Petherick's
    application for funds to, 112;
    annoyance over Speke's behaviour
    in Bandawarogo, 158-9; awards
    Speke Gold Medal, 177; receives
    Speke's telegram about source of
    the Nile, 177, 179; attitude
    towards Speke's opponents, 181-2;
    Petherick's report to, 184; Speke's
    report to, 196-7, its failure to meet
    criticism, 197, and its alienation of
    the Society, 197; as platform for
    meeting between Speke and Burton,
    200; its attitude towards Speke's
    request for recognition, 204;
    sponsors Speke memorial, 225
Gerad Mohamed Ali, Sultan, 22, 24
Gomm, Sir William, 17
Gough, Lord, 16, 41 n
Graham, Major, 50
Grant, James Augustus: his first
    meeting with Speke, 16; his
    character, 17; is invited to join
    Speke's expedition, 111, and the
    Speke family's reactions, 112; in
    Zanzibar, 121; at Ukuni, 131, 133;
    suffers poisoned leg, 137, 141, and

stays at Karagwe, 141; rejoins Speke
    at Bandawarogo, 162; at Mutesa's
    Court, 162-5; leaves Speke's
    expedition for Petherick, 165;
    is rejoined by Speke at
    Kamrasi's, 171; his concern at
    Speke's accounts of the expedition,
    188; offers to visit Emperor
    Napoleon, 192, 207 n; attends
    Speke's funeral, 203; his tribute to
    Speke, 206; his death, 226, and the
    attempts to add his name to the
    Speke memorial, 226-8
Grant Duff, Sir Mountstuart, 226
Gray, Sir John, 193-5
Greenfield, Hume, 197
Greenwood, Colonel, 197
Grey, Sir George, 116, 119, 120

Habr Awal, the, 48-9
Haines, Captain Stafford, 5
Hamed bin Sulayim, Sheikh, 70, 72-3
Hamerton, Lt.-Col. Atkins, 58-9, 61-3
Hammond, Edmund, 113
Hanga, 91
Harar, 7, 30
Herne, Lieutenant G. E., 5, 11, 12,
    21, 31, 33, 35, 39, 43-4, 46
Hillary, Sir Edmund, 177
Himalayas, Speke's activities in the,
    17-19

Imam, 11, 24, 26
Ingham, Professor Kenneth, 97 n
Irungu, 151

Jaifa, 172
Jami Hassan, 46
Johnson, Rev. George, 14
Johnston, Sir Harry: on Petherick in
    Egypt, 108; his errors about Speke's
    death, 209; his description of H. M.
    Stanley and the Victoria Nyanza,
    223; on the Government's
    recognition of Speke, 225
Jordans, 8, 13, 14, 181
Jordans Nullah, 84
*Journal of the Discovery of the Source of
    the Nile*: forged Hindu map in, 189;
    publication of, 189, and reactions,
    190-2; inconsistent sales of, 192
Jukes, Professor, 197
Juma, 141